GERMAN
ROMANTICISM

GERMAN ROMANTICISM

BY

OSKAR WALZEL

AUTHORIZED TRANSLATION FROM THE GERMAN

BY

ALMA ELISE LUSSKY

CAPRICORN BOOKS
NEW YORK

PRINTED IN THE UNITED STATES OF AMERICA

CONTENTS

CONTENTS

PART II

THE CREATIVE LITERATURE OF ROMANTICISM

GERMAN ROMANTICISM

PART I

ROMANTIC PHILOSOPHY AND AESTHETICS

I. THE ROMANTICIST

I. RELATION TO STORM AND STRESS

THE solitude and enchantment of the forest, the rush-
ing mill-stream, the nocturnal stillness of the German village, the cry of the night watchman, splashing
fountains, palace ruins and a neglected garden in which
weatherbeaten statues crumble, the fragments of a demol-
ished fortress: everything that creates the yearning to
escape from the monotony of daily life is romantic. This
yearning lured the German romanticist not only to distant
realms but also to peculiarly native customs, to old German
art and manners. The romanticist would fain have learned
to feel again as a German and to fashion out of this
strengthened national feeling a newer and more virile
Germanism. Though he cast his eyes upon the glories of
the past, the romanticist nevertheless heralded a spiritually
quickened golden age of the future. His dreamy eye
became unexpectedly bright and clear; ironic luminaries
gave a sudden but transient light. Hard upon the glorification of death and the world beyond came the brisk, clear
call to the joyous life of actual deeds, to vigorous self-
contemplation, and to eager activity in behalf of humanity.

German romanticism is so rich, so variegated, so many-
faceted that the more it is studied, the greater becomes
the chaos of antithetical phenomena into which it threatens
to disintegrate. It is difficult for human understanding
to find in it a semblance of unity. Yet it is not merely

3

obsolete usage or convention to speak of romantic poetry
and speculation, or of romantic temperaments, and to
designate by such terms that group of historical phenomena
which appeared around 1800. We feel there is something
unifying in this world of romanticism. We perceive the
romantic quality in the poets who called themselves romanticists and who were so considered in the nineteenth century. This romantic quality is equally evident, whether
we concentrate our attention upon the personalities of the
so-called romantic school or the personalities of the Heidelberg group, or of the Suabians of Uhland's circle, or of
the north Germans, Z. Werner, Kleist, Fouqué, Eichendorff, E. T. A. Hoffmann, or Chamisso. The roots of this
feeling are yet to be disclosed by scholarly research.

The problem is made all the more complex by the fact
that similar emotional effects were produced by others
who were outside the so-called romantic group. The Storm
and Stress period, primarily, seems to be most closely
related to romanticism. [1]

Through Storm and Stress, as well as through romanticism, an intellectual tendency and a certain spiritual attitude,
which for thousands of years had largely determined the
thoughts and feelings of humanity, gained the ascendency
in German poetry. In the philosophy of Plato there appeared an important point of departure and an effective
proof of this tendency in thought and feeling. But it was
Plotinus' metamorphosis of Plato's doctrine and, later,
Neoplatonism (going back to Plotinus) that gave this
tendency its distinctive feature and made of it a philosophy,
which, although representing only an intensification of the
ancient classical creed, nevertheless, was in principle
opposed to the peculiarly classic character of antiquity.

Greek art and poetry, especially the Greek plastic arts,

were the result of a delight in the sense of sight. They sprang from a close, friendly relation to the objective world, which they represented as something intrinsically related to man, the beauty of which gave great delight. Even when depicting the incidental or unique, Greek art and poetry remained close to nature as she reveals herself to our senses. But even Plato depreciated the objective world. Plotinus went a considerable step farther when he made out of Plato's ideal world a world of the spirit. The phenomenal world was of value to him only insofar as it was thoroughly spiritualized. Thus he made the philosophy of antiquity subjective. He seemed, indeed, to suggest the advisability of fleeing from the objective world and many of his spiritual descendents actually did turn their backs upon it.

Plotinus, who in the struggle against Christianity had tried to resurrect the ancient philosophy, was fully in accord with the moods of early Christianity. Hence, at a very early date, the philosophy of this avowed non-Christian became associated with the doctrine of the new faith. The theologians of the Middle Ages came to a definite understanding with Neoplatonism, some being strongly for it and others just as strongly against it. The Germanic peoples, who lived in a harsher, more oppressive natural environment than the south Europeans, found Neoplatonism quite in accord with their own feeling toward life. Christianity with an admixture of Neoplatonism seemed to them like the continuity of the conceptions of their ancient faith. This affinity was most evident in German mysticism during the Middle Ages.

The Italian Renaissance, likewise, is at many points saturated with Neoplatonic conceptions. The nature philosophy of the Renaissance, particularly in its attempt to treat the world as something spiritualized, dealt with ideas and desires which hark back to Giordano Bruno. His Silesian contemporary, the *Philosophus Teutonicus* Jacob Boehme, agreed with him in important places almost to the letter. On the other hand, in pietism, that fruit of the Thirty Years' War, the old German mysticism of the Middle Ages was revived. Thus the Neoplatonic attitude toward the world was brought down through the centuries. In periods which tended toward a reawakening of antiquity it had to battle again and again with an alignment of thought to which the objectification of the phenomenal world was important, even though the spiritualization demanded by Plotinus could not be attained. The opposition generally appealed to the authority of Aristotle. The followers of Neoplatonism were reproached for their tendency to pass on from the spiritualization of nature to superstition and belief in wonders and miracles. As a matter of fact, the nature philosophy of the Renaissance and of Jacob Boehme did give rise to a murky stream of superstition and a mania for miracles. And thus the great heritage of Neoplatonism was threatened with extinction.

Around 1700, however, Plotinus' philosophy was revived in England by Shaftesbury, who continued to speculate upon the idea of the spiritualization of the world in the highest and purest sense. He was himself hardly aware of his connection with Plotinus, probably picking up the thread of Giordano Bruno and deeming Plato alone to be his guiding spirit. His conception of the world was closely related to the philosophy of the German Leibnitz. In the field of aesthetics, however, which was of prime importance for the subsequent rise of German poetry, Shaftesbury was more influential than Leibnitz. At an early date German classicism began to derive sustenance from Shaftesbury. But it left the actual development of the heritage of Plotinus to philosophers who, like Hamann, were in particularly close touch with the religious, pietistic side of German thought and feeling rather than with the rationalistic side. Hamann's pupil, Herder, thus directed the feelings and thoughts of pietism and of Shaftesbury, both descendant from Plotinus, to German poetry, at first, indeed, to the environment of the youthful Goethe, from which the movement of Storm and Stress developed. It is the association with Plotinus and his followers which gives to the arch-classicism of Goethe and Schiller that peculiar and distinctive trait which differentiates it from similar high points in modern European literature, notably from the literature of the era of Louis XIV.

But German classicism rested quite as much upon the philosophy of classical antiquity as upon that of Plotinus. Aristotle is quite as significant in Schiller's later productions as is Neoplatonism. Goethe censured the partisans of Plotinus for valuing the phenomenon less than what is behind it and conditions it spiritually. Beyond the attitude of these two great leaders there was still enough opportunity to carry on the wealth of ideas contained in the Neoplatonic heritage and to utilize it, not only in the interests of German art, but also for the philosophic consciousness of the Germans. German romanticism assumed this task, at first unconsciously, then with avowed, conscious aim.

Even though the Storm and Stress thus seemed to be merely the introduction to romanticism, the final source to which its philosophy and aims may be traced is almost entirely obscured. But romanticism became aware of its spiritual ancestry. Indeed, it is one of the most delightful tasks offered the research scholar in romanticism to trace the gradual dawn of consciousness that it was romanticism which resuscitated the ancient fusion of the Neoplatonic and the Germanic, that it was romanticism which carried on and enlarged the legacy of Plotinus.

It is of the utmost importance for the art of German romanticism that almost everywhere where Neoplatonic philosophy is perceptible there is also a less rigid enforcement of the strict tectonics of Greek classicism. Dissolution of artistic form, abandonment of harmonious simplicity, and the desire to relinquish sharp contours and nice limitations are then apparent. Nor did the Storm and Stress adhere to rigid form. It rejected Aristotle just as did romanticism. German classicism, however, held with Aristotle and strove for quite contrary objectives. Imbedded between the Storm and Stress on the one hand and romanticism on the other, it created upon German soil a literature fashioned in the spirit of the ancient classical conception of form. [2]

Romanticism carried on much that had been sacred to the Storm and Stress but which Goethe and Schiller had meanwhile cast aside, after abandoning the desires and creations of their youth in their bold, consistent ascent to German classicism. But the idea of romanticism can be grasped more clearly if the delicate, deep-lying differences are fathomed which are peculiar to the spiritual and artistic revolution of 1800 as opposed to the earlier revolution in German life and art. Naturally the point of divergence lies where the greatest opposition is revealed: at the time of early romanticism and of the rise of the youthful, seminal ideas of the representatives of the older romantic school. The early romanticists are farthest removed from the Storm and Stress. Although in its later development romanticism approached the Storm and Stress, there never was real concord between the two movements. The fact that romanticism, even in its later days, could never properly be identified with the era of the "original geniuses" of 1770 but retained its originality and independence is due primarily to the leaders of the early romantic movement, who had plainly set forth what hopes and desires, what spiritual demands and artistic possibilities lay slumbering in the heart of every romanticist. Friedrich Schlegel, Novalis, Schleiermacher, and Tieck (the latter less definitely but all the more vividly) had clearly reflected the temper of their generation. The very first fainthearted attempts of these individuals to understand themselves are the sign-posts for modern research.

As early as the beginning of the last decade of the eighteenth century a new form of artistic and spiritual culture began to stir in the letters of Friedrich Schlegel to his brother Wilhelm; a new *Weltanschauung* was detaching itself from the old. Wilhelm Schlegel, the friend of Gottfried August Buerger, still held at that time the point of view of the era of the "original geniuses," and Friedrich sought to defend the new doctrine against his brother. Wilhelm assumed the rôle of one who scorned reason, but Friedrich proved that Wilhelm himself made extensive use of that faculty.

As a conscious man of reason Friedrich spoke to his brother, who, while rejecting reason, was nevertheless saturated with it. And there lies the antithesis that exists between the Storm and Stress and early romanticism. During the seventies, men of culture, with Hamann and Herder at their head, were wont to mock at reason; the early romanticists, along with the critic Kant, sponsored its use. But according to Kant, Hamann and Herder were

themselves men of reason. Friedrich, like Schiller, had
learned from Kant that striving after the eternal and
infinite was a postulate of reason. Soon afterward Schiller
outlined the nature of the man of reason or ideas in his
treatise *Ueber naive und sentimentalische Dichtung,* illus-
trating and clarifying his point by contrasting the idealist
with the realist. As early as 1793 Friedrich had learned
to distinguish between the conscious and unconscious man
of reason, for having himself been set right regarding
the postulates of reason and having been made conscious
of them by Kant, he had discovered in his brother the
same yearning for the infinite as in himself but not the
consciousness of having thereby become a man of reason.

The fact that the cultural leaders of the seventies rejected reason may be ascribed to Kant, as well as the fact
that the youthful Friedrich Schlegel openly and un-
equivocally adopted it. At the beginning of the seventh
decade, Kant, through English empiricism, had become
doubtful of Wolff's metaphysics and, when Herder got
in touch with him, was on the very verge of scepticism.
Something of Hume's scepticism of reason was thus
passed on by Kant to Herder and by the latter, in turn,
to the intellectual life of the time. Had Kant in those
days been less sceptical and had he not turned his back
distrustfully upon all metaphysics, he could not, together
with Socrates-Hamann, have become Herder's teacher.
Hamann's antipathy to reason, fostered by Hume, is revealed in R. Unger's far-reaching study (*Hamann und
die Aufklaerung,* 1911) as the focus of his very being.
Kant was at that time inclined, like Hamann, to utter
a Socratic "And see that we can know nothing." To be
sure, Kant speedily passed from this empirical, sceptical
ferment to a new metaphysics. Herder, however, remained

an empirical sceptic all his life, though with the idealistic desires that hold sway in the Faust-natures of the Storm and Stress period as well as in Wilhelm Schlegel (*A*, p. 370 ff.).

That early romanticism, and also Friedrich Schlegel from the very first, grasped this situation clearly is due to the critic Kant. The latter demonstrated the metaphysical wants of the man of reason and taught Friedrich Schlegel not to regard reason as the antithesis of everything mighty and sublime in the human soul. Following Kant, Friedrich took great pains to distinguish the man of reason with his urgent impulse toward the infinite from the "cut and dried sophist," in whom "the very essential and noble instinct for intelligible conceptions and for clear understanding" is "unnaturally strong" (to Wilhelm, p. 142). Friedrich Schlegel combated such veneration of reason, if on no other account than that it seemed one-sided, for as early as 1793 he likewise had formulated his demand for versatility (p. 125).

The concatenation of reason and the urgent desire not to destroy by sheer ratiocination the subconscious in man is, according to Ricarda Huch, the essential characteristic of early romanticism. That the Storm and Stress would of necessity have a different point of view is quite clear from its understanding and appraisal of the concept "reason." [3]

Schopenhauer defines the concept of the metaphysical desire thus: the human soul would fain overlook the whole of experience in its deepest interrelations, survey all phenomena in their totality, and become aware of the unity which comprises them all. This is as much the desire of the adherent of the Storm and Stress as it is that of the romanticist. But the romanticist alone realized that this

Concat.

desideratum is set by reason, while the representative of the Storm and Stress, like Hamann, scoffs at reason. Yet it is nothing but a rational desire to attain the desideratum of metaphysics when Faust expresses his wish to apprehend what in the last analysis holds the world together and to behold intuitively all seminal and creative power.

Ricarda Huch delineates in masterly fashion the daring hope of the romanticists to illumine even the most obscure phases of life. The romanticists actually and deliberately beheld visions; they did not merely have presentiments of them. They were not satisfied with experiencing emotions alone but they subjected them to analysis. Thoughtfully they pondered over their instincts. The Storm and Stress, on the other hand, did not dare to give a name to emotion, convinced as they were that there is nothing in a name but empty vapouring, befogging the divine inspiration. Like Rousseau they feared emotion would be destroyed if they sought to form a definite conception of it. The romanticist had no such fear, though constant analysis and self-analysis did undermine his temperament. The representative of the Storm and Stress was and remained a youthful, virile, and mighty "fellow," swept along by a single violent emotion, to which he resigned himself with misgiving, but unwilling, nevertheless, to interpret his own dreams. Ecstatic enthusiasm prevented him from dissecting his emotions; or, like Werther, he burrowed down into his grief and lost himself there. The romanticist, on the other hand, was always seeking to interpret; he always had a secret to disclose. His emotions were weakened and subdued by these disclosures, but he himself became spiritually refined (*A*, p. 346 ff.).

This marked tendency to analyze the emotions made romanticism especially productive in two fields: the contemplation of art and the comprehension of religion. In both instances it was necessary to illumine the very depths of the subconscious. Although the power of spontaneous artistic creation was fully acknowledged, the desire for thinking artists was never before so strongly voiced; and no predecessor had grasped as keenly as Schleiermacher the very essence of religion. He was able to do so because he had the ability in true romantic fashion to transform emotion into conceptions and to grasp its peculiarity and its antithetical relation to intellectual activity. For though the romantic penchant for analyzing does not hesitate even before emotion, neither does it degenerate into rationalism.

Hence it was possible for romanticism to establish a point of contact with Friedrich Heinrich Jacobi. This emotional philosopher (an opponent of Kant), whose novel *Woldemar* was rejected by Friedrich Schlegel in 1796 with cutting acerbity, nevertheless, in 1793 received prominent mention in the latter's letters to his brother. Contrary to Wilhelm's judgment (p. 126), Jacobi's earlier novel *Eduard Allwills Briefsammlung*, 1792, was consigned by Friedrich to the literature of rationalism and Jacobi himself considered a rationalist. Hence early romanticism could attach itself to Jacobi and yet not be fully in accord with him. Fichte, Schelling, and Schleiermacher built upon Jacobi's foundation but also crossed swords with him.

None of the romanticists was as close to Jacobi as Schleiermacher. As early as 1802 Hegel expressed his conviction that Schleiermacher was a magnified Jacobi (*Kritisches Journal,* 2, 1, 134 ff.). The point of contact was in religion, a field which romanticism reserved for the emotions only. "On account of the wealth of their inner life and their 'mysticism'," says Dilthey (*Leben Schleiermachers,* p. 332), "they found themselves opposed to all

Religion = emotions only.

the learning which surrounded them, and the depth and freedom of their emotional life, and the keenness of their thought did not easily permit them to compromise. Both remained conscious of the connection between their mysticism and their individuality. Both saw a higher realism founded in this mysticism as opposed to idealism in its various branches." But Jacobi was, in the light of Rousseau's teachings, far too much opposed to all reflective thinking to enable him to join the romanticists. Like Rousseau he says, "There is light in my heart but when I seek to bring it into my head, it is extinguished." Jacobi destroys every link between faith and knowledge and places them in absolute and fundamental antithesis toward each other. He, too, would grasp the absolute, infinite meaning of the world; his metaphysical urge is very strongly developed. But in this endeavor thinking is only a hindrance to him; faith alone points the way—a faith which has its being solely in individual emotion. He is convinced of the irreconcilable antithesis existing between philosophic thought and true mysticism. Hence Schleiermacher replied quite correctly to Jacobi (to Brinckmann, July 19, 1800, 4, 73 ff.), "The seeming controversy between the newer popular philosophy and mysticism gave him the false impression that there really could be a quarrel between philosophy and mysticism, whereas, as a matter of fact, every philosophy leads to mysticism of some sort. . . . If Jacobi only wished to decree that philosophy and mysticism lie wholly apart and that their seeming connection is due solely to the fact that they touch at a tangent, he would cease quarreling uselessly with philosophy."

Temperaments such as Jacobi's, perforce, very soon made clear to the romanticists, schooled as they were in

Kant, that the metaphysical urge of rational beings also held sway in heads that played off their strong emotion against any edifice erected by reason. Schleiermacher went to school to Kant as well as did Friedrich Schlegel; but neither tarried long there. Romanticism is unthinkable without Kant, but its antithesis to him, primarily in the field of ethics, gives it its peculiar right to existence.

2. HERDER AND ROMANTICISM. THE ORGANIC CONCEPTION

The romanticists, like Schiller, were diverted from Kant's ethics by their conviction that a human being could be raised to the highest ethical level only through the harmonization of reason and morality, not merely through one-sided reason. It was Shaftesbury who led both Schiller and the romanticists to this conviction. At this point the romantic world once more approached the generation of the seventies, for Hamann vigorously stressed the necessity of totality and demanded that everything that man might attempt in word and deed should proceed from his united faculties; detachment is objectionable. Herder, however, as well as the whole Storm and Stress movement, understood by his demand, in the first instance, the endeavor to go forth into life, away from dull reflection, not to linger over pen and ink but to rise to creative deeds. Again it devolved upon Kant's discriminating, guiding criticism to clarify the issue and to prepare the weapons with which Schiller and the romanticists, striving to transcend him, attacked Kant himself. German culture, through the hostility of Hamann and Herder toward reason, was threatened with the danger of repudiating all logic. Romantic totality, however, demanded not only men of emotions, and natures inclined

toward deeds, but thinkers and contemplators as well.
Thus Schiller saw in the representative of the Storm and
Stress a man of intellect and of the senses who was
unable to rise to complete harmony of human talents and
activities. The conception of aesthetic education, itself
derived from Shaftesbury and beyond him from Plato
and Plotinus, [4] was therefore formulated by Schiller with
constant regard for Kant's moral demands of reason.
And when romanticism formulated its ideal of culture, it,
too, was at great pains to grant its genuinely romantic
conception of "culture" not only sparkling, shifting emotional moods, but to give it also a strong intellectual
foundation. In both instances one perceives that the point
of departure was Kant's lofty, intellectual demands upon
humanity and from this point a way was found to the
"nature" and "emotions" of the Storm and Stress. In
both instances, finally, there was set up against Kant's
moral demand, which was valid for all humanity, a code
of ethics for the exceptional, the noble natures, and the
highly gifted personalities. Such men were likewise
honored around 1770. [5]

Romanticism, like the Storm and Stress, defended the
prerogatives of superior personalities as conceived by
Shaftesbury. To be sure, the desire of each individual to
live his life completely led, around 1770 and again around
1800, to capriciousness and licentiousness. But the dire
consequences which occasionally resulted should not arouse
prejudice against the respect for the greatness of the idea
which in both instances lay at the root of the cult of
personality. It was the high regard for the personal attri-
bute which is the birthright of every individual. Hence
Hamann prized the idiosyncrasy of individuals as well
as of nations; out of this premise grew Herder's under-

standing of all that is peculiar in art and life. The significance of all that is individual was brought out most forcibly by the romanticists, particularly by Schleiermacher. In the field of ethics, contrary to Kant, they insisted upon the right of personality. As art critics they vied with Herder in assuming the empathic attitude toward the most wilful personalities. Wackenroder, affectionate and clinging, led the way; the all too variable Tieck followed him faithfully; and Wilhelm Schlegel well-nigh outdid himself in universal receptivity. At the same time, in the spirit of Herder, they strove to comprehend art phenomena in their historical connotation. In history they also created a field for the right of personality when they indicated where and why personality was not free, but rather hedged in by forces of historical development. For the romantic conception of history was to view all that is postulated historically in its relation to the whole, but at the same time not to deny to it its individual value. [6]

But not only in their understanding of individuality did Herder and Schleiermacher come in contact with each other. Two years before Schleiermacher wrote his *Reden ueber die Religion*, Herder presented views in his last collection of *Christliche Schriften,* under the heading, *Von Religion, Lehrmeinungen, und Gebraeuchen*, which directly approached Schleiermacher. To be sure, the latter by means of his deeper grasp on the religious life differentiated more keenly between religion and dogma and set the religious emotions in antithesis not only to metaphysics but to ethics as well. But Herder, going back to Lessing, pronounced religion to be one thing and dogma another, and religion he termed the essence of Christianity. This, on the one hand, promulgated the fundamental idea of Schleiermacher and, on the other, summoned back to life the point of view of Lessing, than whom, Friedrich Schlegel said (to Novalis, December 2, 1798, p. 86), no one had a more prophetic vision of the new and genuine religion.

Herder's significance for romanticism is naturally to be found in another field also. At first glance it actually seems as though romanticism would have been an impossibility without Herder. This seems incompatible with the meagre recognition which he received from the romanticists and with the knowledge of the unbridgeable antithesis which exists between the two. Can it be that the mere contrast between the two generations kept Herder from receiving due thanks? Another conjecture might be nearer the truth. Many of Herder's intellectual achievements had already been so generally appropriated that in using them one scarcely gave thought to their author. The younger generation all too soon forgot that Herder had blazed the trail to Shakespeare, to indigenous poetry, to the Middle Ages, and to the folk-song and that he had even prepared the way for romantic orientalism. His "sensitive aesthetic" was hateful to Wilhelm Schlegel (*Berlin Lectures*, 1, 47, 16 ff.). And whereas Friedrich Schlegel in an early essay on the history of civilization claimed for the *Ideen zur Philosophie der Geschichte der Menschheit* that it "very delightfully champions deeply cogitated experiences rather than one-sided reason," Wilhelm's final decree in 1803 was that it was a book in which were to be found neither ideas, nor philosophy, nor history, nor humanity; he recognized in it not the beginning of something new but the climax of erroneous modern historiography (Haym, *Die Romantische Schule*, p. 911). And Wilhelm Schlegel once deemed Herder's *Plastik* one of his favorite books!

Schelling was more conscious of the thanks that he

owed Herder than any of the foregoing. Purposely he
fashioned the title of his first publication in natural philosophy after Herder's masterpiece. For he recognized
everything of Herder's that he used, even when he received
it at second-hand. To be sure, it was through the lecture
given in 1793 by Karl Friedrich Kielmeyer, professor in
the Karlsschule in Stuttgart, entitled *Concerning the Interrelations of Organic Forces in the Ranks of the Various
Organizations; the Laws and Consequences of These
Relations*, that Schelling was induced to conceive of nature
and humanity as a single mighty, unified organism; but
he himself traced Kielmeyer's train of thought back to
Herder. As a matter of fact, in Herder's treatise *Vom
Erkennen und Empfinden der Menschlichen Seele*, 1778,
and *Gott*, 1787, delicate threads may already be found
which lead to Schelling and Novalis. Herder helped build
the bridge from Spinoza to natural philosophy and thus
he contributed his share to usher in the reversion to the
realistic philosophy that set in with Schelling. In 1802,
in the sixth part of *Adrastea*, Herder sought tardily to
deduce in his way the consequences of the premises which
he himself had given Schelling, but in doing so did not
admit to himself or to others that Schelling, outstripping
him, had long before disposed of that very matter. For
Herder did not recognize in Schelling's nature philosophy,
couched as it was in scholarly, formal diction, his own
property and contributions. And thus, once more, two
people who were destined for intimate and profound
mutual understanding went their separate ways, coldly and
unsympathetically. But in view of the strong connections
between natural philosophy and Herder's thought, one can
conceive how a man of J. W. Ritter's type could seek
refuge in Herder's arms after the death of his friend

Hardenberg and find absolute peace in his society. In his *Fragmente aus dem Nachlasse eines jungen Physikers* (1810, 1, XXXI, ff.) Ritter erected a memorial to this friendship. Still another romantic natural philosopher, Gotthilf Heinrich Schubert (*Selbstbiographie*, 1854, 1, 278 ff.), approached Herder in the latter's declining years.

Out of romantic natural philosophy developed also the fulfillment of one of the youthful Herder's wishes. In the third collection of *Fragments Concerning German Literature* he had once discussed the possibility of a new mythology, having been stirred by a blustering, disdainful word of Hamann's (*Schriften*, ed. by F. Roth, 2, 280).. More clearly and specifically than Hamann, Herder wished to create out of the "ocean of devices and details which engulfs us" and out of the "new world of discovery which surrounds us," a new mythology. Later the idea emerged again in Herder's mind (see p. 68 f.).

But there was another reason why the romanticists did not accord Herder the recognition that was due him. The organic conception of nature and of art is the key to romantic philosophy. Herder had helped to forge this idea but Schelling alone seemed wholly to have recognized his share in its creation. The other early romanticists gave Goethe the credit. As a matter of fact, Goethe's contribution was fully as great as Herder's (36, p. XXXV ff.). The early romanticists, who, contrary to Schelling, approached the organic conception of nature and of art from the aesthetic point of view rather than from that of natural history, found this conception more fully developed for their purposes in declarations made by Goethe during the period following his Italian journey. Karl Philip Moritz's treatise *Concerning the Plastic Imitation of the Beautiful*, inspired by Goethe, moved them very deeply.

Hence Wilhelm Schlegel in his Berlin lectures (1, 102 f.) paid rather extravagant praise to Moritz. Tersely and in a fashion easily intelligible to every one, the organic conception of nature and of art was here presented as the romanticists interpreted it, not only from the point of view of its application to aesthetics but also of the reasons underlying it, later put forth by Schelling. Unqualifiedly it was admitted that Moritz alone had determined in the highest sense the principle of imitation in the arts. Yet Moritz was only one of many who had worked on the evolving conception of an organic work of art. But Wilhelm Schlegel mentioned only him and in so doing used the comparison of an artist with Prometheus, who also imitated nature "when he fashioned man from earthly strain and animated him with a spark stolen from the sun"—a comparison which since the time of Shaftesbury has been frequently used in connection with the aesthetic problem of the organic conception and which is particularly familiar in Goethe. [7]

But Schelling, too, soon derived greater inspiration from Goethe's work in the natural sciences than from Herder. And so finally, from the scientific point of view as well as from the aesthetic, Goethe was everywhere acknowledged as the sole inspiration of romanticism although Herder had diligently striven toward the identical objectives.

readily assuming different shapes or forms!

3. ROMANTIC TRAITS: THE PROTEAN, MAGIC, YEARNING
FOR THE ABSOLUTE

Two favorite conceptions of early romanticism are reminiscent of Shaftesbury and beyond him of Plato and Neoplatonism: the conception of human totality and the organic conception as applied to nature and art. Both are common to classicism and to romanticism. Both seem to attest the fact that romanticism has a foundation just as sure and safe as classicism. Harmonious, balanced personalities, human beings whose inner lives have the assurance of a process of nature: this was conceived by romanticism as the ultimate goal in the art of living. But did not the romanticists very often both in their outer and inner lives represent the very opposite of such self-assurance?

The early romanticist was too much of a philosopher to think that this goal of harmony ever could be attained. Friedrich Schlegel knew as well as Schiller that spiritual harmony is an ideal that can be approached but not reached. The modern cultural world is too full of antithesis to permit the individual with conscious effort to arrive at that inner harmony which was once bestowed upon man as a gift of the gods. Since, however, harmony is the union and synthesis of antitheses, the romanticist believed that he could approach his ideal of harmony by turning from one antithesis to the other and returning again quickly to the first. To vibrate thus between extremes was contrary to classical ethics. But the romanticist believed that by so doing he could best escape the danger of one-sidedness, which classicism likewise sought above all things to avoid. And so he became protean, a dualist from principle. Friedrich Schlegel recognized in contradictions the sign of many-sidedness and of genuine love of truth. That is romantic. Tieck's William Lovell declared he was more changeable than Proteus himself or a chameleon. The fundamental idea was that contradiction could be avoided as long as one continued differentiating with increasing nicety. Hegel's philosophy was announced with its doctrine of antithesis, of constantly turning thesis into antithesis. The way had been prepared for it ever since Kant, Fichte, and Schiller had accustomed their readers to set up antitheses and to resolve them into higher unity and thus to think in triadic rhythm. Friedrich Schlegel himself very soon employed the Kantian categories—harmony, multiplicity, and totality—for ethical purposes and wished to lead man from harmony to multiplicity in order that he might thus approach totality (to Wilhelm, October, 1793, p. 124). In his philosophic lectures in 1804–6 (Windischmann, 1, 76, 93 f., 108) he was still occupied with these conceptions. His pupil, Adam Mueller, came forth in 1804 with a book called *Die Lehre vom Gegensatze*. Neither could Schelling's nature philosophy dispense with the conception of antithesis, for which it used, like Goethe in his research in natural science, the term "polarity."

In these conceptions, harmony and multiplicity, both of which Friedrich Schlegel wished to satisfy in order to arrive at totality, there are concealed postulates which still persist in undiminished strength: on the one hand, the yearning to encompass the world in mighty grasps and, on the other, the desire to experience life in its most secret charms, free from systematic obligation. These are the antitheses between which the romanticist was constantly vibrating; these are the poles which he would fain have synthetized. The impulse to give to all experience a conceivable explanation and at the same time to experience all things without mental preoccupation was perhaps most strongly developed in Novalis and it caused him much grief. The mental heritage of the speculative seventeenth and eighteenth centuries, acquired on one side from Descartes, Leibnitz, Spinoza, and Kant and on the other from Bacon, Locke, Berkeley, Hume, and the French materialists, was no inconsequential burden to posterity.

Naturally Faust's dictum, "Insofar as I am static, I am enslaved," lies at the bottom of the glorification of antithesis and the protean nature of romanticism. The soul wishes to preserve its freedom. Infinite determinability, which also in Schiller's estimation was an advantage, is most truely safeguarded to him who is most capable of protean mobility. In the final analysis, however, the protean mobility of the romantic spirit is based upon the consciousness of being able at all times to rise above itself. Herein lies also the root of romantic irony. Novalis once declared that the mobility of the ego consisted in unrestricted rising above itself. Fichte's doctrine of intellectual perception justified the romantic fraternity in their custom of objectively observing at all times the play of their own ego. It was not new to the eighteenth century to divide the ego into an observing subject and an observed object. The new idea was this: the romanticist did not stop at observing, but went a step farther and sought arbitrarily to guide the ego, to urge and determine it, and to promote in it any desired mood.

Not by way of philosophic speculation but rather through direct observation of himself and others, Tieck first depicted this fundamental trait of the romantic personality with all its artistic peculiarities and likewise with all the dangers which threatened it, in the character of William Lovell (1795–6). Friedrich Schlegel asserted (*Athenaeumfragment* 418) that this novel presented an "absolutely new character." With this recognition Schlegel made Tieck and his comrades aware of the typical significance of Lovell's character. Here for the first time a romantic nature was poetically conceived and its spiritual life drained to the dregs, to the point where self-annihilation and destruction are to be found. Lovell did not merely morbidly exaggerate the habit of dividing the ego into an observing subject and an observed object. A subjective conception of the outer and inner worlds in which both depart from reality was also peculiar to him. Friedrich Schlegel promptly emphasized the determining trait: "Lovell is a fantast in every good and bad, in every lovely and disagreeable sense of the word." Schiller's treatise *Ueber naive und sentimentalische Dichtung* describes the character of the fantast: he deserts nature out of pure wilfulness in order to be able to give the stubbornness of his desires and the moods of his imagination fuller sway. "But just because fantasticality is not an abnormality of nature but rather of freedom and hence arises from a tendency which is in itself quite praiseworthy and capable of infinite perfectibility, it also leads into a progressively more abysmal depth which can end in nothing but self-destruction" (12, 263). Schiller's statements agree thoroughly with Lovell's life and nature. Lovell was a solipsist: "Things exist because we thought them"; "We are the fate which supports it (the world)"; "Virtue exists only because I myself exist, a reflection in my inner mind"; "Virtue exists only because I thought it" (6, 178). Novalis did not always avoid similar solipsism successfully. The illimitable power which he, upon the authority of Fichte, ascribed to the human will shows how much he had in common with Lovell. Jean Paul, who enriched the gallery of problematic natures of this period by more than one portrait, followed from the start the spiritual upheavals which were occasioned by the dual partition of the ego and hence had already arrived in *Hesperus*, 1795, and *Siebenkaes*, 1796–7, at the artistic formulation of the *Doppelgaengermotiv* which later was used in so many

varieties by E. T. A. Hoffmann. [8] Roquairol in *Titan*
(1800–3) is just a step removed from Lovell and is such
a typical figure that his characteristics can still be traced
in Byron or in Benjamin Constant's *Adolph*, 1816.

Jean Paul and Hoffmann were thinking of Fichte's
"intellectual perception" when they portrayed the spiritual
woes of the dual ego. To Novalis this intellectual perception became a sort of magic which would enable humanity
to determine itself even physically. Fichte's second introduction to the *Wissenschaftslehre* (1, 463) calls intellectual
perception the immediate consciousness that I am doing
something and what I am doing: it is that by which I know
something because I am doing it. "I cannot take a step
nor move hand or foot without the intellectual perception
of my consciousness in these actions; only by means of
these perceptions do I know that I am doing it; only by
means of them can I differentiate between my actions
(and in them, myself) and the empiric objects of my
actions." Novalis gave Fichte credit for having taught
and discovered the active use of the mind (Minor, 2, 193);
but he questioned whether Fichte had discovered the laws
for the active use of the organs generally. He thought
that just as we set our minds working at will, just as we
indicate the activity of our mind in gestures, and express
it in deeds, just so we ought to learn to move, and limit,
and harmonize, and distinguish our internal organs. He
conceived the possibility of establishing arbitrary command
over various parts of the body generally considered involuntary. He deemed it not impossible that a human
being then could, independently of nature, replace lost
limbs or will himself to death. This gave rise to bold,
preposterous hopes; human self-determination was here
given the greatest latitude. The man who harbored this

idea was himself for a long time trying to die by sheer force of will. Could arbitrary determinability in the romantic sense, or the desire to rise above oneself and to observe and guide at will the play of one's own spirit have been carried to greater lengths? Yet Novalis believed that he was merely developing Fichte's ideas and possibly also those of Hemsterhuis.

Fichte's doctrine of the ego which posits the non-ego was corroborated and strengthened in Hardenberg's mind by the conception of his favorite philosopher, Hemsterhuis, that reality is the creative result of our outer and inner organs. Among these organs that of morality stands out preëminently with Hemsterhuis. As well as including the "moral sense" of the English, the moral organ points to Locke's inner experience, but at the same time it is the germ of an infinite meliorism and an approach to the deity. The hopes which Hemsterhuis places in the moral organ appealed to Novalis. These two philosophers, who gave man such great power over the empiric world, kept strengthening Novalis in his tendency to make ecstasy (it plays an important part in the teachings of Plotinus and Neoplatonism) the measure of human strength and of the efficacy of the human will. He became a magician in the strict sense of the word and at the same time derived support from the idealistic philosophy of his time; hence he called his system "magic idealism." [9] Only a poet could tread such precarious paths and accept as deeds of the will what obviously was nothing but the work of fantasy. W. Olshausen (*Friedrich von Hardenbergs Beziehungen zur Naturwissenschaft seiner Zeit*, 1905, p. 70 ff.) quite rightly shows that everywhere herein may be observed traces of the secret, inner impulse of artistic, genial creative ability. And so Novalis turned from philosophy back to poetry. As a poet he could satisfy the insatiable passion to condition and determine reality. As soon as he recognized this fact, philosophy and poetry became one and the same thing to him. The aestheticizing of philosophy, which to Friedrich Schlegel and particularly to Schelling became an article of faith of prime importance, was in the case of Novalis, too, by no means anything in the nature of a renunciation. "Poetry is what is absolutely and genuinely real. That is the kernel of my philosophy. The more poetic, the more true," he says (3, 11; cf. 376). The philosopher prejudices none of his rights and renounces nothing by becoming a poet, for poetry is truth. A. G. Baumgarten had once applied Leibnitz' psychological interpretations to aesthetics and made art the prelude to knowledge. Schiller's *Artists* carried the idea farther and sought to intimate that man could enter the land of knowledge only through the morning portal of the beautiful. But Novalis, like Schelling, prized poetry yet more highly; it is entitled not only to a propaedeutic meaning; it is not merely a means to knowledge; it is knowledge itself.

The conception that poetry is absolute reality, that it is equal to truth, not only pointed to a philosophic conviction beyond mere things, that beyond the phenomena of the empiric world lay the true world, but actually recognized in poetry a means of grasping the absolute. Here the infinite became finite; here the absolute became experience.

The weightiest reason for striving for the infinite is the knowledge that man has been given a designation which surpasses the limits of human existence. Yearningly the romanticist gazed beyond mere temporal life and sought the way from the finite to the infinite. Well did William Lovell know (6, 128 f.) how tormenting can become a yearning which will not be satisfied. Yet the romanticist did find in love the means to quiet this yearning. As early as May 17, 1792, Friedrich Schlegel admitted to his brother (p. 46) his yearning for the infinite. And even at this time he linked this yearning with the conception of love. The heart thinks to find in the loved one the infinite treasure it seeks; this yearning, this love permits man to penetrate the absolute and eternal. Similarly Fichte recognized, in its philosophic connotation, the conception of yearning. Fichte explains it in the *Grundlage der gesamten Wissenschaftslehre* (1794, p. 303) as the "impulse toward something entirely unknown which reveals itself only in a sense of need, in a feeling of dissatisfaction or emptiness which though craving to be satisfied does not indicate how it possibly might obtain satisfaction." To Fichte this yearning was the presupposition of all knowledge and morality; it was the original, wholly independent expression of the striving inherent in the ego. By defining this yearning Fichte gave romanticism the means of recognizing its innermost self, inasmuch as the impulse of the man of reason toward the infinite and eternal has always been accepted as the distinguishing mark of the romantic generation. It is furthermore romantic that the man of reason is fully aware of these relationships. Wherever the romanticist perceived yearning, he found the metaphysical desideratum, the impulse toward the infinite. And so love moved into the circle of the metaphysical desideratum—first of all, a spiritual love in the sense of Plato and Plotinus, an enthusiasm for recognition, a spiritual, creative impulse striving to draw us toward the divine, a yearning love for the divine, a religious love for the infinite such as Schleiermacher championed. This mystic love, which was quite familiar to German mysticism, did not stop within the confines of religion. It was also associated with the love of man for woman. And so romantic yearning expanded into an all-embracing bond joining knowledge, religion, and passion. Hence Novalis' fairy-tale about Hyacinth and little Rosebud led the lover into the arms of his beloved when he sought to disclose the veiled picture of Sais and to fathom the absolute truth. Hence Novalis could present all romantic yearning for infinity symbolically in his dream of the Blue Flower. But all of this was already portended in Friedrich's letter to Wilhelm (May 17, 1792) in which yearning for the infinite was specified as a source of love. In this romantically conceived religious love for God and for woman the romanticist's yearning for the absolute found rest. The infinite was thus, according to the romantic creed, demanded and mentally encompassed by reason, made finite in poetry, and experienced in love. It was the creed of a yearning which, about to soar into illimitable spaces beyond mere temporal existence, could, nevertheless, find twofold satisfaction and peace in this world: in love and in poetry. Love was here conceived in the divine and human sense; it was religious love for God as well as sheer human love. [10]

These preliminary deductions indicate the line of development which the romanticists followed. Their desire to grasp the ultimate basis from which the world has come stumbled at length against the firmly-wrought walls within which Kant had set the limits of human understanding. They realized that their consuming yearning for the infinite and absolute was destined forever to remain mere yearning. Out of this disillusionment grew the doctrine of romantic irony; it indicates that the romanticist was fully aware of the unbridgeable antithesis between his metaphysical demands and their fulfillment. Nevertheless,

Fichte

he looked about him for the means by which he could be brought closer to eternity. The vigor of his spirit was no longer to be restrained by the consciousness that he wanted and demanded more than would ever be given him. From various sources came ways and means to reach the absolute. In love and in poetry the temporal embraced the eternal, the finite the infinite. The romantic ironist became a prophet and a seer.

Such aspirations are not compatible with calm, staid philosophy; romantic thought soars continually into the world of fantasy, just as the philosopher follows hard upon the heels of the romantic artist. If the romanticists, Schelling included, had not been poets, they would not have been capable of the enthusiasm which is implied in their doctrine of experiencing the infinite. As early as July 21, 1791, Friedrich Schlegel glorified this enthusiasm in a letter to his brother Wilhelm, and, quoting Goethe's *An Schwager Kronos*, he declared: "When we are positively incapable of any enthusiasm, it is time for us to depart this life."

The nearer the early romanticists thought that they were approaching infinity, the more frequently the conception of enthusiasm appears in Friedrich Schlegel's remarks. In the last articles in the *Athenaeum* this conception appears repeatedly. Novalis, indeed, had the idea of a "culture of enthusiasm" (3, 44). The fourth thesis, moreover, which Friedrich Schlegel presented before the faculty at Jena was entitled *Enthusiasmus est principium artis et scientiae*.

In his humorous treatise *Der Philister vor, in, und nach der Geschichte* (1811, p. 13) Clemens Brentano appealed to the enthusiasm which would fain soar beyond the infinite: "Let us take the word student in its broader

nearer to infinity = more enthusiasm!

sense . . . of a person . . . who is engaged in researches in eternity, in science, or in God, who happily mirrors in his soul every beam of light, a worshipper of the idea per se, and the Philistines are his opposite."

Like the majority of his contemporaries, Brentano had freely expressed, both seriously and satirically, his attitude toward the tendencies of early romanticism. Even if the later romanticists had not spiritually drawn closer to the Storm and Stress, they were all (particularly Brentano) much too deeply imbued with the genuine protean character of romanticism to have hung slavishly upon every word of the older generation. When, like the latter, they attacked Philistinism, they (especially Eichendorff) were delighted to ferret out a trace of it in the very camp of the romanticists. Many of the catchwords of early romantic speculation seemed to them colored by Philistinism. But in spite of all this, the quotation from his treatise on the Philistines shows how closely Brentano's thought was linked with the attitude of the early romanticists. In these final and ultimate demands all the romanticists agreed.

Just one more proof. It may be found in a man whom the myopic like to consider antithetical not only to early romanticism but to romanticism in general, namely, Uhland. In a youthful treatise he set forth his conception of all that was romantic just as it is here presented in accordance with the creed of the early romanticists: "The spirit of man feeling, indeed, that it will never experience infinity in all its splendor and wearied by the vague groping of its desire, soon fixes its yearning upon temporal images in which there seems to be a dawning vision of the celestial. . . . This mystic manifestation of our innermost feelings in an image, this projection of the world spirits, this incarnation of the divine, in a word: the presentiment of infinity in our perceptions is what is romantic" (*Werke,* ed. by L. Fraenkel, 2, 347 f.). How closely this is related to the thought of Friedrich Schlegel, Schleiermacher, and Schelling will presently be confirmed by a more minute consideration of the early romantic theory.

II. THE FIRST AND SECOND STAGES OF THE EARLY ROMANTIC THEORY

1. FRIEDRICH SCHLEGEL'S EARLY CLASSICISTIC EFFORTS

IT is quite self-evident that a group of writers that is primarily interested in vital problems should bring up again and again in its aesthetic theories the problem of existence. It seems to be one of the irreconcilable antitheses in romanticism that when it pursued art it did so for art's sake and yet scarcely concealed the vital problems which have been developed in the previous chapter. It is but rarely that one finds romanticism applying single-mindedly the formula *l'art pour l'art*. To be sure, it refused absolutely, just as did classicism, to enslave art for inartistic purposes. Inasmuch as it seemed to extend the field of poetry into infinity and sought to turn life into poetry and to bring poetry into life, there followed naturally and inevitably the depiction of life in poetic garb.

Even when the youthful Friedrich Schlegel set forth towering ideas in literary and cultural history, one feels that what was actually hovering before him and primarily engaging his attention were the problems of the romantic conception of life. But so slowly did he trace the spiritual development of the history of mankind and its poetry that others, chiefly Schleiermacher, Schelling, and Novalis, were able to approach, before he did, the solution of the problems with which he himself in letters to

34

his brother had long before grappled. This much is true at least, that before he had time to publish them himself many of his own ideas were returned to him at second-hand, having meanwhile been developed by others. Hence for a long time he was considered to be by no means an original thinker but merely a zealous, rather over-zealous, appropriator of the ideas of others. As a matter of fact, not he, but his brother Wilhelm, played this rôle. [11]

The romantic theory was at first developed by Friedrich Schlegel from the point of view of literary aesthetics. He took up a catchword of Herder's and would fain have become the Winckelmann of Greek literature; besides smaller essays he presented the grandiosely conceived fragment of his *History of the Poetry of the Greeks and Romans* (1798). But he did not wish merely to characterize and describe. He always stressed systematic, constructive historiography. He gave new interpretation to the historio-philosophic problems which Rousseau, chiefly, bequeathed to the eighteenth century.

Rousseau, not always and not in his maturest manifestations but rather in his most effective youthful essays, recalled to the overcultivated world the simplicity of primitive existence. For a long time, thanks to Rousseau's impetus, the philosophy of history revolved about this one problem. But the contentment of the primitive social order, or rather lack of order, did not seem at all plausible to German thinkers. German idealism very soon renounced the desire to lead humanity backwards to a doubtful contentment which contained no trace of culture, and sought rather to lure it on to culturally higher spiritual perfection. Kant, Fichte, Schiller, and Hemsterhuis, also, point in this direction. Not contentment but moral goodness, not a spiritless, golden age of the past, but a spiritually quickened golden age of the future is what Schiller hoped to attain (11, p. LXII f.). No one had more implicit faith in this ideal than Novalis.

To be sure, it had to be admitted that, according to Rousseau, culture had made humanity one-sided and inharmonious. The only alternative, if one would not complacently accept this disadvantage, would be to envisage this lost harmony in the future, to make of it an ideal toward which man must ever strive but which he can never hope to attain. This cultural historic interpretation lies behind ethical views which are peculiar to romanticism as well as to classicism. As a romanticist Friedrich Schlegel should have been in conscience bound to take the part of the disunited but spiritually richer variability of modern culture rather than that of the simple harmony of the old. Curiously enough his essay *Ueber das Studium der griechischen Poesie* (1797) presents exactly the opposite point of view. Not of his own accord but largely through Schiller's inspiration he later arrived at a fuller appreciation of modern culture. Before he acquiesced to this impetus, however, he underwent a period of "revolutionary mania for objectivity." Not until he surmounted this did the romanticist in him become fully conscious.

The essay *Ueber das Studium der griechischen Poesie,* like the sketches *Ueber die Grenzen des Schoenen* and *Vom Wert des Studiums der Griechen und Roemer,* attempts to determine the relation of ancient and modern art and culture. In the second half of the eighteenth century, under the influence of Winckelmann's interpretation of the ancient, not only Herder, Goethe, Schiller, and von Humboldt, but also Garve, Forster, Bouterweck, and many others tried to solve this problem. In place of Rousseau's antithesis of a state of nature, primitive, to be sure, but harmoniously content, over against a cultural state which was chary of contentment and lop-sided, there entered into the discussions of the ancient and the modern the antithesis of ancient unity and modern disunity. Winckelmann's conception of the noble simplicity and quiet grandeur of all that was Greek had made it possible to substitute for the continuity of primitive peoples, which was found in Rousseau's antithesis, the artistically ennobled harmony of Greece, which was a worthier ideal for the highly educated son of the eighteenth century than the intellectual poverty of primitive peoples. The spiritual advantages of the primitives, such as their absolute harmony, were preserved to the Greeks in their capacity as idealized primitives. Furthermore, the Greeks of Sophocles' and Phidias' time were regarded as in a stage of unconscious, instinctive art, which makes the conformation of the Greeks to Rousseau's primitives still more pronounced. Friedrich Schlegel, like Schiller, proceeding from these premises, applied Kant's historic rule to the ancients and the moderns, and found in the former nature and in the latter art, that is, artfulness. He took these conceptions so seriously that in his essay *Vom Wert des Studiums der Griechen und Roemer* he attributed to the ancient cultural development a circular motion and to the modern a continuous straightforward one. For according to Herder, natural, organic development runs in circles; whereas, in conscious artistic development Kant had discovered the inevitability of continuous ascent.

When Friedrich Schlegel compared ancient and modern, he not only interpreted but sought to fathom the nature of both by contemplative study. And thus, wholly in the spirit of a subtle observation of Goethe's (*Italian Jour-*

ney, May 17, 1787) and probably inspired also by an observation of Bouterweck's, he reached the conclusion that modern poetry had a preponderance of the individual, the characteristic, and the philosophic, and an eagerness for whatever was interesting, piquant, and striking. As soon as the "interesting" was recognized as the distinguishing feature of modern poetry, Friedrich Schlegel could, in accordance with Kant's *Kritik der Urteilskraft,* declare that modern poetry indeed was not concerned with the beautiful; for according to Kant, the beautiful arouses a disinterested satisfaction. Thus ancient poetry alone would have the prerogative of belonging to the world of the beautiful. The modern in comparison seemed *manieriert* (affected)—an expression borrowed from Goethe's usage (33, 54 ff.; cf. *Jahrbuch der Goethe-Gesellschaft,* 1, 41 f.-*A,* p. 294). It was also imitative of Goethe when Friedrich set classical poetry as the representative of objectivity over against this affected poetry of the "interesting." Christian Gottfried Koerner, Schiller's friend, who at this time was wholly under the influence of Goethe's aesthetics, also loved the conception of objectivity; and from Koerner Friedrich Schlegel derived much inspiration in his early years. At length Greek poetry revealed itself in its historical development as the "everlasting natural history of good taste and art" on account of its conformity to nature and its organic ascent, undeterred by any extraneous aims.

This process of derivation accorded to the spirit of Greece and its poetry the unique distinction which, shortly before, and probably under the influence of Wilhelm von Humboldt, Schiller's letters *Ueber die aesthetische Erziehung des Menschen* (1795) had demanded. It really was not quite just of Schiller to mock in the *Xenien* at Friedrich Schlegel's Graecomania and to presume to see the profound truth which he himself had proclaimed to the world turned topsy-turvy by Schlegel, for Schiller himself had meanwhile assumed another point of view. The treatise *Ueber naive und sentimentalische Dichtung* (1795-6) discussed the advantages which accrued to the modern poet in spite of all the greatness and significance of ancient poetry; the modern sentimental poet had the advantage over the ancient naïve poet because of his broader intellectual culture and because humanity had achieved a greater development in reason and ideas.

For Friedrich Schlegel's proportion: "The ancient is to the modern as the objective is to the interesting" corresponds to Schiller's proportion: "The ancient is to the modern as the naïve is to the sentimental." Owing to the date of publication of these closely related studies by Schiller and Schlegel, it was falsely assumed that Schlegel had merely developed Schiller's hypothesis. As a matter of fact, Schlegel's interpretation had been finished long before he ever read Schiller's treatise. Neither is Schiller's proportion based upon the artistic manner and aesthetic impression of ancient and modern poetry, as is Schlegel's. Schiller based his upon natural feeling and decided that in the case of the ancient poet, who in the eyes of the eighteenth century had a natural point of view, this feeling was naïve while in the case of the modern poet, who by reason of his inharmonious culture yearned for the harmonious unity of nature, this feeling was sentimental. This was the observation of the eighteenth century frame of mind, which was decidedly sentimental, that is, filled with a yearning for nature.

The sentimental being who is consumed by yearning is, moreover, very closely related to the romantic, yearning man of reason. Schiller's treatise determined the artistic significance of these kinds of people and poets. And Friedrich Schlegel learned from Schiller that he had not been quite fair to the sentimentalists, the moderns, whom he had stamped as the advocates of the interesting, the non-beautiful. The romanticist had treated the coterie to which the romanticists themselves belonged less kindly than the classicist Schiller. It is to Schiller's credit, therefore, that he helped romanticism to the consciousness and knowledge of its own significance. Hence Friedrich Schlegel's mania for objectivity vanished immediately and after the publication of his treatise *Ueber das Studium der griechischen Poesie* he joined at once and unreservedly the ranks of the moderns, the romanticists.

The bitter words which Friedrich Schlegel heaped upon the moderns in his study grew merely out of disguised affection. He treated them so badly because spiritually they were so close to him. For among them were his very favorites, Dante and Shakespeare. He still made exceptions for both of them among the moderns. But even now he was buoyantly hopeful for the new and rising German poetry. His hopes were based upon a "remarkable and mighty symptom," Goethe's poetry, which was in his estimation the "dawn of genuine art and pure beauty" (Minor, 1,114). The explanation of this is found in Friedrich's letter to Wilhelm, February 27, 1794. "It seems to me the problem of our poetry is the synthesis of the essentially modern and the essentially ancient; if I add that Goethe, the first representative of the new era in art, has begun to approach this goal, you will understand very well what I mean" (p. 170).

This citation also reveals the fact that at first Friedrich Schlegel still clung too firmly to the classic principle of

harmony to allow him to consider favorably the adoption of the genuine romantic trait of vibrating between
antitheses. If our goal be not indeed harmonious objectivity, let us at least strive for harmony between ancient
objectivity and modern subjectivity—that is what he
meant to say in 1794. Here too he was very close
to Schiller. It remained for Fichte to lead him on to new
points of view.

2. FRIEDRICH SCHLEGEL'S ADOPTION OF ROMANTICISM. ROMANTIC POETRY, ROMANTIC IRONY, TRANSCENDENTAL POETRY

In a trice Friedrich Schlegel, after his "affected hymn
in prose to the objective in poetry," adopted the romantic
point of view (*Lyceumfragment* 7).

The Fichtean elements of the early romantic creed developed above (p. 26 ff.) would perforce place a higher
estimate upon modern poetry. Fichte's conception of "intellectual perception" increased the significance of the
conscious, self-directing creative artist. Fichte also emphasized absolute human freedom and variability. Ethically
Fichte interpreted these qualities much more strictly than
the romanticists; the latter merely found substantiation
for their protean variability and the ease with which they
swung from pole to pole when Fichte's lecture *Ueber die
Bestimmung des Gelehrten* (1794) declared: "To master
the irrational, to govern it freely according to its own
laws is the ultimate purpose of humanity. This purpose
is quite unattainable and must forever remain so if man
is not to cease being human and to become divine. But
he can and must approach this goal; hence the never-ending approach to this goal is the true destiny of humanity."

In the *Athenaeumfragment* 116, 1798, Friedrich Schlegel transferred all these traits from humanity to romantic poetry. Romantic poetry is a progressive universal poetry; it is still in the process of becoming; that, indeed, is its peculiar nature—that it can only become and never can be completed. No theory can set it forth exhaustively and nothing short of a divining critique might dare to attempt to characterize its ideal. It alone is infinite just as it alone is free and recognizes as its highest law that the sovereign will of the poet recognizes no law above itself. Point for point were reiterated the demands which Fichte made upon man and his progressive universal activity—to be sure with the added clause which turned rigid self-discipline into spontaneous activity of the will. But in the same *Fragment* Fichte's intellectual perception was used to determine the nature of romantic poetry: the reflection of a thinking, active person upon his thoughts and deeds, the ability to see himself as in a mirror. For, according to Friedrich Schlegel, romantic poetry was most capable of hovering upon the wings of poetic reflection, midway between that which was presented and him who presented it, unfettered by any real or ideal interest, intensifying this reflection and multiplying it as in an endless series of mirrors. Such a poetry of intellectual perception enabled the romantic artist primarily to raise himself at any time above his own creation and his own creative act and to observe both with a critical eye. It admitted, in a word, of romantic irony.

The *Geschichte der Poesie der Griechen und Roemer* was already mindful of the Socratic irony "which links that which is most holy with the frivolous and joyous" (Minor, 1, 239, 15). The *Lyceumfragmente* 42 and 108 gave more specific definitions, while the most outstanding

varieties of irony were still more completely developed
by the essay *Ueber die Unverstaendlichkeit* (2, 392 f.).
Friedrich Schlegel's aphoristic remarks concerning irony,
from the standpoint of the subsequent development of
romantic thought, received the most thoughtful elucida-
tion in the fourth discourse of K.W.F. Solger's *Erwin*
(1815). The antithesis which naturally exists between
Schlegel's suggestions and Solger's subjective conception
of irony is prone, since Hegel's time, to be over-estimated.
Romantic irony was very intimately associated with
Fichte's intellectual perception and the demand to raise
oneself above oneself, which the romanticists deduced
from Fichte's formula. At the same time, however, it
was the result of a dawning consciousness that a rational
human being can never wholly satisfy his metaphysical
desires; in short, it was a frank confession that, involved
in the finite as he is, he can never exhaust the infinite.
Even for the romanticist there remained between the infinite and every attempt to put it into words an insuper-
able gap. The human spirit becomes aware of its inadequacy and with wise self-limitation offers its pronouncements in a way which in itself already admits this inadequacy. The admission of constant inadequacy, however, is the first proof that humanity does not persist in
vain self-reflection but is lifted by means of its spirit
beyond the shortcomings of its understanding. It is—
in Fichtean parlance—the final resort of man in his effort
to master the non-ego by means of the ego. Hence Friedrich Schlegel could very well say that self-limitation is
the ultimate, inevitable requisite of an artist and a human
being (*Lyceumfragment* 37).

By means of romantic irony, the consciousness of the
most unlimited spiritual freedom rises from such self-

limitation. By what appears to be a case of utter self-renunciation the romanticist attained the greatest variability and the most unlimited self-determination. It is the same high level of unhampered human nature which Schiller visualized in his discourse *Ueber die aesthetische Erziehung des Menschen,* in which he recognizes in the activity of the play instinct the purest, most vigorous expression of human nature, and declares that man is wholly human only when he is at play. Romantic irony also transforms the most difficult spiritual and intellectual thought-processes into play. Schiller's theory of the play instinct, however, has its source in Fichte's philosophy exactly as does the doctrine of romantic irony.

Romantic irony enables humanity to hover free and unfettered over all things in the universe. By means of it the variability which was indispensable to the protean romantic nature was preserved. By means of it the romanticist was reared to "urbanity" and kept from all "illiberality." The problem of culture in the romantic theory here took on its most peculiar trait: the harmony toward which classicism strove being unattainable in its entirety, one must seek to approach it by way of the utmost versatility (cf. *Lyceumfragment* 55).

A conspicuous trait of romantic culture, saturated as it was with irony, was wit. There are unnumbered reflections upon it in Friedrich Schlegel's notes. From the conception of wit which was peculiar to the eighteenth century and which is nearest kin to the "esprit" of the French, he proceeded to a form of wit which became an indispensable element in romantic philosophy (*Athenaeumfragment* 116, *Lyceumfragment* 16). The *Athenaeumfragment* 220 distinguishes between purely poetic wit which resolves expectancy into nothing (Friedrich Schlegel had Kant's definition of laughter in mind—*Kritik der Urteilskraft,* § 54) and the much more significant philosophical wit. The philosophical type of wit, which Friedrich Schlegel would like to have made, even in the case of Bacon, Leibnitz, and Kant, the source of very important discoveries, was valued all the more highly by him inasmuch as philosophy was nothing to him but the spirit of universality, the science of all the sciences which in their flux integrate and again disintegrate—a chemical reaction in the field of logic. His *Fragmente* and those of Hardenberg are the best evidence of the expectations both entertained in respect to the daring combinations yet to be produced by a logical chemistry of this sort (cf. Olshausen, p. 42 ff.).

In accordance with the assumption set forth above, romantic poetry is nothing less than "transcendental poetry" (*Athenaeumfragment* 238). Just as transcendental philosophy is critical and presents the creator as well as the creation and embodies, moreover, in a system of transcendental thought a characteristic of transcendental thinking, just so transcendental poetry relates "the transcendental elements not infrequently prevailing in modern authors and the preliminaries to a poetic theory of imagination to the artistic reflection and lovely self-portrayals which are found in Pindar, the lyric fragments of the Greeks, and the ancient elegies, and, among the newer poets, in Goethe." In all of its various manifestations transcendental poetry should portray also itself and be at all times simultaneously poetry and poetry of poetry.

"Poetry of poetry"—another of Friedrich Schlegel's difficult catchwords. The *Athenaeumfragment* 238 is concerned with a type of poetry which makes itself the object of presentation, in which the poet himself is seen at his task. Indeed, it was a favorite form of romantic irony to put the poet himself as well as the art of poetizing into poetry and to allow the poet and the reader to rise above the poetic creation by continually destroying its technical correctness and its illusion. Poetizing once more conceived in the sense of Fichte's intellectual perception! The poet observes his own creative act and weaves it into poetry; the reader, likewise, should freely and consciously enjoy poetry as poetry and only as poetry. The theory, sponsored likewise by Schiller and Goethe, that a work of art should not produce an absolute illusion but should rather keep the reader and observer aware of the fact that they are in the presence of art and not of reality, was here most consistently adhered to (cf. W. Schlegel's *Berlin Lectures*, 1, 262, 15). From this point of view Goethe's *Wilhelm Meister* seemed to the critic Friedrich Schlegel to be poetry of poetry (Minor, 2, 171, 30 ff.).

But to Friedrich Schlegel poetry of poetry was also something quite different, something much higher, as was presently revealed in the *Athenaeumfragmente;* "Goethe's purely poetic poetry is the sheerest poetry of poetry" (Number 247). Here poetry of poetry appears as the antithesis of poetry of poetastry. Here Friedrich Schlegel touches upon the solution of the most difficult problem in poetics, the question of the nature of the poetic. In this Fichtean phase of his theory, however, he could not as yet give a satisfactory answer. Later he found one. (See p. 70 ff.).

In the theory of romantic irony lay also the basis for the theory of genius. An unconscious, dreamily creative genius cannot be thought of as springing from such soil. All the advantages which Friedrich Schlegel had claimed in the days of his objectivity for the artist who created instinctively vanish. The conception of genius cherished by the Storm and Stress was definitely put aside. Genius must have a hold upon itself, must be under self-control. "An artist in the heat of inspiration is, to say the least, in an illiberal condition for communicating his ideas." (*Lyceumfragment* 37). And so Friedrich Schlegel can only bemoan the fact that there are artists, who, while they probably do not think too highly of art (for that would be quite impossible), are, nevertheless, not quite versatile enough to rise above their greatest effort (*Lyceumfragment* 87).

Gradually subjectivity assumes the place which objectivity had held in Friedrich Schlegel's first period. The poets who, as opponents of the Greeks, played decidedly less exalted parts in those days are now, since the significance of the modern has been thoroughly grasped, elevated to quite different rôles. That *Athenaeumfragment* (247) which designates Goethe's purely poetic poetry as the sheerest poetry of poetry calls Dante's prophetic poem the only system of transcendental poetry and still the highest of its kind, and furthermore declares that Shakespeare's universality is like the core of romantic art, and finds in Dante, Shakespeare, and Goethe the mighty triumvirate of modern poetry.

The *Discourse upon Poetry* (1800) does not add greatly to this verdict. Cervantes, Ariosto, Sterne, Jean Paul, and others merely serve to explain more fully the nature of this now fully recognized modern romantic poetry. A new definition of romanticism is developed: that which presents sentimental content in fanciful form is romantic (Minor, 2, 370, 43). It is still reminiscent of the definitions in the *Athenaeumfragmente* which were inspired by Fichte. The hopes which the essay *Ueber das Studium der griechischen Poesie* placed in the immediate present now find a new foundation; even here there is allusion to transcendental idealism and to Fichte (2, 353, 2). But Friedrich does not here have only Fichte in mind; the men who practically condition the third stage of his romantic theory are ushered in: Schleiermacher, Schelling, and Novalis.

III. THE THIRD STAGE OF THE EARLY ROMANTIC THEORY

1. SCHLEIERMACHER'S EARLY INFLUENCE

IN the spring of 1799 Schleiermacher finished his first independent publication, *Ueber die Religion; Reden an die Gebildeten unter Ihren Veraechtern*. The book was the result of studies in Spinoza which he had pursued together with Friedrich Schlegel. The latter, critically concerned, supervised the printing with great care. Spinoza's pantheism or acosmism asserted that the infinite encompassed all that was finite. From this dogmatic assertion Schleiermacher educed his religious postulate that all that is finite is to be found in the infinite. For the infinite, he contended, is grasped only in the religious process; if the mind is concentrated upon the infinite, religion ensues. Schleiermacher based his assertion upon an investigation of the psychological process of perception and determined the moment in which the conception of the universe, together with a mighty effusion of emotion, is awakened in man. From this point of view, man becomes religious when he is permeated with a feeling of dependence upon the universe. Religion to Schleiermacher was, moreover, neither metaphysical nor moral; it was perception of the universe. He had two ends in view: first, to isolate the essentially infinite, eternal, single from the flux of finite things lest it be submerged thereby; second, to grasp the presence of this infinite, eternal, single principle in finite things and to reconcile the contradiction between the infinite and the finite.

49

That which is individual is likewise infinite; it is the expression and reflection of infinity. Individuality in the higher sense, human individuality, springs from the union of the infinite and the finite. Every human being represents an individuality. But in each individuality only those faculties are potential which determine the nature of humanity; hence every human being is a compendium of humanity itself. And when a man has found infinity within himself, religion is achieved. The radius along which we proceed from infinity in order to become specific and individual beings is the voice of conscience, which imposes upon every one his particular task and through which the infinite will is carried over into the finite world.

Through self-perception we attain perception of the infinite. Self-perception becomes the organ of moral culture. It reveals in individuality the expression and reflection of the universe. "Whenever I gaze upon my inward self, I am immediately in the realms of eternity. I behold the activity of the spirit which no world can change, which time cannot destroy, which itself creates both world and time." Thus read Schleiermacher's *Monologen* (1800), which proceeded from his religious views to the formulation of his ethical convictions.

The crux of Schleiermacher's ethics is: the aspiration of every human being is to win for the ideal inherent within himself free play and ample development, and to have love and understanding sustain it (Dilthey, *Schleiermacher*, p. 454). The aim of his ethics is the achievement of the free individual will. "To become ever more intensively that which I am is my only will. Every action is a special development of this one will. Come then what may!"

Schleiermacher's ethics matured in his posthumous

study *Entwurf eines Systems der Sittenlehre*. The demands of the *Monologen* are here reiterated, when in the complete development of the individual, who is manifesting his inner life in full harmony with his various faculties, is sought the ethical task of humanity. Every being has his individual task and fulfills it by perfecting himself. In this absorbing aim recourse must be had to every phase of the cultural life of society. The moral law is thus seen to be the inevitable inner function of an intelligent being. It is not in fundamental antithesis to the law of nature, as Kant conceives it to be. Interpreting ethically the evolutionary idea of Leibnitz, Herder, and Schelling, Schleiermacher allowed one feature in the process of becoming perfect to pass over from nature into history. His idea was not to destroy the lesser aims but to bring them to a level with the higher. A certain kinship with Schiller's attempt to mitigate Kant's rigor is not to be denied.

The *Reden* had such a tremendous effect upon the romantic fraternity that only the most discerning observation can differentiate Schleiermacher's contribution to the romantic theory from Schelling's. Henceforth the problem of the infinite and of the universe was of primary importance to the romanticists. This was the point of departure for the attempts to put man and infinity in close alliance. Schleiermacher indicated one of the ways by which, in the romantic sense, the absolute became accessible to man (see above, p. 28 ff.).

2. SCHELLING AND THE ROMANTICISTS

a) *Aesthetic philosophy and the organic conception*. Three phases of Schelling's philosophy are important for

cultural history and for the poetry of romanticism: (1)
his natural philosophy, particularly as presented in the
Ideen zu einer Philosophie der Natur, 1797; in the treatise, *Von der Weltseele, eine Hypothese der hoeheren
Physik,* 1799; and in the *Entwurf eines Systems der Na-
turphilosophie,* 1799; (2) his aesthetic idealism, which is
presented by his *System des transcendentalen Idealismus*
(1805); (3) his system of identity, which he first explained in his essay *Darstellung meines Systems der Philosophie* (1801) and subsequently in a series of supple-
mentary essays. In the first phase Schelling linked Fichte's
Wissenschaftslehre with Herder's and Goethe's vitalistic
conception of nature; in the second, he boldly entered the
field of aesthetics and arrived at conclusions which suggest Schiller; the third stage was conditioned by Spinoza.
Schelling's natural philosophy regards nature as one
vast system which has proceeded from reason. Nature is
assumed to be an unconscious form of rational life having
the tendency to generate conscious forms. Nature is the
Odyssey in which the soul, finally at rest after much diva-
gation, finds its abiding place, that is, finds itself. Philosophic knowledge of nature here conceives the whole process of nature as a purposeful coöperation of forces,
leading from the lowest forms of existence to the highest
forms of animal life and of consciousness. Nature must
be envisaged as a vast organism, the component parts of
which are ordained to generate life and consciousness.
The philosophy of nature is thus the account of the soul
in the process of becoming; the different phases of natural
life are the "categories" of nature, inevitable intermediary
forms, in which reason progresses from unconsciousness
into consciousness.

Nature, likewise, is intelligence in the process of becoming. In the development through which it must pass, the isolated incident is regarded not as an end in itself but merely as an inevitable means to an end. The individual in nature is but a passing moment in which the alternating play of forces comes to a halt only immediately to begin again. There is antagonism in nature between antithetical forces. But the basis of all natural processes is not only dualism and polarity but also the synthesis of these antithetical forces. Thus Fichte's triadic rhythm of thesis, antithesis, and synthesis becomes the principle of deduction in natural philosophy. At the same time a favorite idea of Goethe's is put to account (cf. p. 23, above).

The antithesis between nature and reason had remained indispensable to Kant's and Fichte's metaphysics, even though they, too, had to recognize the postulation of nature by reason. Schelling did away with this antithesis by characterizing nature as a process of reason.

Nature philosophy is the doctrine of the becoming of the ego; transcendental idealism is the doctrine of the ego itself. Neither in theory nor in practice does the ego reach its highest development; in both it is unbalanced. This lack of balance is removed only in the aesthetic function of the ego. For genius is the unconscious-conscious activity of the ego; its creation, art, is the finished presentation of the nature of the ego. Art displays the absolute balance between unconscious and conscious activity which is otherwise not possible in experience and which is thinkable only in infinity. It is only in art that the sensual and spiritual worlds merge; for genius is the intelligence which operates in the capacity of nature. Thus art becomes the highest instrument of philosophy because it solves the problem which is the crux of philosophic thought. Every true work of art is a manifestation of the absolute world unity, expressed in a perfect form. In such a work of art the antithesis between the impulse of thought and of will is removed.

Art is the consummation of man's mundane existence; it is the maturest manifestation of the ego, which, in turn, is the fundamental basis of all reality. Hence aesthetic force becomes dominant in Schelling's philosophy. In Schelling's system of identity that level is finally reached toward which nature had gradually struggled in the earlier phases of his philosophy. Through his treatment nature became independent and assumed equal rank with the ego. By this time, nature and the ego sought derivation from a common source. Spinoza's doctrine suggested to Schelling that nature and spirit represented the two methods of manifestation of the absolute; and like Spinoza he soon called the absolute God.

The absolute is to Schelling neither ideal nor real, neither spirit nor nature, but rather the undifferentiated union of all antitheses. At the same time the absolute admits the possibility of being differentiated within itself and becoming a system of varying phenomena. According to Schelling absolute reason develops along two lines: in the one nature predominates, in the other, the spirit. In none of these particular phenomena does the absolute achieve perfect form; in the human organism, for example, the physical predominates, in the best products of an artist the ideal is most prominent. Hence the perfect display of absolute reason is possible only in the universe, in the sum total of all phenomena. The universe, furthermore, is the most perfect of all organisms and the most consummate work of art; it is identical with the absolute organism and the absolute work of art.

The nature philosophy of the Renaissance had likewise conceived of the universe as an organism and a work of art. Hence, Schelling, in 1802, made Giordano Bruno, the greatest of the Italian nature philosophers, the advocate of his doctrine and developed his aesthetic pantheism in the dialogue *Bruno; oder ueber das natuerliche und goettliche Prinzip der Dinge.*

At this third stage Schelling's philosophy cast off the Fichtean form; he no longer proceeded from the ego but from nature, from that which had formerly been posited and made real by the ego. Nature now demands to be judged independent of subjective consciousness.

To determine how much of Schleiermacher's *Reden* and *Monologen* was derived from Schelling, naturally only the work of the latter's first period, that is the period of his nature philosophy, need be considered. Schleiermacher's point of departure, from which he wrested his realistic delight in the finite, was religion. This point of departure was foreign to Schelling. Furthermore, Schelling's realism emerged in the third stage of his development, in the philosophy of identity. This realism of his may have been previously developing, it may have even announced its presence, but surely Schleiermacher professed his realism before Schelling; perhaps he, along with others, led the way for Schelling. Like Schleiermacher, Schelling, too, in his earliest essays, was working upon the problem of the visible presence of the infinite in the finite. Again one gets the impression that Schelling's transcendental idealism and philosophy of identity more nearly approximate Schleiermacher's conception and emphasize more strongly the problem of reproducing the infinite in finite form than does natural philosophy. Perhaps this was the result of Schleiermacher's influence.

Certain it is that Schelling's verdict on individuality meanwhile underwent a change which brought him over to Schleiermacher; at any rate his nature philosophy promulgates a theory much less favorable to individuality than did Schleiermacher's doctrine of personality.

The turn toward aesthetics which takes place in the second and third phases of Schelling's romantic development is to be found in the *Reden*. Schleiermacher specifically emphasizes the relationship which exists between the religious process and the aesthetic impression (*Reden*, Ed. 1, p. 149; Dilthey, *Leben Schleiermachers*, p. 304). At this point, to be sure, Schelling derived nothing from Schleiermacher; the parallel between the universe and a work of art was suggested to him in more detailed fashion elsewhere. The hasty remarks of Schleiermacher were far surpassed in potency by Goethe, one of the chief sources of Schelling's philosophy. To interlink artistic creation and the observation of nature was self-evident to Goethe, particularly after his Italian journey (cf. *Jahrbuch der Goethe Gesellschaft*, 1, 21 ff.).

It is a very difficult task to determine how far the romanticists were indebted to Schelling for the conception and application of the organic hypothesis. Unquestionably no one developed it as logically in all its phases as did Schelling. But equally certain it is that Friedrich Schlegel's line of thought was from the very first directed to the same end. Very soon he applied aesthetically the conception which has a long previous history in the philosophy of art of the eighteenth century and which was handed over to Schelling, as well as to Friedrich Schlegel, in highly perfected form by Goethe, Herder, and Moritz (see above, p. 20 f.).

The distinguishing trait of the organic conception is

the desire to grasp each phenomenon as a whole, and, whether the world itself, or just a part of it, is being studied and evaluated, to concentrate on the idea of the whole, the unit. The *Athenaeumfragment* 116 and the definition of romantic poetry which it essays (see above, p. 42 f.) are built upon the idea of a unified whole, and that without any inspiration from Schelling. "Romantic poetry is a universal progressive poetry. Its aim is to reunite the diversified genres of poetry . . . it embraces everything that is poetic, from the greatest system of art, which itself merges other systems, to a sigh, a kiss, which a musing child breathes in artless song. . . . It is capable of the most consummate, most universal culture, not only from within but also from without, inasmuch as it develops impartially all the component parts of each and every one of its products which is to represent a unit." But long before this, Friedrich Schlegel pressed on toward the unit, the whole, in a work of art. In the middle of May, 1793, he wrote to his brother (p. 86) : "There are but two laws in poetry, one of which is: the diverse must inevitably be joined to inner unity, by which must inevitably be determined the being, place, and significance of everything else." Friedrich Schlegel gave a new lease of life to the dry, rationalistic, purely schematic aesthetic categories, unity and diversity. He continued to pursue the course which Herder, Lenz, and Goethe had followed in the Storm and Stress period and which also had been the object of K. Ph. Moritz's speculations. In aesthetics Friedrich Schlegel's knowledge and evaluation of organic unity increased continuously and rapidly until he conceived not only an individual work of art but all of art itself as an organic unit. Proudly he says, in 1804, in the preface to the first volume of *Les-*

sings Gedanken und Meinungen (p. 34): "We have set up the interpretation and knowledge of unity (in art and poetry) as the one most essential fundamental requisite for a critique which is truly to fulfill its noble purpose." Lessing is claimed as the precursor of the tendency. It is self-evident that the organic interpretation of art as a whole meant to Friedrich Schlegel an historical interpretation also.

But the wish to conceive of a work of art as an organic whole has its source in Friedrich Schlegel's metaphysical desires. Like Schopenhauer, Friedrich Schlegel would view a work of art in its deepest interrelations and become aware of the unity which prevails in the midst of its diversity. From the individual work of art he proceeds logically to art as a whole.

Did Friedrich Schlegel, perhaps, meanwhile learn from Schelling to regard the whole world, the universe, as an organism? In the *Ideen* and in the *Gespraech ueber die Poesie* (2, 339. 364) this attitude is presented quite in the form of Schelling's aesthetic idealism. The universe as a work of art! Schlegel surely came to this conviction as soon as Schleiermacher had again brought the universe to his notice. It was only necessary at this time to reawaken in Friedrich the old conceptions into which meanwhile new life had been breathed. For from the beginning he had been in the habit of extending his views of organic unity beyond the confines of aesthetics to the conception of the whole world. His letter to Wilhelm, August 28, 1793, states the parallelisms which are reiterated in the *Ideen,* in the *Gespraech,* as well as in Schelling's aesthetic idealism. Without indeed using Schelling's own expression, Friedrich here anticipated Schelling's conception of the universe as the sum total of all phenomena, and of this universe he predicated all those qualities which he had previously claimed for a work of art.

How much, if anything, Schelling derived from Friedrich Schlegel for the second and third phases of his romantic period will probably never be determined beyond contradiction, for both are based upon Goethe's and Herder's aesthetics and conception of nature. But Schlegel seems to have recognized sooner than Schelling the relationship between Goethe's artistic manner of thinking and his scientific. Goethe himself inducted Schelling into these relationships but not before Schlegel had long since grasped the full significance of the organic conception for aesthetics as well as for the conception of nature.

Thus the doctrine of the *Mittelpunkt,* which plays such an important rôle in the organic philosophy of Friedrich Schlegel, may well be traced back directly to its original source, Goethe (36, p. XLIII) and Moritz. Marie Joachimi (*Weltanschauung der Romantik,* 1905, p. 33 ff.) would make the doctrine of centralism, the *Zentrumslehre,* Friedrich Schlegel's peculiar creed.

The artistic form which resulted from these conceptions is not, according to Plotinus, determined by external laws but by something innate. It conforms to the purpose of an individual work of art only. This attitude toward form leads easily to open, loose construction. It avoids the stringent demands of well-defined outlines. It harmonizes with the aims of so-called German formlessness. It can produce deliquescent forms which have a tendency to vanish altogether. German romanticism did not avoid these final consequences, but Goethe's classic creations, even though based likewise upon organic aesthetics, nevertheless, preserved the regular forms of art. To be sure, Goethe himself, at times, and particularly during the era of romanticism, deviated from such forms of art and did homage to more mutable, less sharply outlined forms.

b) *Schelling's natural philosophy*. To appreciate Schelling's, and later Schlegel's and Hardenberg's natural philosophy, one must cast a glance upon the development of the natural sciences in the second half of the eighteenth century. Novalis and Friedrich Schlegel, and Schelling, too, would have been less daring in their interpretations of natural philosophy, if they had not stood in the presence of new and surprising discoveries which upset man's entire conception of natural processes. When the announcement of new discoveries in the realm of the natural sciences is a matter of almost daily occurrence, the scientific imagination begins to work with feverish haste. Magic and mysticism put in their appearance and, impatient, outstrip the results of research, which, though moving rapidly, is nevertheless too slow for the restlessness and overzealousness of scientific enthusiasts.

In physics the theory of the force of gravity had led Kant, 1755, and most definitely LaPlace, 1798, to their hypothesis of the origin of the solar system. Chladni demonstrated, in 1787, the vibratory condition of plates and discs in acoustic figures. In 1789 Galvani's experiments with frogs gave proof of animal electricity; another electrical phenomenon was thought to have been discovered in the voltic pile until Volta himself proved both forms of electricity to be one and the same. Chemistry was thoroughly transformed by Lavoisier and Priestley, the discoverer of oxygen. Around 1790 there loomed large in the field of the natural sciences another movement which had had its inception approximately a generation earlier: the supplanting of the mechanistic conception of nature by the vitalistic-organic conception. Haller, the great savant of Bern, blazed the trail.

Mesmerism grew out of vitalism. In good faith and in accordance with his best judgment, Mesmer (1733-1815), by drawing false conclusions from perfectly correct observations, developed the doctrine of animal mesmerism. Romanticism down to Justinus Kerner took delight in learning from him. It was a mistake on the part of Mesmer and his adherents to think of predecessors who had relied entirely upon suggestion and hypnotism as holding views similar to theirs. [12] The wealth of new discoveries in magnetism, electricity, and galvanism, which had as yet by no means achieved summary order, opened wide the doors for false hypotheses and arbitrary analogies. The same phenomena caused the dynamic-organic interpretation of natural processes to develop with increasing strength alongside the mechanistic. The vitalistic-organic conception increasingly assumed the leadership, primarily in the organic branches of science.

Goethe was favorable to this conception from the very beginning. He was accustomed to think of himself as a part of nature. Though striving valiantly to remain within the domain of reality and to respect the limits of sense-perception, he, nevertheless, sought to discover the types from which plant and animal life had developed. He was no more inclined to set up phases of development than to seek causes or effects of such phases. Side by side with Goethe's physiological conception there entered into Fichte's works a psychological natural philosophy. For Fichte's triadic schema is just as much a primitive form of evolutionistic thinking as Goethe's doctrine of the types and in last analysis serves to explain the development of spiritual processes.

Schelling at length proceeded from physiological and psychological contemplation to the construction of an evolutionary system and with this in view unhesitatingly manipulated inanimate nature in purely dynamic fashion. Step by step he showed how inanimate nature advances toward the animate. He expressly wished to trace an evolution from the former to the latter. He was not concerned with a theory of descent, nor was it his aim to explain cause and effect. Schelling knew very well (see above, p. 19) how near he here approached the interpretations contained in Herder's *Ideen*. It probably dawned upon him gradually in his association with Goethe how much he was also indebted to the latter. The Fichtean point of view alone was wholly alien to Herder and Goethe: the transcendental-idealistic conception which still directs and dominates Schelling's natural philosophy, the conviction that the ego posits the non-ego, and that without the ego there could be no such thing as nature.

In spite of everything, Goethe, as he admitted to Schelling on September 27, 1800, felt himself decidedly drawn to Schelling's theory, in which he could not fail to recognize his own ideas. "I should like an absolute union," he added at the time. In his poem *Weltseele,* he proceeded to sing dithyrambically of the spiritualization of inanimate nature and of the ascent through nature to the spiritual world (cf. *Goethe und die Romantik,* 1, p. LXXXVII).

The natural historian Goethe did not apply in detail the "categories of nature" of Schelling. He did not go beyond a keen delight in the general conception of natural evolution. But incredulously the sons of a later generation contemplated Schelling's daring juxtapositions, which, to be sure, did inspire many a scientific discovery, but remained, essentially, dreams. One must keep this fact in mind, lest one immediately stamp Hardenberg's yet more daring concatenations as empty paradoxes.

c) *Schlegelizing the natural sciences.* Even to Schelling the natural-philosophic combinations of Hardenberg must have been somewhat disquieting. Hardenberg's *Fragmente,* published in 1802, after his death, contained much material which was merely of ephemeral value but which, having appeared in print, has become fixed as the residue of Hardenberg's thought. Schelling, by applying laboriously and often uncertainly the latest results in physics, evolved an interpretation of nature in which nature appeared, step by step, to be a gradual assumption of consciousness. A human element was thus woven into nature. Novalis and Friedrich Schlegel went even further; they not only transferred spiritual qualities into nature; they saw natural processes of a chemical and electrical sort in the spiritual realm; they sought to interpret what is human by reversing it into the life of nature. Novalis speaks of the tolerance and cosmopolitanism of flowers, propounds the question whether the souls of plant individuals are not, perhaps, ethereal oils; he calls thinking a muscular activity; wit to him is spiritual electricity; logic corresponds to meteorology and he queries, "Can it be perhaps that thinking oxidizes and feeling disoxidizes?" (2, 215). And in accord with his method of applying to nature the relation of the sexes, he maintains, conversely, "Woman is our oxygen" (2, 217). These were very bold concatenations of philosophic wit (see above, p. 44 f.) and attempts to find, by means of mere combination, new scientific horizons.

But rather than Schelling, Franz Baader and Johann Wilhelm Ritter became Hardenberg's props and aids. And he gave them both hearty recognition—with which even modern science is not niggardly in the case of Ritter. Concerning Baader, Hardenberg wrote to Friedrich Schlegel, November 7, 1798, "His deeds of magic reunite that which the sword of stupidity has severed." Apparently Novalis was here thinking of the unifying of the spiritual world and nature. Novalis' letter to Caroline, January 20, 1799, said of Ritter, "Ritter is 'Ritter' (a knight) and we are but squires. Even Baader is merely his poet." Endeavoring to fathom and prove in strictly scientific fashion the newly-discovered phenomenon of galvanism, Ritter published, in 1798, his *Proof That Galvanism Continuously Accompanies the Life-Processes in the Animal World*. Herein, also, it was attempted to prove that nature is the most perfect organic system. From this new proof of the complete unity of nature, Novalis boldly proceeded to the hypothesis of a "galvanism of the spirit."

The close spiritual contact of these two friends [13] throws some light upon the esoteric conception of "galvanism of the spirit." Friedrich Schlegel, who is the only one to transmit the expression to us, does not seem to be very clear himself about the purport of the conception (*Aus Schleiermachers Leben,* 3, 77. 81). Fragments of Hardenberg's are of not much more assistance (2, 214). E. Spenle (*Novalis,* 1904, p. 205. 210) conjectures that Novalis was led on to Mesmer's "magnetism" by Ritter. Ritter was first and foremost among the natural philosophers to pursue those mystical bonds between nature and the human soul which at that time were thought to exist in the phenomena of hypnotic sleep and he expected to find in them revelations concerning the secrets of the animate and inanimate worlds (*Fragmente aus dem Nachlasse,* 2, 81). In the state of trance (spiritistically speaking) and in hypnotic sleep (medically speaking), Ritter, and with him Novalis, (*Lehrlinge zu Sais,* 4, 26 f.) thought he had discovered a state of "involuntariness" in which the soul in most unhampered fashion beholds the absolute. Thus the consciousness of a human being in this state of involuntariness (according to Fichte, the "intellectual perception" of a person in the hypnotic state) became the key to knowledge. Here the line drawn from Fichte converges with the line which proceeds from the mysticism of the vitalists and from Mesmer. The marvelous results which were expected of Novalis' "magic idealism," the intensification of Fichte's "intellectual perception" to a magic power of self-enchantment and to the occult control of nature (see above, p. 26), had their physical basis and their natural-philosophic probability—so the romantic magicians, Novalis and Ritter, thought—in animal magnetism, in hypnotic sleep, or, as they themselves called it, in the involuntary "clairvoyance" of somnambulism (cf. Ritter, p. 83, 85).

And so one understands why Novalis attached such great importance to "ecstasy" (3, 186, 219). For its stressing of ecstasy, Novalis thought Fichte's "intellectual perception" was of increasing importance in the search for knowledge. The ecstatic seer has visions which are denied all others. Through his emphasis upon ecstasy, however, Novalis was led inevitably to the source of all mysticism —Neoplatonism. The whole endeavor of the romanticists tended toward a supernatural understanding of divine truth vouchsafed to him who is in immediate contact with divinity itself, a conception which was advanced by Neoplatonism. Even Philo stipulated that for this purpose the soul be merely passive and receptive and refrain from all self-direction. In ecstasy of this sort the divine spirit dwells in man, he says. Beyond this state lies all thinking, according to Plotinus; ecstasy is faith and blissful peace in God.

Hence when Novalis (Raich, p. 102) at length pronounces the names to which he himself thinks natural philosophy is most indebted, there appear first Fichte and Hemsterhuis, and then Spinoza. But he goes on to say: "Plotinus, probably inspired by Plato, was the first to enter the sanctuary with the genuine spirit and since then no one has penetrated as far into it as he." Novalis considers Leibnitz' *Theodicee* but a "glorious attempt in the same field." Goethe it is "who is to become the liturgist of this type of physics." [14]

Nowhere certainly did Novalis again find personal endeavor so intuitively anticipated as in Jacob Boehme and his mystic surrender to divinity. He did not become intimately acquainted with him until the beginning of the year 1800, too late, therefore, to learn anything new from him. Boehme was discovered for the romanticists by Tieck and the latter also introduced Novalis to Boehme's teachings. Hardenberg's poem *An Tieck* (1, 224 ff.) could therefore celebrate the subject of its apostrophe, on account of his relation to Boehme, as the "harbinger of dawn." Tieck himself wove his own experiences into his novel *Der Aufruhr in den Cevennen* (1826), and told of the effect of entering Boehme's world from the world of rationalism. Friedrich Schlegel sums up keenly and tersely what the natural philosophers, as a group, found in the shoemaker of Goerlitz (Windischmann, 1, 482 f.): By applying idealism to nature and by profoundly relating the human soul to it, Boehme had anticipated intuitively the knowledge of the latest discoveries. Friedrich is, of course, thinking of the transmission of the spiritual qualities of humanity to nature. "But much more remarkable and characteristic," he adds, "is the approach of his philosophy to poetry. Boehme throughout adopted the poetic point of view; in this respect no other philosophy compares with his; none has such a wealth of allegory and symbolic meaning. Not even Plato was able to regard Greek gods and mythology as profoundly and nobly as we do now, much less to interpret them as penetratingly as Jacob Boehme interprets the symbolical in Christianity." Therefore Friedrich Schlegel maintains that Boehme is a "perfect idealist," a "greater interpreter" than Plato; of all poets and authors he created the loveliest and most significant allegories.

Boehme actually interprets chemical conceptions psychologically and theosophically with a daring not even surpassed by Hardenberg's fragments. His doctrine proceeds from the assertion that both good and bad are derived from the godhead, that the divine and the anti-divine are both contained in the deity, as is sweetness and bitterness, light and darkness. Sweet is to him like quicksilver and the latter, again, he takes as his symbol of organic nature, of plants, animals, and man; bitter corresponds to saltpetre, to the inorganic kingdom, to darkness. The former in his estimation is heaven, the latter, hell. The intermediate member is living fire, sulphur, which acts in the capacity of a destructive fire of anger and also of a benevolent fire of love. These are symbols which were soon used very freely by the romanticists. The fire in the "centrum" very soon came to be, for Friedrich Schlegel, a form of his favorite conception of the *Mittelpunkt*. "In the 'centrum' hidden the eternal fire lies, struggling ever toward the mighty Father, with sweet and yearning heart throbs, raising tree and floweret to the ethereal skies,"

Tieck says in his sonnet *An Friedrich Schlegel,* a poem which "really fathomed the soul of Friedrich Schlegel" (Joachimi, *Weltanschauung der Romantik,* p. 48).

Friedrich Schlegel's observations about Boehme indicate the particular application which the "Schlegelizing of the natural sciences" (Steffens to Schelling, September, 1799) sought and found. There may be much that is arbitrary and fantastical in Novalis' analogies but in the end all these things lead into the realm of poetry; as a poet Novalis could take the privilege of moulding a poetic "physics" into a "doctrine of fantasy" and of discovering in the most fantastic poet the true magician of physics. The poet, Novalis thought, understands nature better than does the scientist. Was this assertion too daring if one took Goethe to be the liturgist of the new physics?

Philosophy was not merely to serve knowledge; it was to pass over into poetry. Nature philosophy, furthermore, was given the very special task of creating a new mythology.

The aridity of modern poetry was blamed upon the lack of mythology not only by Klopstock and Herder but also by Schiller in the *Goetter Griechenlands.* Friedrich Schlegel in the *Rede ueber die Mythologie* in the *Gespraech ueber die Poesie* points out how mythology could be revivified. From out of the profoundest depths of the soul it must be created. The old mythology is to be viewed from Spinoza's point of view and from the angle of the new physics and is thus to receive new life. The other mythologies, too, should be reawakened, particularly those of the Orient. The medium through which all these treasures are to be resuscitated is none other than the "study of physics," "out of the dynamic paradoxes of which there are even

now bursting forth everywhere the most divine revelations of nature" (2, 363).

Simultaneously, again, Schelling indicated mythology
(in his *System des transcendentalen Idealismus*) as the
intermediate member in the return of science to poetry.
And again it cannot be determined whether or not Friedrich Schlegel came upon this idea through Schelling. Certain it is that Schelling had the idea in mind at an early
date, but it is also certain that Schlegel presented it more
boldly, with greater balance and perspective. Indeed, from
its inception, his nature philosophy, as well as that of his
friend Novalis, was conceived much more poetically and
fancifully than Schelling's. To be sure, Schelling, in his
lectures on the philosophy of art, presented the whole
theme in more opulent and better organized fashion, but
at that time he derived his support entirely from his romantic confrères. Wilhelm Schlegel's Berlin lectures were
much concerned with explaining the conception of the
natural-philosophic mythology (1, 354 ff.; 2, 46 ff.).

The transmutation of natural philosophy into poetry
was, perhaps, the greatest acquisition which poetry derived from the romantic theory. At any rate, here was
systematically conceived and stabilized on a high spiritual
plane what poetry had ever practiced unconsciously, but
which was now, by means of conscious art, abundantly
to enrich German poetry: the vivification and humaniza-
tion of nature.

The new romantic mythology did not stop within the
confines of natural philosophy. The effectiveness of Friedrich Schlegel's and Schelling's mythological program and
the great debt which German poetry owed it can be learned
from F. Strich's work *Die Mythologie in der deutschen
Literatur von Klopstock bis Wagner* (1910). This book

also gives a detailed account of the previous history of romantic mythology.

The demand for a new mythology gave great impetus to the fancy of the romantic poets. To the Storm and Stress poet, free creative fancy was far less significant than the ability to feel deeply the weal and woe of life. The idea of transcendental poetry approached the romantic tendency toward free creative fancy. It assured facile mobility and unrestrained extravagance. Nature philosophy, however, offered a new and promising field. The flight of romantic fancy could properly rely upon the ideas which proceeded from Fichte. But inner legitimacy and the ability to engender something organic and alive were guaranteed to fancy by the romanticist through the natural-philosophic spiritualization of the world. The result of both was "poetry of poetry" (see above, p. 45 f.). Through natural philosophy, however, this conception acquired a new meaning.

3. POETRY OF POETRY. ROMANTIC MONISM

Schleiermacher's *Reden* had a tremendous effect, not only on Schelling, but on the romantic fraternity generally. In the first place they kindled Friedrich Schlegel's and Novalis' love for the universe; they strengthened Novalis' and Tieck's tendencies and anticipated kindred desires in Friedrich Schlegel; they led Friedrich Schlegel into the field of ethics and thus provided the hypothesis of *Lucinde*.

Friedrich Schlegel's third collection of fragments, the *Ideen,* was sustained by Schleiermacher's doctrine of the universe. Herein was expressed what is now called the monism of romanticism (M. Joachimi-Dege, *Deutsche Shakespeare-probleme,* 1907, p. 212 f.). Because, as Schelling also subsequently presented it, the infinite revealed itself everywhere in the finite, because the glory of the universe could be recognized in each of its phenomena, the romanticist learned to love reality. Platonically the classicism of Schiller retained the distinction between the "real" world and the "true" world. The romanticists were well aware of the distinction, but for them it was impossible to see the true world in the real world and to rejoice in it. So whereas Schiller laid claim for the poet to the true world in opposition to the real one, Schlegel was convinced that poetry did not achieve the highest reality (Minor, 2, 327). For to him the real was not what was ordinary and common, which was all that Schiller saw in reality; for Schlegel reality has been ennobled by its palpable alliance with the infinite. Thus the romanticist enjoyed the pleasures of life and found life good. He began to love the finite world insofar as infinity was found reflected in it. Just so Plotinus became enthusiastic over the world insofar as it was permeated by the divine spirit.

Love for the infinite, yearning for it, had long been peculiar to Friedrich Schlegel. This mystic philosophy of love was furthered by the impression of Schleiermacher's *Reden*. In the finite world this yearning for the infinite found satisfaction in love for a beloved woman. Again Schleiermacher turned over to his romantic comrades, Friedrich Schlegel as well as Novalis, ideas which were by no means new to them, but more clearly and deeply cogitated: that which was merely human and commonplace was deified and elevated to infinity. Even the most human love appeared as an innate divine power.

Poetry also, thanks to Schleiermacher, was conceived anew. At last it becomes possible to say what constitutes the poetic and upon what "poetry of poetry" is founded. "All the sublime achievements of art are but remote imitations of the infinite achievement of the world, the one work of art which is forever perfecting itself," says Lothario in the *Gespraech ueber die Poesie* (2, 364). Ludoviko answers, "In other words: all beauty is allegory. The ultimate, simply since it is inexpressible, can only be said allegorically." To which Lothario says: "Therefore all the inmost mysteries of all arts and sciences appertain to poetry."

This anticipated the conviction which Schelling held in 1801 that no work of an artist could rival the absolute work of art, the universe. Here Schleiermacher's religious adoration of the universe was used to fathom poetry. Poetry of poetry depends upon the relation to the universe, to the infinite. All poetry, therefore, is allegorical or, better still according to our usage, symbolic. By means of an image poetry reveals the infinite. Wilhelm Schlegel's Berlin lectures (1, 90) proceeded to explain: "The beautiful is a symbolic representation of the infinite"; and, indeed, it was a deliberate and intentional conversion of Schelling's definition: Beauty is the infinite finitely presented. Wilhelm Schlegel thus reverted to the formula of his brother.

Inasmuch as the glory of the infinite, according to Schleiermacher, rests upon all that is finite, the domain of poetry is immensely extended. "Well, is everything poetry?" one of the women participating in the *Gespraech* may well ask in humorous consternation (p. 354). In the preamble of the *Gespraech* (p. 338, ff.) the illimitable sphere of poetry is extolled in mighty cadence.

But poetry of poetry is now a poetry which embraces this poetic quality of the world. Romantic poetry does this most consummately. Hence Friedrich Schlegel demanded that all poetry should be romantic (p. 373). And inasmuch as this poetry was so closely related to the romantic conception of yearning, Friedrich Schlegel furthermore demanded that romantic poetry present a sentimental content. This term, however, he warned, did not denote "the usual disreputable meaning of sentimental when the term connotes almost everything that in stupid fashion is touching and lachrymose and full of those familiar noble emotions in the presence of which characterless people are prone to feel so inexpressibly contented and important" (p. 370 f.). Friedrich Schlegel thus interprets what he means by sentimental: "That which appeals to us when emotion is supreme—not sensual but spiritual emotion." And in spinning out the meaning of this conception, he presents the profoundest thoughts which he ever uttered on poetry and romanticism: "The source and soul of all these emotions is love and in romantic poetry the spirit of love must be visibly hovering invisible everywhere . . . the gallant passions which one cannot escape anywhere in the poetry of the moderns are the very least, or rather they are not even on the outer fringe of the spirit of love; at times, indeed, they are absolutely nothing except something very unlovely and loveless. No, indeed, it is the same sacred breath that affects us in the tones of music. It cannot be grasped forcibly or mechanically, but it can be gently enticed by mortal beauty and disguised therein; and the magic words of poetry can be penetrated and spiritualized by its force. But in that poem in which it is not, or cannot be, everywhere, it is, indeed, not at all. It is an infinite being and by no means does its interest center upon and cling to persons only, or events, situations, and individual inclinations; to the true poet all of this, with whatever ardor it may beset his soul, is but an indication of that which is higher, infinite, a hieroglyphic of the one everlasting love and of the divine flush and ebullience of plastic nature" (p. 371). The deepest secrets were to be revealed and with delicate touch Friedrich Schlegel succeeded in lifting the veil which concealed them. He sought to formulate in words what poetry meant to the modern man. And almost all of those conceptions which we have come upon up to this point, the conceptions by means of which the romanticist sought to interpret the world, make their appearance. Poetry and the poetic were very closely bound up with the mood of yearning. Yearning aims at something higher, at the infinite. That striving after the infinite which was peculiar to the rational-minded romanticist was reflected in poetry. Thus poetry became analogous to love in the romantic sense. In it man approached infinity; in poetry the absolute became experience to him; in nothing finite, considered from Schleiermacher's point of view, was the infinite more immediately present than in poetry. At this point in romantic thought there was indicated most impressively that, and why, life and thought, nature and philosophy had to become poetry for the romanticist.

If poetry is an image of the infinite, it is the duty of the poet, and of the artist generally, to submit to the world his vision of the infinite. The artist thus becomes a mediator. "A mediator," says the forty-fourth *Idee*, "is one who perceives the divine in himself and effaces himself in order to announce it and to present it to all people in morals and manners, in word and deed." But only he who has his *centrum* in himself is sufficient for the task. "Whosoever is lacking in this respect must choose a definite guide and mediator outside of himself" (*Idee* 45). "He only can be an artist who has a religion of his own, an original conception of the infinite" (*Idee* 13). Thus Friedrich Schlegel proceeded with Schleiermacher's conceptions. Genius here acquired a new trait. The romantic-ironic traits of genius which lent their possessor something liquescent, uncertain, and vacillating found their complement in the demand that the artist be a comprehensive personality, an "organic spirit" (*Athenaeumfragment* 366) and have a firm *centrum*.

And so the rays which came from Schleiermacher's, Friedrich Schlegel's, and Schelling's deification of the infinite converged. Though Fichte had procured for the romanticists illimitable self-direction and arbitrary freedom and at the same time drawn the line of cleavage for the realm of spirituality and that of nature, it was not only this dualism that had to make way for a monism that revelled in reality. The illimitable and unrestricted sovereignty of the will, too, was no longer permitted to hold sway undisturbed. Organic unity and totality, union and synthesis of component parts into a comprehensive whole having a firm and sure *centrum:* these new hypotheses give the romanticist his authoritative power. They demonstrated how finite man represented in himself the eternal and infinite in a form peculiar to none other than himself.

The new conception of genius took from this term much of the excessive clarity of consciousness which had developed in the early romantic doctrine as an outgrowth of Fichte's "intellectual perception." Here was presented the way in which romanticism could again approach the Storm and Stress doctrine of unconscious genius. The eternal, the infinite, the divine becomes real in a work of art. "The immediate cause of all art is God," Schelling may therefore say, pursuing the mediator idea of Friedrich Schlegel, in his lectures on the philosophy of art (§23) at the beginning of the nineteenth century. But genius is to him "the eternal conception of man in God and of the immediate cause of his productions" (§63). Proceeding from such statements the later romanticists could arrive at a conception and evaluation of "nature poetry" which was much more closely allied to the vague presentiments of the Storm and Stress poets than to the attempts of the early romanticists to grasp the purposeful wisdom of great artists, notably Shakespeare.[15]

But the new doctrine could also quiet the painful yearning for the infinite. The anguish of the rational human being, who can never reach his ideal, finds rest in the monistic blending of the infinite with the finite. His yearning love for the eternal, the absolute, God, the universe— it can find peace in love for the finite, in love for this world. Hence Hardenberg's Hyacinth finds perfect, untarnished joy in Rosebud's embrace (4, 24).

But in spite of all, romantic poetry remained essentially poetry of yearning. The romantic poet sings much less of fulfilled than of unfulfilled longing, be it mere spacial longing for the far-away, or the yearning to grasp the eternal and divine, or merely yearning for the loved one. The romanticists, primarily Novalis, found for the nuances of these yearning moods the most delicate modes of expression.

IV. THE PROGRAMS OF ROMANTIC
ETHICS AND RELIGION

I. SCHLEIERMACHER. "LUCINDE." THE EDUCATION
OF WOMEN

THE efforts of the romanticists to establish a new code of ethics were bound up from the beginning with Schleiermacher. In order to judge these romantic tendencies fairly, it is well to keep this connection in mind. The lofty ideal which Schleiermacher proposed for his ethics also demanded an understanding evaluation of the daring ethical paradoxes of the romanticists. It was Schleiermacher, chiefly, who aimed with cutting acerbity and the most pointed epigrams at the prevailing morality.

In opposition to the moral philosophy of the Enlightenment, the romanticists demanded a new moral code. Hence the majority of their ethical expositions, to which Nietzsche's efforts bear strong internal and external resemblance, have also Nietzsche's overstrained and exaggerated polemic character. In ethics the intrepid innovator is inclined to lay on his colors rather more luridly than in the fields of aesthetics or natural history. In this field the transvaluation of all values proceeds with great clatter. Many a resounding slap is heard here, whereas the literary and natural-philosophic revolutionaries enter the lists with weapons less forceful and violent. The idea is to flout the "economists of morality." Romanticism marched into battle against the "Philistine."

As revealed in the *Monologues* and in the *System of Ethical Doctrine,* Schleiermacher's ethics is striking first of all because of its antithesis to Kant's rigor. Like Schiller, Schleiermacher, too, would offer a distinct moral code for exalted personalities and marked individualities and have it clearly understood that some select characters can very well abandon the persistent self-examination which is inherent in the observance of the categorical imperative. If, as a result of this, his exceptional characters, his "beautiful souls," are ruthlessly thrust out of the even tenor of a quiet life, Schiller would retain for them the support to be derived from the categorical imperative. Schleiermacher had in mind an organic morality, a cognizance of the voice which speaks from the depths of human individuality, a cognizance of the law which is as natural and inevitable in an individual as existence itself. Friedrich Schlegel likewise was striving toward an organic morality of this sort. But in the early romantic period he arrived neither at a clear understanding of his aims nor at an unequivocal formulation of them. Furthermore, his ethical observations were concerned far more with the destruction of existing ethical values than with the presentation of new constructive values.

The Storm and Stress waged war against the self-same rationalistic morality out of opposition to which the romantic moral code developed. Hence one is here prone to overlook the subtle differences. At first glance Heinse and the author of *Lucinde* seem to be nearer akin than they really are.

The Storm and Stress, primarily Heinse, was headed for the high seas. All barriers were to be let down. The "heart" was to be the sole law-giver, that is, the passing fancy, the mood of the moment, not the law of a distinct personality which had been deduced through reflection and self-scrutiny. A philosopher of enjoyment, Heinse rejected all that was bourgeois in love. Marriage he presented only as a "hard yoke," "death in life," a "habit and a law," which "is only for the rabble simply because it is rabble and cannot govern itself." Heinse would have none of this "barbaric legislation"; he wanted a republic where at least man and woman and their love were sacred and free. Such glorification of free love quite naturally meant primarily for woman a complete revolution in the existing state of affairs. Thus Heinse, at the end of *Ardinghello,* developed the principles of his ideal republic where love was to soar on high with the utmost freedom. [16]

Though the other champions of Storm and Stress did not rise to these demands for utterly lawless freedom in individual life, and though Goethe, in *Stella,* and Schiller, as champion of "freethinking passion," stopped at a more moderate concession of exceptional instances, there sprang, nevertheless, from the collective poetry of the period a hymn glorifying strong, titanic womanhood. But Heinse alone consciously depicted the happiness of the unmarried woman who, like a goddess, complete mistress of herself, lived in companionship with the most sensible, handsome, witty and talented men and reared her children joyously as the voluntary children of love. Even in destruction, the titanesses of the literature of the day, Adelheid von Walldorf at their head, testified to the intense and seductive effect which the conception of a type of womanhood which courageously disregarded all bounds had upon the youth of the time.

Romanticism heralded the liberation of woman and waged war against the existing status of marriage. But it did not seek the exaltation of woman in sexual licentiousness and it contended for the genuine and true marriage as opposed to the false and conventional one. The oft-quoted statement of Friedrich Schlegel, "One cannot understand what might seriously be said against marriage *à quatre*," does not contain the distinguishing characteristics of romantic thought in regard to marriage. As a matter of fact, the thirty-fourth *Athenaeumfragment*, from which this quotation is taken, denounces prevailing marriages with moral austerity because they are for the most part merely "concubinage." The experiment of marriage *à quatre* and divorce generally ought merely to be transitional phenomena. Optimistically Friedrich Schlegel hopes that the time will come when all marriages will be true marriages. Fichte's "natural right" (1796, *Werke,* 3, 336), in which the conception of marriage closely approximates Friedrich Schlegel's views, and which may have served as their model, is substantially more revolutionary. The same spirit breathes through Schleiermacher's *Idea of a Catechism of Reason for Noble Women* (*Athenaeumfragment* 364). "Observe the Sabbath of thy heart that thou honor it and if they would hold thee, free thyself or go to ruin!" Thus Schleiermacher admonishes the maiden in love and also the woman who is legally bound to an unloved husband. To be sure, he offers the warning, "Thou shalt not contract a marriage that must needs be broken." To him marriage is something sacred; he would relinquish the existing marriage only to exchange it for something better. Friedrich Schlegel's *Lucinde* has exactly the same point of view (1799). It mocks at adultery and scorns the man who sees only femineity in women and likewise the woman who sees in a man merely the measure of his natural qualities; but it also does honor to "genuine marriage," the prerequisite of which is everlasting love. Schleiermacher's apology for *Lucinde,* the *Vertrauten Briefe* (1800), was really not adding anything in this respect when it proposed "to set forth in clear, firm strokes a philosophy of life which would determine for the new order of society the essential character of woman, love, marriage and friendship, modesty, and the artistic presentation of love" (Dilthey, *Schleiermacher,* p. 497). Not out of opposition to Friedrich Schlegel's novel but rather in thorough accord with it, Schleiermacher also believes that marriage alone gives rise to a vigorous, effective life.

The attacks which Friedrich Schlegel's *Lucinde* suffered proceeded less from opposition to its conception of marriage than to its artistic presentation and its analysis of love. Certain it is that Friedrich is not a skillful narrator; he cannot compete with his model, *Wilhelm Meister's Lehrjahre,* nor yet with the *Ofterdingen* of his friend Hardenberg in the matter of artistic presentation of epic events. He sought to set forth a product of "wit," a product of the sovereign will of the poet which recognizes no law above itself. *Lucinde* is bound up with Fichtean elements of the romantic theory in another sense also. It is consistently occupied with self-reflection; it is a novel of "intellectual perception." This novel was to present love in all its phases, just as Goethe's *Meister* reflected the theater, and *Sternbald,* painting. And so the climax is reached in an impressionistic, mimic rendition of the "most delightful situation." This realistic presentation, to which Friedrich Schlegel clung with characteristic stubbornness, may well repel any one who wishes for such subject-matter the artistic style of Goethe's Roman *Elegies.* However, the last thirty years have given us many at-

Schlegel — Lucinde

tempts in the shape of novels to comprehend life in all its phases. A serious and sympathetic attitude (which for these later novels has been taken as a matter of course) ought to prevail in respect to *Lucinde,* also. One could also easily find in the most modern literature counterparts of the "pedantry" of *Lucinde* which is so frequently harped upon. [17]

The aim and purpose of the entire book is to throw light upon love in all its phases. And so it takes into consideration also that manifestation of love which is not concerned with matrimony or propagation but is an end in itself. Only that person can here take offense who is not cognizant of the romantic conception of love. A supersensual, sensual wooer, the romanticist makes love his religion, and religion, moreover, as Schleiermacher understood the term. "Today," Julius writes to Lucinde, "I found in a French book this expression concerning two lovers: 'They were the universe to each other.' It thrilled me and made me smile when it occurred to me that what was here expressed so thoughtlessly, merely as a hyperbolic figure of speech, was literally the case with us" (p. 243 f.). The romantic conception of love made it possible to combine the exalted and the vulgar, the spiritual and the sensual. As Schleiermacher nicely points out, "They know the body and the soul and their unity and that is the whole secret." This, anticipating Schelling, is the metaphysical prerequisite of the idea of a cultural morality, which through the spirit ennobles sensuousness, fancy, and passion and does not confine them by sheer legal authority.

Love in this sense, and "genuine, true" marriage, also, assumes that woman be spiritually elevated, which is demanded in *Lucinde* as well as in Schleiermacher's *Katechis-*

mus. Women should receive an education; they should come spiritually closer to men and enjoy the same privileges that men do. "Let thyself covet the education, art, wisdom, and honor of men," says Schleiermacher's tenth commandment. This is a wish which from the start animated all of Friedrich Schlegel's profound research.

Here too, Friedrich Schlegel proceeded from antiquity. In two essays which do not deny their relationship to Plato and Hemsterhuis, he speaks his mind: *Concerning the Feminine Characters in the Greek Poets* (in 1794) and *Concerning Diotima* (in 1795). Socrates appears as the champion of the opinion that the perfection of both sexes is one and the same, and Plato and the Stoics testify that the destiny of the male and the female sex is identical. Inasmuch as Schlegel, in agreement with Plato, and in opposition to Rousseau, demands public education for women and then participation in the education, duties, and rights of men, he hopes to ward off an unbalanced masculinity and an unbalanced femininity. The classic-romantic ideal of the harmonious being is applied to the woman question in opposition to Schiller's classicism, which isolated woman in the one-sidedness of the naïve. Wieland, setting forth such examples as Aspasia, approved far more of the ambitions of women for an education. As a critic, Friedrich Schlegel rejected Schiller's *Wuerde der Frauen.* Wilhelm Schlegel wrote a witty parody on Schiller's poem (2, 172). The *Athenaeum* spoke out even more strongly for the educational demands of women. The *Fragmente* are much concerned with that theme. In the essay *Ueber die Philosophie: An Dorothea,* in the second volume of the *Athenaeum* (1799), Friedrich Schlegel forges the link between his aims to educate women and Schleiermacher's conception of religion. In

Friedrich's estimation, love for the universe seems to be a trait rather peculiar to women. To them, he thinks, belongs the subjectivity, the quiet animation of all their endeavors, which to him is essentially the predisposition toward religion or, indeed, is religion itself. And he carries out his statement rigorously: religion is the true virtue and happiness of women; he would train them in philosophy, not poetry; poetry is more akin to the earth whereas philosophy is more sacred, more akin to divinity. And "women stand less in need of the poetry of poets because their innermost being is poetry" (*Idee* 127).

2. THE ESTABLISHMENT OF A NEW RELIGION. HARDENBERG'S RELIGIOUS POETRY

The phenomenon which was observed in natural philosophy and in the deification and aestheticizing of the universe also appeared in the field of religion. It is extremely difficult to say accurately who first gave the impetus. In this instance it is even more difficult than usual because the circle of religious enthusiasts was greater. Schelling, of course, does not come into consideration; it was Friedrich Schlegel and Novalis who, at about the same time as Schleiermacher, were concerned with becoming more religious and gaining new life from Christianity. Neither did Tieck lag behind. He was able to contribute his mite to the religious enthusiasm of the romanticists from an entirely different angle—the contemplation of the plastic arts, which he had carried on with his prematurely deceased friend, Wackenroder.

On November 15, 1799, Dorothea wrote to Schleiermacher from Jena, "Christianity is here *à l'ordre du jour.*" Shortly before, Friedrich Schlegel had reported to his friend how the *Reden* had affected Novalis: "Harden-berg has studied you with the keenest interest and is en-tirely taken in, permeated, inspired, and enkindled. He claims he can find no fault with you and so far agrees with you. Still that is just so-so" (3, 125). This testimony indicates that the *Reden* had a great influence, that they fell also upon well prepared soil, and that the romantic group had already proceeded too far along the road to religion and Christianity to accept Schleiermacher's dog-mas without reservation.

As a matter of fact, a whole year before this Friedrich Schlegel had already written to Novalis (October 20, 1798): "As far as I am concerned, the aim of my literary projects is to write a new Bible and to follow in the foot-steps of Mahomet and Luther." Novalis answered on the seventh of November: "In my study of science in general and its embodiment—I mean in books—I too happened upon the idea of the Bible—the Bible as the ideal of each and every book." Friedrich Schlegel's letter of the second of December recognizes in the "coincidence" of their "biblical projects" a "most remarkable sign and wonder" of the "understanding" between the two friends and also of their "misunderstanding." For Schlegel had immedi-ately read out of Hardenberg's letter that only in a cer-tain sense did Novalis find in the Bible the "dominant literary form, and hence the ideal of every book." Schle-gel himself had "a Bible in mind which not only approxi-mately and in a certain sense, but literally and in every spirit and sense would be Bible." The project is not literary but biblical and absolutely religious. "I propose to es-tablish a new religion or rather, to assist proclaiming it; for even without me it will come and triumph. My religion is not of the sort that would want to swallow up poetry

and philosophy." Darkly Friedrich Schlegel intimates the
condition upon which he may count upon Hardenberg's
absolute consent: "It really amounts to this: whether you
can decide, at least in a certain sense, to think of Christianity as an absolutely negative quantity." And prophetically
he exclaims to his friend, "Perhaps you even have the
choice of being either the last Christian, the Brutus of the
old religion, or the Christ of the new gospel." This new
gospel was already showing signs of life, thought Friedrich Schlegel. Schleiermacher was occupied with a book
on religion. Tieck was studying Jacob Boehme. And the
synthesis of Goethe and Fichte—the prerequisite and
point of departure for romantic natural philosophy (see
p. 53)—could produce nothing but religion. Finally, on
January 20, 1799, Novalis pronounced Friedrich's conception of the negativity of the Christian religion to be
excellent. "Christianity is thus raised to the dignity of
being the base for the projecting force of a new world-
edifice and a new humanity." "Absolute abstraction, annihilation of the present, apotheosis of the future—of this
real and better world; this is the gist of the fiats of Christianity and thus it links itself with the religion of the antiquarians, the godlike nature of antiquity, and the reëstab-
lishment of the ancient world, like a great second wing.
Both hold the universe—the body of the angel—in everlasting equilibrium." Friedrich Schlegel agreed that Christianity was a religion of the future, just as that of the
Greeks was a religion of the past. "But is it not even more
a religion of death just as the classic religion was a religion
of life?" "Perhaps you are the first person in our age
to have an artistic sense for death" (p. 130).

It is clear from these passages in their correspondence
that Friedrich Schlegel and Novalis had long ago passed

beyond Schleiermacher's suggestion. The personal meeting of Hardenberg and Tieck (in the summer of 1799) can only have reassured Novalis and urged him on his way. Novalis had, at an early age, in his *Herrnhuter* environment, come in contact with Zinzendorf's idea of "connection with the historical Christ" and had become pietistically intent upon the fathoming of His "mediatorship." Hence Novalis was the only one in the romantic group sufficiently endowed with the creative strength to express readily in poetic form what religion and Christianity meant to him. There ensued his spiritual songs, which were at the same time revelations of the new religion, of the deification of the universe, of yearning love for eternity, and wonderfully simple expressions of the true believer, to whom the figure of Christ is a guide-post pointing to supermundane realms.

Friedrich Schlegel recognized immediately in Hardenberg's Christian songs their great artistic and human worth (to Schleiermacher, November, 1799): "He also read us some Christian hymns; they are the most divine that he has ever done. There is nothing like them, poetically, except the most intimate and profound of Goethe's early lyrics."

But the germinal ideas contained in the letters exchanged between Friedrich Schlegel and Novalis around the beginning of 1799 became far more clear and profound, artistically, in the *Hymns to the Night* than they had been in the spiritual songs. Sorrowful experience is bound up with this newly achieved religious feeling. Christianity as "the basis for the projecting force of a new world-edifice and a new humanity"; its demand for "an absolute abstraction, annihilation of the present"; the resulting "apotheosis of the future, of this real and better world": all this is woven into the *Hymns* as is also the relation of Christianity to antiquity, to the "religion of the antiquarians." Here also is answered Friedrich Schlegel's question whether Christianity is not even more a religion of death than the classical religion was a religion of life. Antiquity, rooted entirely in this life, in the terrestial, was terrified by death, whereas Christ has reconciled the world to the idea of death. Death throws open to the believer in Christ the portals of a higher and better world; the Cross has made man a citizen of eternity. Schleiermacher's conception that religious emotion draws us close to infinity is exchanged in the *Hymns* for the forms of the Christian creed: the death of the Savior as mediator has opened to mankind the way to eternity. The thought of infinity, symbolized in the conception of an other-worldly life, consoles the poet for the loss of his beloved. He is deprived of his loved one only for the short space of his earthly sojourn. Human existence extends much further, extends, indeed, beyond the limits of temporal being. And it is death that frees man from the fetters of this earthly life.

But here, to be sure, only one side of Schleiermacher's religion is appreciated: the infinite raises us above the finite—and not the other side: the finite is dear to us because it is a symbol of infinity. The *Hymns* are not to be regarded as poetic presentations of romantic monism and romantic joy in life. Novalis wrote them, consumed with the idea which the death of Sophie von Kuehn had aroused in him, the idea of voluntary death, consciously achieved. Later he once more became reconciled to the mundane world, upon which, according to Schleiermacher, there is reflected some of the glory of eternity. Wilhelm Schlegel suggests the mood of the *Hymns* in the eighth poem of his *Totenopfer fuer Auguste Boehmer* (1, 136):

> You seemed, divorced from life,
> Already to move with the tread of spirits
> And without death recovered from mortality.
> You conjured up within you by a spiritual act,
> Like a wizard with sign and gesture,
> For your soul's communion, the vanished being.

Death, consciously willed, is also the aim of the "higher being" in Jean Paul's *Die unsichtbare Loge*. This "higher being" is characterized by "elevation above the earth, the conviction of the insignificance of all earthly striving . . . the wish to die and the vision beyond the clouds" (Hempel, 1, 184). In Emanuel in *Hesperus,* Jean Paul portrays a character of this sort. At the same time Novalis suggests Boehme's conception of "fragility."

Through the Fall of Man fragility came into the world; previously all things were only "their ether." When the fragile form passes away, the soul again becomes ether and beholds all splendors in undimmed glory. The torment of passion vanishes with the bursting of the bonds. As is the case in nearly all mysticism, there is also in these conceptions of Boehme's something of Neoplatonism and of Christianity. A similar combination is at the bottom of the *Hymns;* hence the resemblance to Boehme. Direct acceptance of Boehme's doctrines is apparent only in *Ofterdingen*. The whole novel with its continuations was meant to depict the gradual ascent of man and his deliverance, step by step, from the bonds of earthly life. For the gradations of this striving to ascend, Novalis meant to use Boehme's conception of the three-fold birth. The first and second steps are not pure in the sight of God: the first, the elemental, the level of death; the second, the sidereal, which belongs to both worlds. On the third level, the animal plane, humanity, mature for rebirth, comes into being. Man, to achieve salvation, must pass through each of the three births.

It is evident that this symbolism could easily be associated with the upward trend of the evolutionary stages of natural philosophy. These two presuppositions gave rise to the fictions which were meant to close *Ofterdingen* and which sound strange indeed without this explanation: Heinrich becomes a stone, then a musical tree, then a golden ram, finally a human being. Feminine self-sacrifice enables him to proceed from one step to another. Heinrich von Ofterdingen, too, is lured upward by the eternally feminine.

Boehme's doctrine of fragility, which he accounted for through the Fall from Grace, and his doctrine of the return of the soul to God, found the same response in the soul of Franz von Baader as in Hardenberg's. Windelband (*Geschichte der neueren Philosophie,* 2, 350) recognizes in Baader's philosophy a combination of Boehme's mysticism and the ideas of Kant and Fichte; that is, he finds it rich in etymologies and analogies, and thus he already suggests the close relationship between Hardenberg's and Baader's lines of thought.[18] Through Baader Schelling, also, was strengthened in his inclination toward theosophy, which is apparent in his *Freiheitslehre,* and which was inspired by his pupil, Eschenmayer. By way of the theosophy of the *Freiheitslehre* Schelling went on to irrationalism. Windelband shows (op. cit. p. 338 ff.) how far Schelling followed in Jacobi's footsteps and how he thus became a forerunner of Schopenhauer and Feuerbach. Friedrich Schlegel, when he grew older, likewise did homage to theosophy; he, too, inspired by Boehme, taught that through the Fall of Man infinity entered into the finite and that the finite was destined to return into infinity when the individual subjects himself to the positive, divine law. And so Friedrich Schlegel and his romantic confrères enacted the *salto mortale* into the depths of divine compassion of which the former had once accused Jacobi (Minor, 2, 91). It is not surprising that henceforth Jacobi was a fellow-worker on Friedrich Schlegel's periodicals, just as Hamann, the typical irrationalist of the eighteenth century, experienced at the same time a rebirth in romanticism. But the irrationalism of romanticism, which was hastening to its close, was differentiated from Hamann's by means of its decidedly Catholic character.

3. THE TURN TO CATHOLICISM, TO THE MIDDLE AGES, AND TO THE ORIENT. FRIEDRICH SCHLEGEL'S LATER INTERPRETATIONS OF THE EVOLUTION OF HUMANITY

Novalis did not halt at the revelations contained in Schleiermacher's religion, which dealt chiefly with the infinite and the universe. In his *Hymns* and his spiritual songs he had already utilized the manifold symbols of Christianity. He did not pause, as Schleiermacher did, at the cleavage between morality and theology, on the one hand, and religion, on the other, but went on into the sphere of confessional faith. Even in the Christian creed he sought to separate that which appealed to him from that which did not. When he wrote of the spiritual songs, Friedrich Schlegel also told Schleiermacher (3, 133 f.) of the essay *Christianity or Europe,* written by Novalis, and traced it directly to the "tremendous effect" which

the *Reden* had had upon its author. One must keep firmly
in mind the explicit mention of this essay to Schleiermacher (2, 40 f.) if one would not misinterpret its purpose. It depicts a phase of development in cultural history
according to the pattern outlined by Schiller's classicism,
Friedrich Schlegel's romanticism, and Fichte's philosophy
of history. Primitive, monotonous harmony is followed by
disharmony, which in turn gives way to boundless versatility. But the old terms have new combinations. The first
one is used to denote, instead of ancient Greece, the Catholic Middle Ages. In a few pages Novalis sketches a picture
of "those glorious, splendid days when Europe was a
Christian country, when *one* Christianity inhabited this
continent, so important in the history of the human race."
These "genuinely Catholic or genuinely Christian days"
are tinted with that peculiar romantic hue which was destined for decades to give to the Middle Ages the same sentimental glorification which the eighteenth century had
given to antiquity. The dissension which followed such a
golden age was indispensable for in this way only could
there be cultural development. But in spite of this, Novalis
did not spare Protestantism, the cause of this dissension, a
single accusation. Luther had mistaken the spirit of Christianity. The contention that the Bible is of sovereign validity mixed philology, the alphabetic science, with religious
matters and enervated the meaning. Hence there are very
few high lights in Protestantism—Boehme and Zinzendorf, perhaps. The Order of the Jesuits, however, in contrast to Protestantism, is given a good report. The Jesuits
are represented as the universally active champions of
Catholic religious culture. The Enlightenment fares so
much the worse. In Novalis' opinion, the disciples of the
Enlightenment hate and disparage the Bible, Christianity,

and religion just as much as fancy, feeling, love of art and morality, the days of yore and the coming ages. In the struggle against the Enlightenment, there will arise, in due time, a new harmony. The natural sciences and politics indicate that a new era is at hand—natural science, of course, in the sense of natural philosophy, and politics, because Hardenberg hopes that Christianity is beginning to become virile and active again and to erect a visible church regardless of territorial boundaries. The essay closes, hoping for these "holy days of eternal peace."

With this essay there was established for decades not only the romantic conception of the Middle Ages; it anticipated also the ultimate political-religious stand of romanticism. It was but slowly and gradually that Friedrich Schlegel came around to the same objectives. In 1799 he still contemplated Novalis' disquisition with such an air of superiority and romantic irony that he encouraged Schelling's inclination to offer a word against Novalis. He wrote to Schleiermacher (3, 134) that since Hardenberg and Tieck "are going to such excesses," Schelling "was seized with a new attack of his old enthusiasm for irreligiousness" and added that he subscribed to him heartily. "Apropos of this he sketched an epicurean creed in the Hans Sachs-Goethe manner." *Das epikurisch Glaubensbekenntnisz Heinz Widerporstens (Aus Schellings Leben, 1, 283 ff.)* is a protest on the part of one who venerates nature, to whom "only that is genuine and true which can be felt with the hands," against the spiritualism of those who are seeking God and who lose themselves in the universe. The antithesis, however, is much more subtle than one would think at first glance. Although it all seems to be based upon a keen enjoyment of sensuality, the spiritualism of Schelling, nevertheless, crops out in the *Glaubensbekenntnisz.*

But Schelling, exaggerating, shoves the romantic group into the approximate position of F. H. Jacobi.

The whole thing is a bit of over-done raillery, which does, however, call attention to a chasm, easily bridged as yet, but bound to become ever wider and wider. The romanticists still viewed such antitheses and their humorous presentation wholly from the point of view of pure intellectuality, if not of wit, so that they were inclined to print Novalis' avowal alongside Schelling's in the *Athenaeum*. It would have been entirely in accord with their *philirony* to emphasize in such a manner the antitheses in their own creed. But Goethe, whose advice had been sought, vetoed the plan—Goethe, who in his innermost heart agreed with Heinz Widerporst rather than with the romantic religious group, and who must have found in Schelling's poem flesh of his flesh and bone of his bone.

The spiritual freedom and *philirony* disappeared on the part of all the moment when romanticism proceeded from the discussion of its ideas to deeds. When Friedrich Schlegel entered the Catholic camp, Hardenberg's doctrine was put to practice. But around 1800 Friedrich Schlegel was still so far removed from this step that his immediate interpretations of the history of civilization were quite remote from the fabric of Hardenberg's essay. It is only after his conversion that Friedrich Schlegel's philosophy of history approached the essay *Christianity or Europe*.

At the time of the *Athenaeum* Friedrich Schlegel's first interpretation of world history in the romantic sense was out of focus. The disharmony of modernity had followed the harmony of antiquity; but romanticism, either because it represented, like Fichte, in the sense of romantic irony, the most unhampered and versatile mobility or because it experienced with Schelling the organically inevitable process of becoming progressively conscious, was leading away from this disharmony into new harmony. This interpretation changed the moment when the Orient loomed upon Friedrich Schlegel's intellectual horizon. Novalis likewise referred repeatedly to the Orient in his last productions.

There must be a distinction made, however, between the vague suggestions which bring to mind Hardenberg's favorite book, Jung-Stilling's *Heimweh* (1794), and the undisguised, unequivocal references to the Orient and the East. Jung-Stilling thought of Christ and the Christian creed when he spoke of the East and the Levant; the second spiritual song of Hardenberg's, *Fern in Osten wird es Helle* (1, 64), had the same idea. Ambiguously, even if not in the nostalgic sense of Stilling, *Idee* 133 says: "I am now speaking only with those who are already looking toward the Orient." Similarly, in the conclusion to the *Ideen,* the dedication to Novalis says: "Every bit of wisdom garnered from the Orient is the common property of artists. I name you instead of all the others" (2, 307).

The Orient and India appear more comprehensible in the essay *Die Christenheit oder Europa* (2, 37, 39) and in *Ofterdingen* (4, 142). Friedrich Schlegel is really thinking of Eastern culture when he says in the *Gespraech ueber die Poesie* (2, 362): "It is in the Orient that we must seek the most typically romantic." Similarly in Hardenberg's *Fragment:* "Greater simplicity—fewer but better distributed masses of nature, life, and man in the Orient. The oriental people, the oriental age, etc., are very different from ours" (3, 298). This observation was repeated by Friedrich Schlegel, who used it and developed it.

The essay which, somewhat in the nature of a manifesto, opened the first volume of Friedrich Schlegel's *Europa* sought to draw the Orient into the scope of world's history and discovered in it a combination of the antitheses which hold sway and have held sway in Europe. What arises from a single source in the Orient should separate in Europe and follow a more artistic development. Excellent qualities contained in the antithesis, classical antiquity and the modern romantic age, are blended in India into consummate beauty or exist side by side without mutually excluding each other. In this way the spiritual self-annihilation of Christianity and the most voluptuous, wild materialism of the Greek religion find their highest prototype in India. Hence Friedrich Schlegel is inclined to find the European separation of classicism and romanticism unnatural and objectionable. Catholic art and modern philosophy indicate to him that the union of classicism and romanticism is indeed conceivable; the Catholic church had appropriated the artistic grace and splendor, the poetic versatility and beauty of Greek mythology and Greek customs, while philosophy—not only critical idealism but even Spinoza—was so far in accord with ancient philosophy that it seemed to be merely a continuation of it. Such concord between ancient and modern philosophy is indeed comprehensible, inasmuch as the rift, the ever-widening rift, in the unity and totality of human power and thought had its inception in antiquity. The break has now, to be sure, reached its limit. "Man can sink no lower." At this point Friedrich Schlegel is more pessimistic than ever about the present. A revolution would have to come from the Orient: "We cannot have forgotten, whence every religion and every mythology has always come to us, i.e., the principles of life, the roots of all conceptions" (p. 36).

To join the classic and the romantic, to set aside the

barriers which separate the two conceptions, was the natural result of Friedrich Schlegel's disposition. He had always had totality in mind; great versatility was his aim from the beginning. The conception of romantic "universal poetry" indicated such a program; the *Gespraech ueber die Poesie,* moreover, had amplified the conception of poetry almost illimitably. To join antitheses, the ability to attune himself at any time to any pitch, had been Friedrich Schlegel's favorite tendency ever since he had conquered his "mania for objectivity." Now it was a question of audaciously combining ancient and modern, classic and romantic, in a poetic production. He tried out his new theory in *Alarkos* (1802). Even the meter essayed the combination of antitheses. The Spanish rhythm joined the trimeter in a work of art. The multiplicity of forms, copied from Spanish models, which the romantic drama used, gave rise to further extension which still lingers with artistic effect in Goethe's *Faust,* notably in the third act of the second part.

Henceforth Friedrich Schlegel repeatedly traced the influence of Indian philosophy upon European, obviously in the book *Ueber die Sprache und Weisheit der Indier* (1808, p. 204 ff.) and in the fifth lecture on *Geschichte der alten und neuen Literatur* (1815, 1, 187 ff.). The problem of the development of humanity played a part in all of his later works, for example, presently, in the Paris-Cologne lectures. In these deliberations the re-definition of the conception "romantic" achieved new forms. The Christian, or rather the Catholic, element in the philosophy of Friedrich Schlegel's last phase of development became more and more pronounced. As a result, his conception of what was romantic became very elastic, alternately expanding and contracting. At the same time the problem of harmony was repeatedly reconceived in his various deliberations. Presently, harmony and romanticism complemented each other; again, they were poles apart. The term "romanticism" had the broadest connotation around the middle of the second decade of the nineteenth century.

At this time Friedrich Schlegel was following up in his Vienna lectures on *Die Geschichte der alten und neuen Literatur* (1815, 2, 128 ff.) his assertion in the *Europa* that the union between classic and romantic is conceivable and that Catholicism brings it to pass. In connection with Spanish poetry he repeats the thesis that romanticism has no quarrel with what is ancient and truly antique. But here romanticism, as far as Friedrich Schlegel is concerned, is based upon the "feeling of love which along with Christianity and through it holds sway also in poetry." Ideas which already bobbed up in the *Gespraech ueber die Poesie* here receive an increasingly strong Catholic coloring. Gradually Catholicism evolves as the safe retreat of totality toward which Friedrich Schlegel had aspired since the days of his youth. The *Legend of Troy* and the Homeric poems are now ranged alongside this Catholic romanticism as, indeed, is "everything that is truly poetic in the Indian, Persian, and other old oriental or European poetry." Even in the ancient tragedians he now senses sympathy with this feeling. Indeed, the romantic, which has completely become universal poetry, has only two antitheses: the so-called ancient, which has been falsely set up among us, and which without real love for the ancient merely imitates its form, and the modern, which thinks it affects life by confining itself to the present and limiting itself to reality.

An appendix to the edition of 1822 (2, 128) goes still

further: the harmony in Catholic poetry is rated above the ancient. What the ancients separated, the strict symbolism of the mysteries and the essential mythology or the "new, sensuous hero poetry," is here united. Everything in it is thoroughly symbolic. Shakespeare also rose to this symbolism, which is rooted in the natural mysteries of the soul, but Calderon carried it on to Christian transfiguration.

They were the old points of view attained around 1800: the presentation of the infinite in the finite, totality, the demand for a conscious poetry; but they now all came to a head in Catholicism. Religion, love, mediatorship—they had all already been used in the *Ideen*, had there become an integral part of the conception of romantic poetry. Now these ideas were conceived more narrowly and accurately, not in the figurative sense but in the Catholic.

In the last analysis, the Catholic creed and Boehme's doctrine enabled Schlegel to formulate, in the light of world's history, the highest type of harmony in the Catholic sense. This problem was minutely considered in the eighteen Vienna lectures of 1828 on the *Philosophy of History* (1829). It is the task of philosophy to restore that divine image in man which has been lost. Humanity lost control over nature and fell to a level below it, by choice, through the Fall of Man. It was the prerogative of Christianity to bring the higher light of divine truth into close proximity to life and learning, after the Jews, to be sure, had proved themselves to be guides to the knowledge of God. The fourth era of the world, at the threshold of which Schlegel put his own age, will usher in the triumph of light over darkness. The prerequisite to this whole interpretation is faith in Christ and in the mystery of grace involved in the divine salvation of the human race. Without this faith, the entire history of the world would be "nothing but a riddle without a solution, a labyrinth without an exit, a great junk heap of fragments, stones, and particles of an uncompleted edifice, of the great tragedy of mankind, which would then have no significance" (2, 9).

In the course of this development, which was the final revision of the old interpretation of Schiller and the early romanticists, there appeared a plane of harmony, a particularly favored age, which was possessed of all the advantages with which Friedrich Schlegel, in his youth, and Schiller had endowed Greek antiquity. This period was the pre-Ghibelline Middle Ages. Friedrich Schlegel was thinking of the time when the German racial character and Germanic vigor and heroic strength were completely harmonized and welded together with Roman civilization by means of Christian love and religious sentiment. This happy fusion produced the exalted yet gentle characters of Charles the Great and of Alfred. As soon as the religious strength of Christian sentiment weakened, the elements which had brought harmony into humanity disintegrated once more. Romanticism had its roots in this disruption; it contained the germ of Dante's great work as well as of the painting and architecture of the Middle Ages.

And yet these were merely old theses from the days of early romanticism. Some of Friedrich Schlegel's assertions, however, agreed fully with Hardenberg's essay *Die Christenheit oder Europa*; in both instances the Middle Ages, the time when church and state proceeded hand in hand, were conceived as an era of harmony just as Greek antiquity had been in the letters *Ueber die aesthetische Erziehung des Menschen* or in the treatise *Ueber das*

Studium der griechischen Poesie. Reaching across a generation Novalis clasped hands with the friend of his youth, who meanwhile had become a partisan of Rome. Novalis' presentiments, hovering daringly above the earth, had now become the motifs of Friedrich Schlegel's history of philosophy.

There was, however, no irreconcilable contradiction in this, Friedrich Schlegel's final interpretation of the history of the world and his perception of what was romantic, outlined in the Viennese lectures on the *History of Ancient and Modern Literature*. It was a question rather of the antithesis which from the beginning had been inherent in the romantic interpretation of the conception of "totality." Like Schiller, Friedrich Schlegel, in his early "objective" days, had designated the Greeks as representatives of a harmony which dissolved all antitheses completely. Then there occurred to him as the ideal of human totality the idea of protean mobility, of the ability to spring from one antithesis to the other and to combine the most contradictory situations into unity. This ideal was at the base of romantic poetry; this ideal he found again in the Orient, and found it in such a wealth and profusion of antitheses, that antiquity itself, by way of contrast, seemed out of balance. Hence in the Viennese lectures he discovered romantic elements wherever there was similar profusion. In 1828 he returned to the simple harmony in contrast to which the romantic perhaps seemed richer but also more disrupted. And now he ascribed this harmony to the Middle Ages, in which Germanic heroism and the romantic church went hand in hand—harmony in the classical sense.

Hardenberg's essay *Die Christenheit oder Europa* had anticipated this point of view. For this very reason his essay indicated a decisive step toward the subsequent

Catholic turn in romanticism. Its glorification of the Catholic Middle Ages prepared the way for the period of conversions.

Another preparatory step was provided by the early romantic transfiguration of Christian painting. Novalis' essay, too, did not fail to reveal the effects of the hymns which were sung to Christian painting by its idolators among the early romanticists.

V. TIECK'S AND WACKENRODER'S PARTICIPATION

NOVALIS had not created his picture of the Catholic Middle Ages unaided and uninfluenced. His new friendship with Tieck here bore its first fruits. Tieck turned Wackenroder's ideas over to romantic thought. Perhaps the most noteworthy fact in the whole history of the development of German romanticism is that one of its main tendencies, which was destined very soon to spread its jungly growth over every other aspiration of early romanticism and to appear to the contemporary and subsequent generations as its pivotal point and to endow it with its most enduring cultural and artistic issues, should have proceeded from a most delicate, sickly youth who was doomed to an early grave, who had little or nothing in common with the leaders of the early romantic movement, and who, in his inmost soul, was uncongenial to the romanticists of the protean type. Yet Friedrich Schlegel, who knew him but slightly, hit the nail on the head when he wrote to his brother (p. 307) in the beginning of November, 1797, that "in this whole school of art"— that is, Tieck's circle—he "liked Wackenroder the best" and added : "He doubtless has more genius than Tieck but the latter certainly has more understanding."

In none of the other early romanticists was the soulful, temperamental side developed so strongly, even disproportionately. Hardenberg felt a much greater impulse to struggle from unintelligibility toward clarity. Nevertheless, he is certainly the nearest to Wackenroder; and the spell which Tieck cast over Novalis at their very first meeting rested without doubt upon those of Tieck's characteristics which the latter's association with Wackenroder had aroused. Tieck himself, however, found again in Novalis much of what he had lost through Wackenroder's death, for, adaptable and flexible as he was, he approached Novalis with the same appeal that had, at an earlier time, won over Wackenroder, namely, the emotional. Wackenroder, a morbidly sensitive person with but a slight tendency toward self-analysis and "intellectual perception" in the Fichtean sense, was of all the early romanticists, most closely related to the Storm and Stress. Hence, by virtue of his association with Tieck, he was in a position to foster those favorite projects which the Storm and Stress and romanticism held in common: interest in old German life, art, and poetry.

He was a pupil of Hamann and Herder and shared with his teachers the ability to assume an empathic attitude toward individual types of beauty and to understand and appreciate, in particular, national individuality artistically expressed. Not the distorted glorification of what happened to be his own, but the genuine desire and talent for versatile empathy was as peculiar to Wackenroder as to Herder. In the *Herzensergiessungen eines kunstliebenden Klosterbruders* (1797, p. 106 ff.) we read: "We, the sons of this century, enjoy the advantage of standing on the summit of a high mountain and of beholding many countries and many spans of time spread out about us and beneath us. So let us avail ourselves of this good fortune and let our eyes rove over all epochs and all peoples and let us strive to discover what in all of their manifold emotions and products of their emotions is essentially human."

Wackenroder was brought to an understanding of the older German literature by his teacher, Erduin Julius Koch. As early as the beginning of December, 1792, he admitted to his friend Tieck: "There I made many an interesting acquaintance with old German poets and discovered that this study, pursued sympathetically, is very attractive." Tieck answered (December 28) rather dishearteningly, with the same criticism which Schiller afterwards made of the collection of *Minnelieder* prepared by Tieck: he complained of the "astonishing monotony" of the minnesingers. But Wackenroder was not led astray; as a matter of fact, Tieck was converted, during the summer semester of 1793, which the two friends spent at Erlangen, to mediaeval German studies and specialized, before long, on chap-books. Wackenroder, meanwhile, proceeded from old German poetry to old German art; there was enkindled in him the same love which in, and after, Strassburg had made the youthful Goethe the admirer of Erwin von Steinbach and Duerer. "True art can develop not only under Italian skies, among majestic domes and Corinthian columns but also among pointed vaults, intricately ornate edifices and Gothic towers," the *Herzensergiessungen* maintain (p. 129). Similar reflections had opened the way for Heinse to Rubens.

Penetrating first with loving devotion the art of German antiquity and then Duerer's painting, Wackenroder created for himself a picture of the German past—an idealized one, to be sure, but, nevertheless, a vivid one, born of deepest sympathy. "When Albrecht Duerer was wielding his brush, the German was still a distinctive and noteworthy character of genuine stability in the ensemble of the nations in our part of the world; in his pictures, the

genuineness, uprightness, and force of the German character are faithfully and clearly impressed not only upon
facial expression and externalities in general but upon
the very spirit" (p. 121 f.). This is the mood in which
German life in the old days was seen in Hardenberg's
essay *Christianity or Europe*, later in *Ofterdingen*, and in
the early poetry of Tieck. This mood was repeated with
consummate artistry when Moritz von Schwind created
his *Tale of the Seven Ravens* or his *Beautiful Melusine*
or the frescos from the life of Saint Elizabeth at the
Wartburg. Here there reigned life and spirit as from some
far-off beautiful world. It was not the historic mediaeval
era but an imagined one; it was, however, not akin to
the "Middle Ages of the chivalrous dramas and romances
with their faceless, vague personages and their monoton-
ously virtuous sentiments" (W. Scherer, *Jakob Grimm,*
second edition, p. 60 ff.). For the delicate soul of Wackenroder endowed the German Middle Ages with a nimbus
which was denied the clumsier fingers of the dramatists
of chivalry, even Maler Mueller. It is of more importance,
however, that Wackenroder's beautifying glance led the
Schlegels and Novalis, likewise, to steep the Middle Ages
and all that was German in this spirit.

Before Wackenroder, through the agency of Tieck,
influenced Hardenberg, there was not even a trace of the
glorification of the Middle Ages to be found in the Jena
group. To be sure, there was from the beginning a decided
consciousness of German strength. Still Friedrich Schlegel's thirty-eighth *Lyceumfragment* says: "There is
nothing to criticize in the prototype of Germanism which
several distinguished native discoverers have set forth,
except its setting. This Germanism does not lie behind
us but rather ahead of us." As for the *Ideen* (No. 135),

Wackenroder's confession of faith was but partially incorporated into them. Here there prevails that conception
of German might and of German art and manners which
was manifested in Friedrich's youthful letters to Wilhelm :
it is not the Germanic which is emphasized, Klopstock's
Teutonism is not proclaimed, but rather, homage is done
to the creators of modern German culture. This vindicated
the point of view which Novalis was prone to take : Germany is at the point of assuming spiritual leadership in
Europe. Around 1800 Schiller also subscribed to this belief
and would fain have celebrated the greatness of Germany.
"The German," Novalis once said (2, 124), "has been
the underling for a long time. He may very well grow
up to be the master of all masters. He is experiencing
what many stupid children are said to experience : he will
be alive and clever when his more precocious brothers
and sisters shall have long turned to dust and he alone
will be the head of the house." Friedrich Schlegel and
Novalis were by no means intent upon idealizing the
German. The difference which still existed between them
and Wackenroder at the time when the *Athenaeum* was
discontinued is indicated by *Idee* No. 120 : "The spirit
of the ancient heroes in our German art and learning
must be ours as long as we continue to be Germans. A
German artist has no character other than that of an
Albrecht Duerer, a Kepler, a Hans Sachs, or a Jacob
Boehme. This character is just, true-hearted, thorough,
accurate, and profound, and at the same time inoffensive
and somewhat awkward. Only among the Germans is it
a national peculiarity to pay divine honors to art and
learning for their own sake." Friedrich Schlegel and
Novalis still had their eyes too firmly focused upon facts
to admit of Wackenroder's idealization. Friedrich Schle-

gel's poem of admonition, *An die Deutschen* (*Athenaeum,* 3, 165 ff.), had the same point of view. On the contrary, however, his two songs written in 1802, *Bei der Wartburg* and *Am Rheine* (*Europa,* 1, 1, 8, 15), were already thoroughly imbued with the spirit of Wackenroder and of *Ofterdingen.*

Romantic studies in early German literature were born of this mood. Wackenroder's friend, Tieck, led the way. Though Friedrich Schlegel concerned himself very little around 1800 about old German literature, Wilhelm betrayed some information and here and there interpolated a significant word or two on old German poetry; Hardenberg, however, had Wilhelm direct him to the literature of Heinrich von Ofterdingen (of which the former, by the way, made no use). Meanwhile Tieck was the first to appear, in 1803, with a collection of Middle High German poems, the *Lovesongs of the Suabian Period.* Though the ragged translation into modern High German may be unbearable to many people, the introduction (*Kritische Schriften,* 1, 185 ff.) was positively the first attempt, and a very successful one, at that, to characterize the poetry of the German Middle Ages and to give it an ordered place in the range of romantic poetry. Jacob Grimm was profoundly moved by Tieck's sketch. It was not Tieck's knowledge nor his clever and occasionally quite felicitous summaries, nor yet a remark about the author of the *Niebelungenlied* which anticipated Lachmann's researches —it was probably none of these specific things that overwhelmingly influenced Grimm; it was rather the general view of the German Middle Ages which was maintained throughout in the spirit of Wackenroder and Novalis. The Middle Ages, for Tieck, were a period distinguished by a peculiarly intimate, receptive, comprehensive feeling for

poetry. "Knighthood at that time joined together all the
nations of Europe. The knights traveled from the far
North to Spain and Italy. The Crusades made this bond
still closer and gave rise to a wonderful relation between
the Orient and the Occident. From the North and from
the East came legends which mingled with the native
legends. Great episodes of war, magnificent courts, princes,
and emperors who patronized the art of poetry, a tri-
umphant church which canonized heroes—all these propitious circumstances united to create for the free,
independent nobility and the wealthier citizens a resplendent life in which yearning, aroused, combined freely and
spontaneously with poetry and found reflected in the latter
a clearer, more definite picture of contemporary reality.
The faithful sang of their faith and its miracles, lovers
of their love, knights described chivalrous deeds and con-
tests, and loving, believing knights were the chief auditors"
(1, 195 f.).

The high idealization of the Middle Ages undertaken
by Tieck was toned down several degrees by Wilhelm
Schlegel in his Berlin lectures, 1803–4. He, too, would
like to have the old German poetry brought within the
scope of romanticism; doubtless he learned much from
Tieck's preface. He sought particularly, however, to
describe and fathom more closely "the wonderful relation
between the Orient and the Occident," since Friedrich
Schlegel's new fund of knowledge gave him the means of
comprehending the Orient more accurately. He traced the
romantic spirit of the German Middle Ages, the "chivalrous spirit," as he called it, this "more than glorious,
positively enrapturing phenomenon, hitherto unparalleled
in history," back to the "combination of the elemental,
sincere heroism of the German North with Christianity,

this religious, oriental idealism." More concisely and at the same time with more comprehensive vision, Wilhelm Schlegel took the same point of view, in 1808, in the first of the Viennese lectures on dramatic art and literature. Here he set forth an hypothesis in cultural history which not only reduced the "chivalrous spirit" to a genuinely romantic formula, but also deduced the characteristics of what was romantic in general from the combination of the Northern and Christian elements and, proceeding from this point of view, conceived anew the antithesis of classic and romantic. Human nature, being self-sufficient to the Greeks, was conscious of no shortcoming and did not strive toward a perfection which it could not attain by virtue of its own strength. According to the Christian view contemplation of the infinite has destroyed the finite. "Life has become a world of shadows and darkness and the never-ending day of real existence does not dawn except in the world beyond" (p. 16). This religion makes plain that we are aspiring to happiness unattainable here below and that no external circumstances will ever be able to satisfy our souls wholly. Thus there ensue songs of melancholy when the soul breathes its longing for the home from which it has become estranged. "The poetry of the ancients was that of possession; ours is that of yearning. The former stands rooted in the present; the latter sways between memory and presentiment." Melancholy is the very being of Northern poetry.

This conception of Germanic poetry persisted for a long time. Even down to the time that Richard Heinzel and Wilhelm Scherer sought to fathom the essence and style of Germanic literature, there are traces of Wilhelm Schlegel's impression of the nostalgic poetry of the Middle Ages. It had great influence on the early romantic writers.

Wilhelm Worringer (*Formprobleme der Gotik*, second edition, 1912) advances the theory that a similar mood lay at the bottom of Germanic art.

The friends of German antiquity at the beginning of the nineteenth century, spun out, primarily, the thread of Wackenroder and Novalis, the theory of the "straightforward and genuine heroism of the Germanic North"; they idealized the German Middle Ages. First and foremost came the Heidelberg group, among whom was Goerres. And yet, in celebrating things Germanic, they felt themselves borne along by another, a newer current, for they had become national and were friends of the German nation.

Germanic studies were as much influenced by Wilhelm Schlegel's Berlin lectures as by Tieck's *Minnelieder*. Friedrich H. von der Hagen was an auditor of Wilhelm Schlegel's and willingly admitted his debt of gratitude. [19]

Tieck's interest in Catholic art and poetry brought the romanticists into touch with the Spanish writers also. Tieck secured for them the greatest poet of Catholicism, Calderon. Calderon began to rival Shakespeare in the estimation of the romanticists.

Shakespeare had always been in the foreground as far as the Schlegels were concerned; Tieck had arrived at him independently. As early as 1796 the latter brought forth his arrangement of Shakespeare's *Tempest*, adding to it a *Study in Shakespeare's Treatment of the Supernatural*. Without knowing the author, Wilhelm Schlegel, in the *Jenaische Allgemeine Literaturzeitung* (*Werke*, 11, 16 ff.), expressed his qualified approval. Marie Joachimi–Dege's *German Shakespeare Problems in the Eighteenth Century and in the Age of Romanticism* (1907) shows how the united efforts of the group lead to further ap-

preciation and how, presently, the romantic theory of
poetry is brought to maturity by way of Shakespeare and
how, finally, every new theoretic acquisition is turned to
Shakespeare's account.

Unfortunately Tieck did not, as he had planned, produce
a comprehensive work on Shakespeare, nor did Wilhelm
Schlegel summarize in separate form what he and his
comrades recognized and found in him. Hence the crown-
ing achievement of the early romantic studies in Shakespeare is that partial translation of his dramatic works
which Wilhelm Schlegel, with the help of Caroline, presented to Germany in 1797–1810—to this day the best
translation into German of a foreign classic. In this translation Wilhelm Schlegel was extraordinarily successful
in transforming Shakespeare into a German classic.
Schlegel's rendition of Shakespeare's verse is as familiar
to us and is quoted as habitually and frequently in daily
life as Goethe and Schiller. The completion of Schlegel's
translation, prepared by Tieck's daughter, Dorothea, and
Count Wolf Baudissin and published for the first time in
1825–1833 under Ludwig Tieck's name, insistently demands being done over and has achieved lasting success
only because it was swept along by Schlegel's masterly
performance. [20]

Wilhelm Schlegel was, however, never again equally
successful as a translator. His *Dante*, unfortunately, was
never finished. His *Spanish Theater* (1803–1809), to be
sure, offered the first correct translations of Calderon and
initiated Calderon's influence upon German poetry. Still
Calderon, even after others, like J. D. Gries, had translated other of his works, never became as well known in
Germany as Schlegel's Shakespeare. This contrasting tendency plainly indicates that Schlegel's translation of

Shakespeare is simply the culmination of a cultural sequence which began in the middle of the eighteenth century with J. E. Schlegel and Lessing and in which almost all the distinguished representatives of German culture in the second half of the century took part, whereas the discovery of Calderon is essentially the fruit of romanticism—a much later period. Tieck led the way. Tieck's Spanish studies began in 1793. He resumed them in 1797 in order to translate Cervantes' *Don Quixote*. This piece of work appeared in 1799–1801 and offered Friedrich Schlegel new material for fathoming romantic poetry, first of all, in the *Gespraech ueber die Poesie*. From Cervantes Tieck proceeded to the Spanish drama and lyric, just as, in order to appreciate Shakespeare more fully, he had studied the latter's contemporaries, predecessors, and followers. Now were opened up to him the "enrapturing dreams of Calderon and the marvelous images of the Spanish poets" (*Schriften,* 6, p. XVIII f.). Later he indicated the antithesis which he saw existing between Shakespeare and Calderon: Calderon is closer to antiquity. "In form and in the application of the three poetic unities" he is comparable to the ancients. "What lyric outbursts of passion, love, piety in his romances and canzonet-like verses. What pictures, what fire in these very lyrics, romances, and octaves. Not a drama, scarcely an act is without such creations of splendor; indeed, they are part and parcel of the Spanish drama" (*Krit. Schriften,* 2, 194 f.). Tieck's essay *Das deutsche Drama* (op. cit., 4, 183 ff.) goes still further by declaring that the English and the Spanish stage are diametrically opposed. Tieck, meanwhile, no longer esteemed Calderon so excessively because in the fate-drama he had discovered a dire result of the admiration for the Spanish theater (p. 211 ff.).

How far Friedrich Schlegel still was in his *Gespraech ueber die Poesie* from understanding Calderon is indicated by the supplement which he added to this essay in 1823 for Calderon's benefit. Originally this essay read: "In poetry . . . there was, to be sure, from Lope de Vega to Gozzi, many a worthy virtuoso, but hardly were there any poets and even those only for the stage" (2, 352). Now a statement to the very opposite effect was interpolated: "The only glowing exception is Calderon, the Spanish Shakespeare, a genuine artist and a great poet, who by his depth of imagination and clarity of form stands out in full perfection, unique and entirely isolated in the midst of the chaotic wealth of Spanish dramas" (*Werke,* 5, 246 f.). As late as 1812, in Friedrich Schlegel's Vienna lectures, the forces against Calderon were strongly emphasized (2, 132 ff.). But again in 1822 a whole paragraph (*Werke,* 2, 127 f.) was added which not only raised Calderon to a level with Shakespeare and Dante but also said: "In Calderon the final burst of glory in the resplendent sunset of the Catholic Middle Ages, that renaissance and Christian transformation of fancy, which indeed characterized the spirit and poetry of Catholic mediaevalism in general, achieved its greatest glorification."

Wilhelm Schlegel followed Tieck's suggestion much more quickly. As early as 1803 he began to publish his translation of Calderon. At the same time there appeared in the *Europa* a sort of self-advertisement, the essay *Ueber das spanische Theater* (1, 2, 72 ff.). Even in this, the first explicit romantic utterance concerning the Spanish drama, Calderon is rated high above Lope. Calderon is declared to be just as fertile-minded, just as diligent as an author, and moreover "an entirely different sort of poet—a poet, indeed, if ever there was one" (p. 79). In the third cycle of the Berlin lectures, Wilhelm Schlegel was able to allude to his translation, but even in the first he had already said: "Calderon may serve in the romantic drama as an example of a style just as finished as the Shakespearean but nevertheless quite different from it." The Vienna lectures (6, 384 ff.) had but little to add to the grandiose words of the essay in the *Europa*. [21]

2. ROMANTIC PAINTING IN THEORY AND PRACTICE

Wackenroder's gift for understanding individuality led him not only to Duerer but also to the Italian painters of the pre-Raphaelite era. Here it was not a question of penetrating the German spirit; indeed, it was one of defense rather than of giving information. The struggle against the one-sidedness of the classicists had been started long before Wackenroder's time. Herder, the youthful Goethe, Heinse had preceded him. But Winckelmann's doctrine of the beauty of Greek art as the only means of grace was ever and again gaining new adherents; Goethe, even before the publication of the *Propylaeen* (1798–1800), was more inclined towards it than the world knew. Not unlike Heinse, Wackenroder demanded: "Why do you not condemn the Indian for speaking the Indian language and not ours?—And yet you would condemn the Middle Ages for not building the same sort of temples as the Greeks?" (p. 102).

Wilhelm Schlegel's announcement of the *Herzenser-giessungen* (10, 363 ff.) committed him at the very outset to a conscious effort to be fair to the art of all times. Wilhelm, better schooled in the plastic arts than his brother, promoted, in the *Athenaeum*, the new point of view suggested by Wackenroder. The discourse *Die*

Gemaelde in the second volume (1799) puts Wackenroder's theory into practice and becomes a hymn of praise
to the Italian masterpieces in the Dresden gallery as well
as to many of the more modern paintings of other nations.
Rubens alone is regarded with some doubt. The fame of
Raphael's "Sistine" is really due to this romantic avowal;
nor was Holbein's Madonna overlooked. The whole dialogue emanates from the general examination which the
romanticists, who were almost all gathered together in
Dresden at the time, had attempted in 1798 in their repeated trips through the gallery. The descriptions of the
paintings and the remarks about Raphael are Caroline's.
Wilhelm competed with her in artistic form; he clothed
in the garb of sonnets typical motifs of modern painting,
notably the incidents offered by Catholic mythology.

In the Berlin lectures, Wilhelm Schlegel's contribution
to the history and criticism of art reached its highest
pitch. The historical evaluation for which Wackenroder
had striven with heart and soul was superbly victorious.
Pursuing an observation of Hemsterhuis, Wilhelm Schlegel asserted that all modern art tended to be picturesque,
ancient art, plastic (1, 156 f.). Hence it would be in keeping with the present to cultivate painting at the expense
of the plastic arts and not—as Winckelmann and his
followers wished—to serve the plastic arts only and to
superimpose their laws upon painting. Goethe, otherwise
in favor of clean-cut differentiation among the arts, was,
because of his predilection for ancient art, drawn more and
more to Winckelmann and came to make demands which
forced upon the painter the technique of the sculptor. The
romanticists refrained from similar illogicalities; like
Herder, they kept their eye upon the individual peculiarities of the various arts and guarded against grafting

ancient tendencies upon the modern era. By so doing, to be sure, they opposed the "paganism of Saxe-Weimar," and this opposition grew keener, the more the romanticists espoused, not only for artistic but also for religious reasons, the Catholic motifs in modern painting. Friedrich Schlegel here led the way.

Quite undogmatically Wackenroder had allowed Catholicism to play a part in his historic-individualistic conception. Catholicism, too, is Christianity, he maintained. The religion of the painters of bygone days was, indeed, more to him than an historical fact. He sought to determine the importance of religion in their attitude toward life. He was convinced that the art of the old German masters inexplicably symbolized their lives. "For them life and art had been fused into one mold and by virtue of this devout, invigorating combination their existence followed a more firm and positive course through the fleeting world which surrounded them" (*Phantasien ueber die Kunst,* ed. by J. Minor, p. 8). Thus faith came to be, in his estimation, the decisive factor in the form and emotional content of a work of art.

Hence the *Herzensergiessungen* wished picture galleries to be temples where one might admire great artists in mute and silent humility and in devotional solitude. It was, however, hardly Wackenroder, but rather Tieck, who had a "young German painter" ask: "Can you really understand a great picture and contemplate it with pious devotion without for the moment believing what it represents?" (p. 192). The interrogator, like Schiller's Mortimer, is willingly led by the spell of Catholic ceremonial in Rome into the arms of the Catholic church. Wilhelm Schlegel felt obliged to defend Tieck and Wackenroder from the accusation that their love for art contained a tendency toward Catholicism. The poems which Wilhelm Schlegel himself interpolated in his discourse on painting by no means create the impression that he was wholly unconversant with Catholic ways of thinking. Empathic as he was, he praised Catholic art so unreservedly that subsequently he felt obliged to excuse himself by saying it had been merely the *prédilection d'artiste* for the artistic possibilities of his subject matter. Tieck soon became the champion of Catholic art and formulated the epigram: "A Protestant protests against everything that is good and especially against poetry". (10,275). Novalis' *Christianity or Europe* thus gained support from all quarters.

Friedrich Schlegel's interest in painting, however, began at a time when he had already been drawn very near to Catholicism and conversion. In his *Europa* (1803–05) and in his *Poetic Vade-mecum for 1806* are contained Friedrich Schlegel's most significant observations on the characterization of the plastic arts. He elaborated Wackenroder's ideas and applied them to a much more comprehensive subject matter. He proceeded far beyond the *prédilection d'artiste* and examined Renaissance art less on the basis of artistic than of religious merit. Hence he preferred the "chaste, God-inspired" youthful Raphael to the mature one. Hence his frequent reference to painting as a divine art. Undeniably great credit is due him for his evaluation of the old German works of art which had been collected by the Boisserées.[22] For years his evaluation and historical classification was accepted as final. He was the first to put Master Stephan Lochener's Cologne cathedral picture alongside the "Sistine"; quite in the style of Winckelmann he did honor to this picture (*Europa, 2, 2,* 135 f.). Afterwards, to be sure, Schlegel retracted somewhat of this high praise, although he had learned in the meantime to feel even more strongly Catholic, and proved thereby that his enthusiasm had not been due solely to religious reasons. But the Nazarene school of painters used these confessions of Friedrich Schlegel as a point of departure; from them, far more than from Wackenroder's pen, proceeded that "neo-Catholic artistry," "that lay-brotherish, Sternbaldic mischief," as Goethe sarcastically called it, knowing that in the opinion of his contemporaries he could not maintain his own popularity in the face of this new tendency. Having once more loyally defended Nazarenism in 1819, Friedrich Schlegel in 1825 was able to announce its success. By this time his artistic perception had got so badly out of focus that only one aspect of Wackenroder's still prevailed: the inner light of inspiration. This was now, in Friedrich Schlegel's estimation, of far more importance than the mere gift of vivid imagination or the magic of color.

Propaganda among Wackenroder's followers kept Friedrich Schlegel from applying to the plastic arts his most profound and fundamental art tenets. To Schelling, who was spiritually foreign to Nazarenism, he left the task of training the painter to create organically and to demand of him that he view his subject as a whole and fill in and sketch the details accordingly. Schelling's lecture *Concerning the Relation of the Plastic Arts to Nature* (1807) won Goethe's whole-hearted approval; the basic points of view, whence had developed Friedrich Schlegel's theory of the artistic organism, of the whole and of its parts, and of the alternating union of the two, had been propounded by Goethe himself. And Goethe also could come to an understanding with Philipp Otto Runge, that painter among the romanticists who in his own way had come nearest to Schelling's ideas in theory and in practice.

From an entirely different point of view, Runge, a pupil of
Jens Juels, had been forging ahead toward the same
objectives. Like another pupil of Juels, Kasper David
Friedrich, Runge learned from his master to suffuse the
contours of a landscape in light, to see in a landscape no
clearly drawn outlines, in fact, no definite objects at all,
but rather a general effect in color tones. How unusual
and startling Friedrich's attempts seemed to his contemporaries, and even to a romanticist, is indicated by a remark
made by Kleist (*Werke,* ed. Erich Schmidt, 4, 230 ff.).
It has been said in praise of Runge, that he anticipated
intuitively all of the essential ideas of nineteenth century
painting. As a matter of fact, he was in advance of his
time in his effort to win, like Goethe, a new conception
of light and color by intensive contemplation of nature;
in his organic presentation, which linked him to Goethe
and romanticism; and in his symbolic ornamentation,
which likewise suggested Schelling. Siegfried Krebs (*Ph.
O. Runges Entwicklung unter dem Einflusse L. Tiecks,*
1909) proved that Runge, the artist, inspired by Tieck,
had derived his ideas of the organism and of symbolism,
not from the dogmas of the romantic theorists but directly
from Boehme. Among the romanticists, besides Tieck, the
Heidelberg group was close to Runge. [23]

So-called romantic painting was not determined by
Runge's artistic ideas but by Wackenroder's interest in
the subject matter. The work of Runge and Friedrich
remained a side-issue which did not come to full fruition
until much later. How close this side-issue, in contrast
to Nazarenism, approached Goethe is indicated by the
Epistles on Landscape Painting, which were based upon
Runge and Friedrich, and written by the Dresden physiologist and painter, C. G. Carus, in 1831 and 1833. [24]

Carus linked the theory of landscape painting, or, as he called it, "the art of depicting natural life," directly with Schelling's nature philosophy and the conception of the world-spirit. He felt that a landscape was imbued with a loftier and more potent spirit if one recognized, or at least had an inkling of the active, spiritual force in the broad, expansive surface of the planet. Then one could understand the spiritual bond which, with hidden force, binds the movements and transformations of external nature to the emotional moods of our own souls (cf. his *Lebenserinnerungen und Denkwuerdigkeiten,* 1, 181). Like Friedrich he sought, therefore, a spiritually conceived picture of nature which presented, at the same time, the mobility in the life of the landscape, according to the season, time of day, light, and weather. Neither Friedrich Schlegel nor Carus was to be lured by lovely or memorable scenes; their approbation was reserved for impressionistic landscapes. On the broad plains of Pomerania it occurred to Carus that only an impoverished nature, with oaks, sand, field and swamp, could produce a Ruisdael, whereas the teeming nature of Switzerland for a long time produced nothing in any way similar (*Ibid.,* p. 261).

Meanwhile it has retrieved itself. For this reason, too, Carus and Friedrich are much more closely related to the most recent art movement than are the Nazarenes.

3. MUSIC IN THE LIGHT OF ROMANTICISM. LYRIC POETRY
AND THE ROMANTIC THEORY

Wackenroder led the romanticists not only to painting but also to that art form which is frequently designated as the most romantic of all, namely, music. He was endowed with great sensibility but was not given to self-analysis; hence music and all that it inspired within him must have been the revelation of his inmost soul.

Herder and Heinse seem to have had the same strong reaction to this art. Wackenroder was the pupil of Fasch and of Reichard, the revolutionary writer, and the composer of Goethe's songs, whom the *Xenien* used rather badly. In Reichard's family circle, to which Tieck presently became related, he was surfeited with music. But here Wackenroder, on the other hand, learned not only to apprehend the secrets of music but also to preserve these secrets unsullied and chaste. In those essays in the *Herzens-ergiessungen* and the *Phantasien ueber die Kunst* in which Wackenroder speaks of music, he inveighs particularly against expressing a piece of music in words, "measuring the richer language by the poorer and resolving into words that language which scorns mere words" (*Phantasien*, p. 71). And yet how well he could conjure up in words the mood of the old choral-like church music! (p. 64). But Wackenroder said: "He who seeks to discover with the divining-rod of searching reason that which has its source within will ever have only observations about the emotion; he will never experience the emotion itself. . . . Just as any work of art can be comprehended and grasped spiritually only by the same emotion which produced it, just so emotion itself can be comprehended and grasped only by emotion" (p. 70). An emotion should remain an emotion but even as such it should nevertheless be fully comprehended (cf. above, p. 14). For as an emotion it has a perceptive value which is lost when it is dissected into concepts. Wackenroder seeks to explain what he means: "I shall use a flowing stream as an illustration. It is beyond human art to depict in words meant for the eye the thousands of individual waves, smooth and rugged, bursting and foaming, in the flow of a mighty river—words can but meagerly recount the incessant movements and cannot visibly picture the consequent rearrangement of the drops of water. Just so it is with the mysterious stream in the depths of the human soul; words mention and name and describe its flux in a foreign medium. In music, however, the stream itself seems to be released. Music courageously smites upon the hidden harp strings and, in that inner world of mystery, strikes up in due succession certain mysterious chords—our heart-strings, and we understand the music" (p. 71). Without any pretensions to philosophy, Wackenroder aimed at the same thing as Schelling's aesthetic idealism and the related conceptions of Friedrich Schlegel and Hardenberg: art and philosophy are inextricably bound together and a work of art is the medium of a higher understanding. [25] Wackenroder, outstripping the philosophy of his day, actually got into touch with Schopenhauer, who, for his part, merely expanded Schelling's doctrine. From the artistic point of view, upon calm contemplation every single thing is transformed into its fundamental idea, its eternal form, into the essential and enduring qualities which are peculiar to it. Thus art penetrates into the perception of infinite ideas, the full comprehension of which is not vouchsafed to mere reason. And according to Schopenhauer, music alone of all the arts offers more than an image of conceptions. Music could still exist even if the world itself did not. Music is "just as much the immediate objectification and image of the collective will as the world itself is." "Hence the effect of music is so much greater and more penetrating than that of the other arts: the latter are concerned only with the phantoms of things, but music is concerned with their essence" (*Die Welt als Wille und Vorstellung*, ed. by E. Grisebach, 1, 340).

It was Wackenroder's conception of music, anticipating Schopenhauer, that determined the important rôle which music plays in the life, sensibility, thought, faith, emotion, and poetry of the romanticists. [26]

From the postulates which Wackenroder offered him, Tieck derived his question: Is it not immaterial whether a person thinks in the tones of instruments or in so-called thoughts?" (*Phantasien*, p. 90). This is poetically expressed in the frequently glossed lines:

> Love thinks in lovely sounds,
> For thoughts are too remote;
> In sound alone she would express
> What she would beautify.

Novalis goes further in defining music: "Stories without coherence, but with association, nevertheless, like dreams. Poems, merely mellifluous and full of lovely words, but wholly without meaning or coherence—at most a few intelligible verses—like a mass of fragments of widely-differing articles" (2, 308). This form appeals to him especially for the fairy-tale; it is "like a dream-picture, without coherence, an ensemble of marvelous things and events, i.e., a musical fantasy, the melodious sequence of an Aeolian harp, nature itself." Tieck's *Sternbald* suggests the idea that one could devise conversation musically (Minor, p. 284) and elsewhere propounds the question why the content of a poem should lie specifically in its content (p. 344). And so in *Sternbald*, words vie with music, verses seek to imitate the tone-color of specific instruments, the timbre of the reed-pipe, the post-boy's

horn, the melody of the bugle-horn, the Alpine-horn.
Tieck's *Die verkehrte Welt* carries the experiment even
further, having at the beginning a symphony in words;
the *entr'acte* music is supplied in words also. Brentano's
Gustav Wasa imitates this jest of Tieck's. In the sym-
phonic overture to *Die verkehrte Welt,* however, under
the caption "Violino Primo Solo" we read: "What! It is
not permissible, not possible to think in sounds and to make
music with words and thoughts? What a pretty fix in that
case should we artists be in! How impoverished speech,
how even more impoverished music!" (5, 286).

Tieck in his *Phantasien* also advanced his doctrine of
the relationship between color and music: "For every
lovely painting there is without doubt a complementary
piece of music and the two together have but one soul"
(p. 45). Courageously and steadfastly he proceeded in
this course, lending sound to form and color, and color
to sound. In *Zerbino* the flute characterizes itself: "Our
spirit is as blue as the sky and lures you into the blue
distance" (10, 291). Here the communism of the senses
is specifically meant (10, 251):

The color sounds, the form reverberates, and each,
According to form and color, has tongue and speech.
What has been separated by divine jealousy
The goddess of fancy here reunites.
Sound knows its color
And through every leaf the sweet voice shines.
One family all are color, fragrance, song.
In close embrace, all are but a single friend,
In divine poetry so firmly bound
That in this friend each one beholds himself.

The *audition colorée*, the hearing of colors, was herewith introduced into the garden of romantic poetry. It is hard to say how far the romantic vogue for sounding colors and beaming sounds rests upon actual dual susceptibility on the part of the individual romanticists and how far it is just pursuing a catch-phrase. With consummate subtlety, Ottokar Fischer seeks to prove that Tieck (*Zeitschrift fuer Aesthetik*, 2, 531) and E. T. A. Hoffman (*Archiv fuer das Studium der neueren Sprachen,* 123, 1 ff.) really had the gift of dual susceptibility. Hoffman, according to Fischer, though, of course, inspired by Tieck, was not content merely to accept the formulas of Tieck's *audition colorée*, as the majority of the other romanticists did.

The phenomena of sound and color played an important part in romantic poetry. The color-sensitivity of the romanticists, which gave their style such a peculiar tint, was appraised by W. Steinert (*Schriften der literarhistorischen Gesellschaft*, Bonn, vol. 7, 1910) on the basis of Tieck's nervously vivid color-sensitivity. The rôle which was accorded music in Hoffmann's productions was duly recognized by C. Schaeffer (*Die Bedeutung des Musikalischen und Akustischen in Hoffmanns literarischem Schaffen*, 1909). Hoffman may be accepted as the pivotal point of all types of romantic musical emotion, even though, as E. Kroll proved, (*E. T. A. Hoffmanns musikalische Anschauungen*, Koenigsberg dissertation, 1909) in questions of musical theory and in his attitude toward individual musicians, he adhered to the principles of classical music and assumed the genuine romantic point of view only when he proceeded to subjective interpretations. The musical and acoustic qualities are strongly pronounced in Hoffmann's imagery and language as is also the play of colors and even more particularly the play of light. He compared sound with visual phenomena even more readily than he transformed what he saw into a procession of sounds. Indeed, he even changed sounds into physical beings.

The fact that romantic imagery in general replaces the clear and concise phenomena of sight with the far more uncertain phenomena of sound, may be traced back to the conscious tendency to remove from common reality the more sensual and routine things by comparing them with the less sensual and less known and by placing side by side the familiar, the well-known and the strange, the marvelous, thus lending the presentation dignity and power (cf. Wilhelm Schlegel's *Berliner Vorlesungen,* 1, 290). Hence the romanticist was led to interpret what is visible and perceptible by means of related sounds. He was the more justified in so doing because he really perceived the external world musically. His hearing was better and more subtle than that of other people; dull, faint noises reached his ear more clearly. Visual perceptions therefore assumed a rhythmic quality or a spiritual process took the form of a musical melody, but combination and antitheses in the realm of thought seemed to him like symphonically arranged voices. Friedrich Schlegel's discussion of Goethe's *Lehrjahre* treats this poetic production as if it were a piece of music. He defends Tieck's *Sternbald* against Goethe's accusation that he offered only "musical travels" with the commendation that the book pretended to be nothing but lovely music of, and for, the imagination (*Caroline,* 1, 469). Wilhelm Schlegel says of the songs in Tieck's *Volksmaerchen*: "The language has relinquished all corporeal form and resolves itself into a spiritual exhalation. The words seem hardly to be spoken; hence the whole seems even more delicate than song; at any rate, it is the most immediate and insoluble union of sound and soul, and yet the marvelous melodies can be understood" (12, 34).

There was another cause for the lack of clarity and precision in romantic imagery. The latter dealt with the "new mythology" of romantic "physics." Natural philosophy added to the store of romantic imagery a wealth of symbols, the more profound meaning of which is as vague to us as it was familiar to the romanticists. Goerres developed a crushing wealth of imagery. His efforts were steadily directed toward the interpretation of the most recondite spiritual phenomena by means of analogous phenomena in nature. Romantic imagery was more to him than a mere figure of speech; he actually thought that he was making new discoveries in keeping with the spirit of natural philosophy when he set the ancient and modern worlds over against each other like original and erosional mountains, carrying out the contrast to the last letter. Goerres' arbitrary style was due to the fact that the constant parallels in spiritual and physical processes were the accepted and self-evident thing in his natural philosophy. Any one who cannot orient himself in a world of such perceptions finds only bombast in Goerres' works (cf. *Euphorion,* 10, 792 ff.). As a matter of fact, he wanted to develop the new symbolism of nature. In his effort to create the imagery anew and to develop it from the temper of the times, Goerres is in accord with Jean Paul, his stylistic model. And from Jean Paul the way leads back to Klopstock whose "shimmering" similes point in the direction of romantic imagery.

"More delicate than song, the most immediate and insoluble union of sound and soul"—thus Tieck's lyrics were conceived. The song was to have the effect of music and the words vie with the melody; the sound effect was of more importance to the poet than the formulation of the thought or content. This is especially true of his youthful lyrics; and within this group, the songs of his *Magelone* and then those of *Sternbald* come nearest to his ideals. The sound effect is produced by means of free rhythmic form; this effect may change not only from verse to verse but also from strophe to strophe. Emotional poetry of such subtlety cannot and will not maintain throughout an entire poem a single metrical scheme. The ebb and flow of the mood, the romantic-protean change in the emotional situation is indicated when strophes of varying nature unite in one song. Lyrics such as these, inasmuch as they express so subtly the subjective in life, can also lure the composer, as is indicated by the fact that Brahms set to music the songs of *Magelone* (Opus 33). The lyric form can express passion, but better still it can depict a succession of images as they flit in deliquescent outline through the poet's mind. This is proved by the poem which opens the second volume of the first edition of *Sternbald*. In seventy-five lines, which for the most part are arranged in strophes of four lines each but which also contain some stanzas of five and six lines, the poet, according to his own commentary, "laments in these words his youth, which has fled, and his memories range themselves at his feet in the shape of sounds and gentle pictures." The changing mood is depicted by the flux of the rhythmic structure, which gains speed in a happy mood and is more deliberate in a sad one. But the mood itself is derived from the images which crowd the poet's fancy. Hopefully and joyfully the poem starts:

Hands are beckoning from the clouds,
Red roses on every finger;
They beckon with flattering caresses.
"Whither," you pause and ask, "goes the way?"

Then all the spring zephyrs commence to sing;
The flowers are fragrant and tinkle;
Delicate rustling echoes down the valley:
Be brave and do not fear.

Do you see the moonbeams' shimmer,
The glimmering of the bubbling springs?
The golden hilltops high in the clouds
And dawn's heaven-embracing wings?

Thus love and good fortune approach you
To catch you, as booty, in their golden net;
So gently, so softly, as to leave no escape,
They close in upon you, and soon you are lost.

The mood changes; the disillusionment which has dogged
all youthful hopes is painted in gloomy colors:

It seems as though the springs were silent;
He fancies dark shadows arise
And quench the green flames of the forest;
And flowers withdraw their finery.

The gracious flowers are gone now;
Fruits stand in the self-same place;
The nightingale conceals its song in the forest;
Only echoes reverberate through the solitude.

Poetry of mood and imagery, absolutely unhampered by
any regulations! And yet there was in this endeavor to

give unchecked sweep to the emotions, the desire rhythmically to grasp and reproduce the mood more clearly and accurately than a stricter verse-structure would permit. Here, more than in any other poetic attempts on the part of romanticism, is manifest the desire to free artistic form of all limitations and to recognize only those restrictions which the spiritual content demands. The prototype for this sort of lyric was presently believed to have been discovered in the diversity of the structural forms of the *Minnelieder,* though it approaches more nearly the free rhythms of Klopstock and Goethe. But there is missing the verve with which Klopstock and Goethe animate their free verse. Furthermore it has submitted to the bondage of rime; this however was thrown off in 1805 and 1806 in the two cycles which resulted from Tieck's Italian journey, the *Reisegedichte eines Kranken* and the *Rueckkehr des Genesenden* (*Gedichte,* 1834, 3, 98 ff., 236 ff.). There disappeared with it a trait of romantic lyric poetry which had done service to euphonious word painting and music. Tieck himself declares in his preface to the *Minnelieder* (*Krit. Schriften,* 1, 199) that rime is demanded by "the love of sound and resonance, by the feeling that similar sounding words must be related either definitely or more or less mysteriously, and by the desire to change poetry into music—into something that is at the same time definite and indefinite." Hence romantic lyric poetry teems with rimes; it cannot heap up enough of them; it cannot repeat them too often, and it makes a veritable game of echoing rimes. For similar reasons it favored assonance, which is carried through verse after verse and which, of even greater service in the painting of moods, is frequently carried to the point of bad taste (Tieck's *Die Zeichen im Walde, Gedichte,* 1, 22 ff.).

The uses to which riming was put also lured the romanticists into the field of romantic metrical structure. The first promptings came from Gottfried August Buerger who suggested to his pupil, Wilhelm Schlegel, the translation and the use of the sonnet and also the imitation of the poetry and forms of the Romance nations. This prescribed a program of lyrics severe in form and far remote from Tieck's musically deliquescent plasticity. Indeed, it is hardly possible to conceive of greater contrasts than exist between the sonnets and stanzas of the clean-cut rimer, Wilhelm Schlegel, and the songs of *Magelone* and of *Sternbald*. And yet Tieck could make the Romance forms serve his musical lyrics. Canzonets and ballads were even more amenable to the romantic tendency to give significance to rimes. For it was a favorite device of romantic subtlety to discover the deeper significance of coupling rimes and assonances as well as of romantic strophic structures. Again it was demonstrable how the spirit is reflected in the form, and the infinite in the finite. Such efforts gave rise to a symbolism of rime and assonance, a symbolism of strophic structure. Wilhelm Schlegel was very prompt to try out rime and assonance, though at first only in the rôle of metrist and philologian. His observations on metrics (7, 155 ff.) treated as early as 1794 problems of the spiritual content of the vocal material of speech. The *Briefe ueber Poesie, Silbenmass und Sprache* appeared in *Die Horen* in 1795 (7, 98 ff.); *Der Wettstreit der Sprachen* (7, 197 ff.), aimed at Klopstock, appeared in the *Athenaeum* in 1798 and sought to measure the musical value of the cultural languages. In his Berlin lectures Wilhelm Schlegel, in characterizing Italian poetry (3, 186 ff.), tried to fathom the principles underlying Italian strophe forms, but not without passing from form symbolism into thin air. At the same time, Tieck's brother-in-law, A. F. Bernhardi, in the second part of his *Sprachlehre* (1803, p. 399 ff.) discussed not only the deeper meaning of alliteration, assonance, and rime but also the tone-color and symbolic significance of Italian and Spanish strophes. The last of these romantic efforts is Kaspar Poggel's splendid article *Grundzuege einer Theorie des Reims und der Gleichklaenge mit besonderer Ruecksicht auf Goethe* (Muenster, 1836).

VI. POLITICAL AND SOCIAL TRANSFORMA-
TION. ROMANTIC POLITICAL SCIENCE
AT THE TIME OF THE WARS OF
LIBERATION AND THE REACTION

A T the beginning of the nineteenth century the stream of romantic thought, which up to that time had been rich and teeming, seemed to be exhausted. Hardenberg's death (1801), Friedrich Schlegel's removal to Paris (1802), his brother's Berlin lectures and the entrance into the circle of Mme. de Stael, Tieck's departure for Italy (1804), Schelling's union with Caroline and his call to Wuerzburg (1803): all these things indicate disintegration and the end. The individual threads are drawn out, this or that phase of the romantic theory is extended, but the formative, speculative epoch in romanticism is essentially past. Such a complete change could only have been brought about by an element quite new, which, unnoticed, had developed with surprising force. The romanticists were by no means so worn out that they merely wasted away without substituting immediately for the ideals which they relinquished something else that was progressive and revolutionary. It was not exhaustion and enervation which set in but rather a fervid animation, which broadened the romantic horizon on the one hand as much as it diminished it on the other.

This new element was an interest in political, national, and social affairs. The romanticists began to take a stand against Napoleon; not only in the aesthetic, but also in the political sense, they became conscious of their national peculiarities, and they began to carry out their doctrine of educating the selected individual by recognizing the significance of the masses, that is, the social unit. German nationality henceforth became their program. In 1810 *Turnvater* Jahn published a book bearing the title *Das deutsche Volkstum*. But the inspiration to these tendencies went back almost five years and it came directly out of the stronghold of romanticism.

With astonishing rapidity the Schlegels proceeded from cosmopolitanism to national politics. Earlier in their career they had been interested, in cosmopolitan fashion, in the French Revolution. Even as late as 1796 Friedrich Schlegel wrote his *Essay on the Conception of Republicanism* for *Deutschland,* the publication of the *sansculotte* Reichardt. Abstractly and logically he started from Kant's words, "The civil constitution in every state should be republican" (Minor, 2, 57), and developed them consistently. Then it became the watchword of the *Athenaeum* to abstain entirely from political discussions: "Do not fritter away your faith and love in the political world but rather, in the divine world of science and art, make sacrifice of your innermost self upon the altar of everlasting culture" (*Idee* 106). To be sure there appeared in 1798 in the July number of the *Year Book of the Prussian Monarchy under the Rule of Fredrick William III* Hardenberg's fragments called *Faith and Love, or the King and the Queen*. Friedrich Schlegel, too, was fascinated and wrote to the author: "There are few things that I honor as much, and but few things have affected me so keenly" (Raich, p. 129 f.). Republicanism vanished and the future romantic theory of political science proclaimed itself. But as yet the national-social feeling was missing.

It was Queen Louise and not the German people that charmed Hardenberg's poetic soul just as she fascinated Heinrich von Kleist. To be sure the *Ideen* had restated the national problem and Novalis and Wackenroder had awakened interest in all that pertained to German antiquity (cf. p. 91 f., 104 ff.). That the temper of the day was nevertheless still far removed from native, patriotic feeling is indicated by Wilhelm Schlegel's biting mockery of the patriotism of Klopstock and his disciples, which he characterized as "fanatical, utterly devoid of knowledge of the historical character of the Germans, their present situation, and their erstwhile deeds" (*Berlin Lectures,* 3, 21 f.). More accurately, the new era proclaimed itself when Wilhelm Schlegel maintained the necessity of war for which "many a philosopher had already interceded" (3, 93 ff.). We read, indeed, in the posthumous sketches of *Ofterdingen:* "War is at home on earth. There must be war on earth" (4, 259).

The turn set in the moment when Friedrich Schlegel stepped upon French soil. The two poems *At the Wartburg* and *On the Rhine,* which he published in the first issue of the *Europa* in 1803 (see above, p. 108), praised the old days of German chivalry not alone in the glorifying sense of Wackenroder and Hardenberg; they were as well a nationalistic conception of the moment. The Rhine reminded Friedrich Schlegel of what the Germans once were and of what they could still be (*A,* p. 447 ff.).

Wilhelm Schlegel, too, March 12, 1806, explains to Fouqué in a comprehensive letter of confession (8, 144 f.) : Mere toying, idle, dreamy fantasy has been, predominantly, the chief element in the poetic output of the last epoch; the type of poetry which Germany needs just now, however, is absolutely not dreamy but vivid, direct, energetic, and, particularly, patriotic. "Perhaps, as long as our national independence, yes, even the continuance of our German name is so seriously threatened, our poetry ought to yield entirely to eloquence." And here Wilhelm Schlegel pointed to the two poems of his brother.

In 1807 Wilhelm Schlegel publicly championed these views in the discussion of Rostorf's *Dichtergarten* (12, 206 ff.). And again he could allude to poems which his brother had written. This whole collection, he said, was conceived in the same spirit as his brother's verses:

> The Germans' fame in golden days,
> When knighthood meant devotion,
> Which now, alas, too late they reverence
>
> Should be, before it fades away,
> All stripped of vain illusion,
> The mighty theme of poets' utterance.

Friedrich Schlegel was headed directly toward the lyric poetry of the Wars of Liberation. [27] Immediately after the Battle of Jena, at the very moment when Arndt began to lift his voice, he wrote his songs *Geluebde* and *Freiheit* (9, 180, 182). Henceforth the patriotic lyric was intimately connected with him. The Viennese follower of the Schlegels, Heinrich Joseph von Collin, wrote his *Songs of Austrian Soldiers* for the War of 1809, in which Friedrich Schlegel participated under the banner of the Archduke Karl. Before they themselves entered the war, Theodor Koerner and Eichendorff were visitors in the home of Friedrich Schlegel in Vienna. Of all the Liberation poets, Max von Schenkendorf most accurately caught the romantic-religious spirit of Hardenberg and Schlegel.

Schlegel's *Freiheit,* particularly, spurred him on to his
Freiheit, die ich meine.

Meanwhile, however, the decisive influence toward
social thought was destined to proceed from him who had
occasioned the most one-sided, individualistic manifestations of romanticism, namely, Fichte. In his *Naturrecht*
(1796) Fichte still inclines so strongly toward cosmopolitan points of view that he has no use for nationality. The state is conceived essentially as a medium of
public order. There followed, however, the demand that
the state guarantee all its citizens the fundamental moral
right to make a living by their work. Fichte developed
this basic idea of socialism in his *Der geschlossene Han-
delsstaat* (1800): the state is responsible for the collective
organization of labor. By this time his state had become
a social organism which he attempted to elucidate in the
Fundamental Principles of the Present Age (1806). Napoleon's wars of conquest urged him on. They raised the
question in his mind whether individual nations, as well
as individual personalities, might not also have a special
destiny in the plan of the world; and whether this special
destiny did not entail the duty of its fulfillment and at
the same time connote the right of a nation to political
independence. Fichte reached the conclusion that the German nation had such a mighty cultural destiny, that con-
sidering the inharmonious development of the other
nations she almost alone was meant to fulfill the ideal of
humanity. In the rebirth of the German nation was his
only hope of relief from the chaotic conditions which
prevailed everywhere. The liberation of the German spirit
was revealed to him as the duty which was entailed upon
the nation by its very destiny. To accomplish this the Germans would need to achieve political nationality. The

ground-work for the future must be prepared by educating the nation.

This is the credo of the *Address to the German Nation* (1808). With one blow the idea of nationality and the new social conception were here forged together. There was no longer merely the gesture toward the departed glory of Germany, no longer merely the demand that Germany ought to have the spiritual leadership of the world (see above, p. 107). The duty to develop national consciousness was postulated by the condition of the German nation, by the existing economic situation, and by the pending problems of society. This was the first unconditional statement of the fact that a commonwealth of learning is no substitute for the state and that the annihilation of the political independence of the German nation threatened the very glory of German literature and art. [28]

Likewise from quite another point of view it became customary to think of the German nation as an entity rather than as various isolated, predominant personalities and to consider the duties which the individual has toward this collective society. The Brandenburger Arnim was prominent here. He was devotedly attached to the soil upon which he was born; he had a genuine fatherland. In 1806 he was already gathering war songs for it. But he was elastic enough in his patriotism to include the whole of Germany. All of Germany was to share the joy which he derived from German life and art. Arnim was the first of the romanticists to work consciously not only for the educated but also for the masses, to bring back to the latter their old national possessions and to give them as much as they could assimilate of the learned world.

Arnim derived his conception of German nationality

from history. He felt there was vested in him a tradition which he wished to see preserved. In the *Graefin Dolores* (1, 93) he says, "Only the profligate begins a new world with himself; the good is eternal." "That marvelous condition without actuality" (*Werke*, 12, 29) which the French Revolution brought to a head was objectionable to him. He would have none of the cosmopolitanism which had "made of Europe one delightful humane fabrication" (*Dolores*, 1, 124). This is the philosophic viewpoint of a margravate nobleman; at the same time Arnim had the highest conception of nobility, feeling that a nobleman before all others must practice self-direction and fulfill his duties. Agrarianism was revealed in him in strictly moral, duty-bound form. His pronounced preference for the country prejudiced him against industry and commerce; it supported his antipathy toward the Jews. A strong class consciousness determined his social pedagogy. He wished to rear not people but Germans; he did not strive, as did the early romanticists, for a harmonious development of all the faculties; he called only for patriotic servants who would work to the best of their ability within the limits of their class of society. [29]

Adam Mueller's teachings were closely related to Arnim's ideas of political science. Hence Arnim could undertake with Mueller and with his fellow-nobleman, Heinrich von Kleist, whose patriotic zeal burst forth with equal might in lyric and drama, the joint enterprise of the *Abendblaetter* (1810-11). Reinhold Steig's researches (*Heinrich von Kleists Berliner Kaempfe*, 1901) have established the fact that the *Abendblaetter* in policy, content, and form were the organ of the Prussian junkers in their struggle against the chancellor of state, Count Hardenberg, against his politics, which dabbled in dilettante fashion with the ideas inspired by the French Revolution, as well as against his ideas of political science, which were based upon Adam Smith. Adam Mueller placed his impress upon the magazine: opposition to the Revolution out of principle, in accordance with Burke's conception of the state; essential continuance of Prussia as an agricultural state; no reforms in economic conditions through the principles of Adam Smith. All this was supported by great patriotism and by the desire to shake off the French yoke. Though perhaps, since it was a partisan paper, the junker political interests may at times have come prejudicially to the surface, the publication is nevertheless a characteristic and genuine document of romantic political, patriotic, and national-economic tendencies. For inasmuch as Arnim could agree with practically all of these pronouncements, just so all of Adam Mueller's assertions led up to the credo of romantic political economy as it developed after the year 1800. The conservative agrarianism which Adam Mueller represented prepared the way for the retrogressive politics of the period after 1815. Adam Mueller became the herald of this tendency, in intimate relation with Friedrich von Gentz, Metternich's right hand man, with Friedrich Schlegel, and with Karl Ludwig von Haller. [30]

In this field, also, Friedrich Schlegel led the way. In his Cologne lectures of 1806 (Windischmann, 2, 306–396) he developed systematically for the first time his views upon natural rights and the rights of the state, upon politics and international law. Here, too, we read (p. 369): "Nobility belongs wholly to the agriculturist; the nobleman is but an elevated agriculturist himself." Here too the upper-class frame of mind is revealed in the statement: "The manner in which business is now carried on is highly dangerous to the purpose of the state" (p. 371). But for the present there was still a wide chasm between Friedrich Schlegel and the Berlin patriots. Schlegel had already assumed a mediaeval religious point of view; he was carrying out systematically ideas and dreams contained in Novalis' essay *Christianity or Europe* (see above, p. 91). There was as yet no bridge leading from here to Arnim, Kleist, and Adam Mueller. Subsequently Adam Mueller went over to Schlegel's camp just as did another comrade of Arnim's youth, J. J. Goerres. Goerres, like the early romanticists, had at one time also been enthusiastic over the French Revolution. Then he visited Paris and returned an enemy of the new France. Presently there developed in him, too, a strong national feeling due to ancient German art and poetry. As a Heidelberg comrade of Arnim and Brentano, he strove to reawaken the old German world and at the same time he set up broad and high ideals for the budding study of German antiquity. From 1814 on, his periodical, *Der Rheinische Merkur,* was creating so much commotion in behalf of the Wars of Liberation that the opposition rendered it due honor by calling it the fifth great power. In 1816 it was suppressed by the reaction; the haughty, turbulently temperamental man from the Rhineland, however, continued for a long time to be the champion of liberalism and fought out many a combat with the Prussian bureaucracy. In opposition to the latter, Goerres espoused the cause of militant Catholicism. After his call to Munich (1827) he had been drawn more and more into the stream of the reactionary Roman hierarchy. Finally he became one of the most zealously enthusiastic supporters of the ideal which filled Friedrich Schlegel's old age. [31]

Fundamental concepts of early romanticism were at the

base of Friedrich Schlegel's theories in the field of political science: one great organism was to be erected, in which all parts were to be interrelated—a universal system of theocracy. The organic unity of all things, God, was conceived in the Christian sense; as in Novalis' essay, as in Friedrich Schlegel's subsequent interpretations of cultural history (see above, p. 99 ff.), the Middle Ages appeared as the sublimest embodiment of the organic and harmonious union of spiritual and temporal power. It was now the task of Catholicism to reëstablish this organic harmony. Thus religion became the organic center of life.

In this confession of faith the church ranked first and the state second. All civil authority comes from God. The church fulfills every ideal of the noblest spiritual community; the state needs only to guarantee the external demands of life in such a community. Hence the state limits itself to the mediaeval ideals of statecraft: order and right, peace and justice.

From such opinions romantic political science proceeded rapidly to a point of view diametrically opposed to the national endeavor rife during the time of the Wars of Liberation. A political universality once more erased the national boundaries which at the beginning of the nineteenth century had arisen to replace cosmopolitanism. Austria was to carry out the universal-clerical ideals; its conglomeration of various nationalities seemed to serve the purpose.

On the other hand, the turn toward collectivism which had set in at the beginning of the century was not lost sight of. To be sure the monarch was elevated to being the representative of the great harmonious unity; indeed, the question was pondered whether supreme pontifical

dignity ought not to be added to the regal dignity. Henceforth the authority of the nobles and not the force of
law was to support the state. In other words, a religious
absolutism such as was, on the one hand, merely planned
and, on the other, actually practiced in the days of the
sixteenth century! Precisely in this way, through the
closest union of society in general, the individual was to
gain the greatest amount of freedom and the idea of the
representation of the masses according to social classes
was considered.

Romanticism proved in these final postulates of a
political nature that it had kept pace with the spirit of the
times. Young Germany likewise believed in cosmopolitanism and collectivism. To be sure it was equally as revolutionary and radical-minded as romanticism was reactionary. But contemporary problems were considered
by both parties with equal enthusiasm, even if from antithetical points of view. Though Young Germany represented essentially the extension of the ideas of early
romanticism, nevertheless, in order to reach the pinnacle
of contemporary thought, it was bound, in the last
analysis, to link the current problems of cosmopolitanism
and collectivism with the wealth of ideas which romanticism had formerly advanced, with all the latter's revolutionary ideals—with elements, indeed, which romanticism
itself had long since abandoned. Young Germany, to be
sure, thus overtook aging romanticism, but by this very
circumstance revealed itself to be nothing but an imitation and drove home the fact that to the very last romanticism was well aware of the problems that were demanding solution.

PART II

THE CREATIVE LITERATURE OF ROMANTICISM

I. LYRICS PATTERNED UPON THE FOLK-SONG

THE trend of thought and the poetry of early romanticism are closely interwoven. The paths which led from the speculation and the poetry of the older generation directly to the creative work of the younger were already apparent in the formulization of the philosophy of romanticism. Yet the poetry of early romanticism is by no means always the mere product of theory; not infrequently it anticipates theoretic conclusions. Nor does the poetry of the later romanticists merely develop the forms and ideas which had been prepared by the early romantic circle. The younger romantic generation was far too richly endowed with genuine artistic talent to follow slavishly upon the heels of the older. This keen artistic bent caused the younger group, from the very outset, to run counter to the speculative trend of Friedrich Schlegel, Schleiermacher, and Hardenberg. But in spite of all this the fundamentals of the romantic nature endured throughout the course of the movement. There is evidence that testifies specifically to this close connection. Uhland's study in romanticism (see above, Part 1, p. 32 f.) proves how devoutly various groups of the younger romanticists, such as that of Uhland and of Kerner, steeped themselves in the fundamental tenets of the romantic theory and made them their own.

The connection which exists between the earlier and the later romantic poetry is clearer and less equivocal than the connection between the theory of the early romanticists and the poetry of the younger group. Very few new developments arise in romantic poetry in later years which can not be traced back to the last decade of the eighteenth century.

The most pronounced change took place in the lyric field. Later romanticism presented German literature with an inestimable wealth of lyric poetry. The German national lyric of the nineteenth century was very largely the outgrowth of the transformation which took place in the field of the romantic lyric during the first decade of that century. This does not take into consideration the lyric poetry of the Wars of Liberation (for this was still a product of early romanticism) but rather that type of lyric which is reminiscent of the folk-song.

The poets of the Liberation created no new lyric form; purposely and effectively they poured new wine into old skins. Their songs were to be singable; many of them were designed to be sung in unison to well-known melodies. Hence their songs were prone to be linked together with the existing profusion of soldier and student songs and, especially, with church hymns. When Arnim offered the Prussian soldiers his *Kriegslieder* for the campaign of 1806, he was already adapting Luther's *Ein' feste Burg ist unser Gott* and also the trooper song in *Wallensteins Lager* to the Prussian temperament. He utilized old folksongs as well as war-songs of the seventeenth century. Even as late as 1813, he attempted, like Brentano, to write new words for the Hohenzollern hymn. Theodor Koerner's song of Luetzow's wild ride also uses Schiller's trooper song, merely adding to Schiller's six-line strophe a seventh line. Other songs of Koerner's are set to the melodies of Schubart's *Kaplied* or M. Claudius' *Rheingesang*. Even calm, convivial student songs were made to sound his mighty alarms, just as secular drinking songs and love lyrics had long ago been transformed into sacred hymns. Naturally the faith which his songs put in God causes him also to make use of sacred poetry to serve his ends.

Hopefully and piously Arndt prays: "Oh Lord, Thou art my trust, my weapon, and my shield"; and that, too, sounds like Luther's *Feste Burg*. Arndt is apt to stress the rhythm so forcefully as to do violence to the natural accent and the sense. Syllables that are hardly equal to the burden receive a stressed accent. He knew very well the inciting force contained in the mighty cadence of verses of this sort:

> "Wer soll der Hueter sein?
> Sprich, Vater Rhein!
> Mag dich der Schwerter Glanz,
> Moegen dich Wall und Schanz,
> Mag dich von Tuermen
> Ein diamantner Kranz
> Hueten und schirmen?
> Ach nein! durch Felsenburg
> Dringet die List hindurch,
> Solches schirmt nie genug
> Gegen den welschen Trug."

These rhythms must be declaimed like the counting-out rimes of children; each verse has two stressed accents. (*Gégen den wélschen Trug*).

Theodor Koerner endowed the Liberation songs with the driving force of Schiller's lyric eloquence. Rueckert, when he attempted the rough-and-ready popular style, did not avoid the danger of lapsing into vulgar bawling. On the other hand he harnessed the delicate structure of the sonnet to the difficult task of defending the fatherland, using thus for political clangor a lyric form which had hitherto been used at most merely for petty literary bickering. Nor, to be sure, did the poetry of the Liberation overlook the four-line stanzas of the folk-song.

Eichendorff's martial tone is related to the tone of his songs in praise of wandering. The poem *Auf der Feldwacht* ("Shouldering my arms, I stand here, lost, on duty") preserves quite perfectly the mood of *Das zerbrochene Ringlein*. From afar comes the sound of evening bells, clouds rear themselves like towers against the sky, pictures of memory arise, and the singer is lost in dreams. Schenkendorf also loved dreamy sounds and the shadowy quality of the folk-song. But at the same time he was more concerned than Eichendorff to have his verses attuned to stirring melodies. Many of his Liberation songs have the qualities of folk-songs.

Neither Tieck's musical lyrics (see above, Part 1, p. 128 ff.), nor the formal little works of art in the romanesque style such as the Schlegels created, nor yet the poetry of Novalis, modest, simple-hearted and at the same time full of allusion and connotation though it was, prepared the way for those poems in the folk-song style which were sung by the Suabians, by Eichendorff, Wilhelm Mueller, and Heine. Strange as it may seem, both Wackenroder and Tieck, as well as the two Schlegels, quite unqualifiedly yielded to the editors of the *Wunderhorn* the grateful rôle of reawakening that strain in German lyric poetry which harked back to the folk-song.

Certain it is that Wilhelm Schlegel, at the very end of the eighteenth century, was induced to return to his former teacher, Buerger, and to the ballads in the manner

of the *Goettinger Hain* by the enthusiasm which Wackenroder and Tieck aroused for mediaeval poetry. Speaking,
in his Berlin lectures, of "romances and other folk-songs"
(3, 160 ff., 167), Schlegel expressed, even more pointedly
than in his essay on Buerger in 1800 (8, 64 ff.), the desire
for a collection of German national lyrics such as Percy's
Reliques of Ancient English Poetry. Similarly Goethe at
the end of the century had once more begun to give his
attention to poetry of the folk-song type; but in his and
Wieland's *Taschenbuch auf das Jahr 1804,* he blazed a
new trail with such songs as *Schaefers Klagelied* and
Bergschloss, both of which leaned toward folk-song and
folk-melody. Friedrich Schlegel's announcement of
Goethe's works, contained in the Heidelberg *Jahrbuecher*
of 1808 (*Deutsche Nationalliteratur,* 143, 376, 378),
noted at once the remarkable blending of the song and
romance qualities in these poems: "A song which adapts
itself to some folk-melody or other, and which is not
written in the first person but rather in any other that is
drawn more or less from romantic legends, and especially
when some story or other in this mythological background
is assumed to be known or perhaps narrated in fragmentary fashion—under these conditions such a song
gradually approaches the romance and finally merges entirely with it." Henceforth ballad-like songs in the style
of the *Bergschloss* and the *Schaefers Klagelied* became
favorite romantic lyric forms. The *Schaefers Klagelied*
especially was imitated again and again by romantic singers; the introduction and certain turns in it were used,
sung repeatedly, and parodied. Under Goethe's sponsor-
ship there also appeared in 1806-8 that collection of German folk-lyrics which gave decided impetus to the spirit
of these two songs and which became the indispensable

prerequisite not only of romantic poetry but of the greater part of all modern German lyrics: namely, *Des Knaben Wunderhorn. Alte deutsche Lieder. Gesammelt von L. A. von Arnim und Clemens Brentano. Mit einem Anhange von Kinderliedern.*

This task united Arnim's blythe eagerness to acquaint the German people with indigenous poetry with that predilection for folk-song and poetry patterned after the folk-song which Brentano had very early evinced. There had already been suggestions of this in Brentano's novel *Godwi* (1801-2). The lyric interpolations in this novel indicate Brentano's artistic ability to create mythological material quite in the manner of folklore. Arnim's tendency toward the dreamy, deliquescent tones of the folk-song coupled with Brentano's folkloristic imaginativeness misled the editors into encroaching considerably upon the domain of the folk-song, which they were studying, by appropriating freely of the genuine material that was before them in order to create fabrications of their own. But Brentano is more discreet than Arnim. The former preserves subtle archaisms whereas the latter prefers the language of his day. Arnim does violence to the rhythm of the folk-songs; Brentano either leaves it untouched or makes it more melodious. Brentano aims only to "restore"; oddities of Arnim's own creation occasionally obscure the original.[32] Sharp philologians, such as Johann Heinrich Voss, at once angrily cried, "Deception!" Goethe, however, acknowledged the fact that these violations did make the old folk-songs flow more freely from modern tongues; and the editors could very well maintain that their own fabrications had been mistaken for genuine folk-songs by connoisseurs. Certain it is that those songs in the *Wunderhorn* upon which Arnim and Brentano left their deepest impress were the most effective. A classic example of this is the poem *Zu Strassburg auf der Schanz,* which appeared in the *Wunderhorn* under the title *Der Schweizer.* The Alpine horn motif was here smuggled into a rollicking deserter-song and henceforth became a favorite theme in nostalgic romantic poetry.

The article in the Heidelberg *Jahrbuecher* of 1808, in which Friedrich Schlegel discussed the *Sammlung deutscher Volkslieder* by Buesching and von der Hagen, indicates how little the early romanticists were inclined to applaud the efforts of Arnim and Brentano (*Nationalliteratur,* 143, 361 ff.). Not only was Goethe's discussion of the *Wunderhorn* (36, 247 ff.) ironically parodied in this article but the collectors were also accused of having covered so large a field as to include much that was inconsequential. But the *Wunderhorn* is said very definitely to have gone astray when the editors "made unintelligibility preëminently the essence of the folk-song and instead of passing over such obscurity wherever it may already have existed they are insatiable in seeking it out, which readily leads to absurdity. To be sure, only those collectors are prone to make this mistake who intentionally alter the text and who fancy they can consciously reproduce the folk-song manner in their own poetry."

Nevertheless Arnim and Brentano by virtue of those very efforts which Friedrich Schlegel censured gave to the folk-songlike lyric of romanticism its most peculiar problem. For henceforth poets sought with more or less success and in most various forms "to reproduce consciously the folk-song manner in their own poetry." Soon songs appear which in stanza-structure and utterance simulate the spontaneity of the folk-song; forms evolve which are like those of the folk-song without being bur-

dened by the crudity and unwieldiness of the older manner of speech (Heine to Wilhelm Mueller, June 7, 1826).
Though the folk-song was imitated almost to the point
of annihilation, but few caught its mood without affecta-
tion as felicitously as did Moerike. Heine aimed at "clear
resonance" and "genuine simplicity," and admitted that
Wilhelm Mueller had thus far best achieved these ideals.
Indeed the problem was so enticing that Friedrich Schlegel
likewise tried to solve it. His *Das versunkene Schloss*
(1806) caught the folk-song mood without any artificial-
ity whatever and so delightfully that it stands out conspicuously among the best efforts of a poet who was
singularly prolific in artistic blunders.

Definite groups are clearly discernible among the many
poets of the younger romantic generation who imitated
the folk-song. Striking individualities, however, stand out
sharply also. Even Arnim and Brentano are antithetical
in style; the contrasts which are evident in their treatment of the material of the *Wunderhorn* emerge much
more clearly in their own poems. Brentano is richer in
moods; each of his poems is homogeneous and pure as to
form. Arnim is fascinated by words and phrases which
he has heard. Just as a lover of music hums to himself
in endless repetition and variation a single strain which
appeals to him and haunts his memory, so Arnim spins
out what he has received from others and fills the rhythm
of a poem which has taken possession of him with words,
the sense of which has slipped his mind. Such poetry, as
Bode (p. 584) correctly observed, aims at "the mannerism of literal connection with what is at hand." But Brentano, likewise, never wearies of repeating words and
phrases, and presents them again and again with slight
variations. Hence the refrain plays a dominant rôle in

his lyrics (cf. Richard M. Meyer, *Euphorion,* 5, 1 ff.). This kind of poetry naturally tends toward musical expression, and Brentano's songs actually lend themselves readily to composition. Some of them are surprisingly close in character to the art of Goethe, but others are almost as bad as Arnim's in that they seem unable to come to a stop. Brentano is rich in moods: genuine, warm emotion, tender longing, bitter sarcasm, subtle irony, combinations of yearning and sarcasm; fresh, driving, inciting, rousing poetry but complaining, disturbing, and enervating as well; twittering and trilling one moment and ponderously solemn the next; here the fire of sensuous passion and presently ascetic aloofness from mundane things as indicated by the form and content of his diction. Arnim is more ponderous and awkward. It is only when he sings of loyal steadfastness, or of quiet, contented activity, or of the joy which he experienced as a husband and father with Bettina at his side that he approximates Goethe in power and finish. In such instances the romantic undertone of unfulfilled longing (which is evident in practically all of Brentano's verses) vanishes entirely.

The Suabians are an easily differentiated group, and yet, even in their midst personality is pitted against personality. The Suabian school curriculum gave them a generous dose of classical culture. Hoelderlin, whose poetry, though unaffected by the rebirth of the folk-song, scaled the heights of free verse in masterly fashion, is a pupil of Greece and of Rome. Uhland also may very well trace the clarity and chastity of his style and the broad, clean sweep of his artistry to his early studies in the ready facility of Latin stanza-structure. He, too, like many another of his late romantic fellow-poets, including Heine,

wrote for a time lyrics that were extravagantly sentimental and the pretension of which to antiquity, in imitation of the folk-song, was grossly overdone. But as soon
as he emerged from this, the foundations of his poetry
and art are determined for all time: a keenly pronounced
feeling for the moods of nature and the landscape which
surrounded him, presented objectively and with an un-
deniable tendency toward the epic, narrative style. His
love songs are few in number but they burn fiercely in a
few terse stanzas; similarly his nature poetry dispenses
with all romantic devices for nervous excitation. He is
the poet of placid days and of the lovely contours of the
Suabian landscape. Whatever he made into poetry, he
had seen and studied contemplatively again and again—
with the eyes of the romanticist, however, not with those
of the Philistine. The restlessness and unbridledness of
the romanticist and the improvising, hasty manner of
manipulating verse, he left to his friend Justinus Kerner.
More mobile by far than Uhland, Kerner experiences
greater torments of yearning and more exquisite joys,
keener paroxysms of grief as well as of delight. The folk-
song manner is so natural to him that he was able to
smuggle one of his songs (*Mir traemt', ich floeg gar
bange;* cf. Bode, p. 190) into the *Wunderhorn* as an original. In Gustav Schwab, Wilhelm Hauff, and Karl Mayer,
Uhland's style becomes conventionally petrified. But
Eduard Moerike, the purest, most genuine Suabian folk-
song lyrist, is versatile enough to unite within himself the
excellencies of both Uhland and Kerner. And he had still
greater gifts: "Goethe's depth and popular simplicity, the
charm of antiquity and the romantic wealth of forms,
quaint humor and the childlike, touching enchantment of
legendary lore, tender trifling and pitiless tragedy, pas-

sionate emotional excitement and gentle contemplation"
are the qualities which his biographer, Harry Maync
(second edition, 1913, p. 239), finds in the lyrics of
Moerike.

The two Franconians, Friedrich Rueckert and August
von Platen, are similar to the Suabians in their trend of
thought and in their tendency toward primness in form,
but artistically they are quite antithetical to one another.
Rueckert, an artist in language and riming but by no
means a master of mellifluous rhythm, carelessly pours
forth his exuberant verses; Platen, strict and self-re-
strained in form, ever mindful of clean, clear rhythm,
would fain realize a world of choicest beauty. Both study
foreign models. Rueckert, however, is willingly incited
by the German folk-song and joins the followers of the
Wunderhorn, whereas Platen's ear is better attuned to the
melody of Romance forms or the methodical beat of antique meters. The Suabian, Wilhelm Waiblinger, who felt
himself drawn to his countryman Hoelderlin, and who
therefore moved in the older poet's circle rather than in
Uhland's, was likewise congenial to Platen.

Quite in the manner of Brentano, the Silesian Joseph
von Eichendorff [33] and the Dessauer Wilhelm Mueller
pattern their artistry upon the German folk-song. Both
pretend at times to be romantic vagabonds whose yearning drives them aimlessly onward and at other times they
feign that they are wandering musicians and students.
Eichendorff is closer to nature; masterfully, through repe-
titiously, he delineates the gentle rustling that agitates
the lonely woods or the silent night. He was fond of
riming *lauschen* with *rauschen* and probably no other poet
did so as frequently as he. The following strophes by

Brentano (2, 243), however, prove how nearly the latter
had already approximated Eichendorff's style:

> Hark, the flute again complains
> And the cool springs are rushing (*rauschen*).
> The golden tones are wafted downward,
> Hush, oh hush, let us listen (*lauschen*)!
>
> Sweet desires and mild longings,
> How sweetly they speak to the heart!
> Through the night that is round about me,
> I am reached by the light of these sounds.

"Through the wood with rapid steps, I hurry with my
lute," begins one of Brentano's poems. That is the favorite
pose of the wandering romanticist. In Eichendorff's
stories, characters that are prone to burst into song always
have a guitar in readiness in order that it may accompany one song after the other. Eichendorff and Mueller
and Chamisso, too, share with Brentano the tendency to
attune the spirit of the folk-song to the world about them.
Disharmonies in the mood are thus introduced, which go
on directly to Heine. The latter admits that he is indebted
to Mueller and grateful to him. Heine and Mueller, together with Chamisso, develop the art of proceeding from
an individual song to a song-cycle, of creating an epic
sequence of lyrics. Chamisso had seen and experienced
more than Eichendorff and Mueller and is at the same time
a more original and more individual character; his French
descent lends a peculiar charm to his poetic thoughts,
emotions, and observations, but at the same time it leads
him into linguistic difficulties which he never quite sur-
mounts. Like Mueller and Platen, he ventures into the

political field nor does he tarry within the narrow confines of his own fatherland, as Uhland does, but takes part
in philhellenic poetry, and not unlike the authors of the
Polish songs, leads directly down to the radical lyrists of
the forties. Chamisso's and Platen's songs, lamenting over
the constitution of things in general, already give evidence
of Byron's influence. Their counterparts may be found
among the lyrics of the Suabians, particularly those of
Kerner. But Byronism and *Weltschmerz* are most rampant in Kerner's friend Lenau, who at this point is in
close touch with his antipode, Heine. A German, born in
Hungary, Lenau grafted upon the German lyric the vola-
tile, passionate strain of gypsy music (*A 1,* p. 356 ff.).
Whereas Heine sought to avoid every suspicion of formal
correctness, Lenau, on the contrary, try as he would,
rarely attained to linguistic and metrical smoothness of
expression. His style, however, is so original that perhaps
not one of his contemporaries, excepting Heine, is so
readily recognizable in imitation. All these lyrists, headed
by Wilhelm Mueller, Chamisso, Lenau, and Heine, revel
in the exotic; they sing of Poles and Greeks, Corsicans
and Biscayans, not only from political motives but rather
because they yearn romantically for the colorfulness of
the remote. In this respect they are very similar to Byron
and to the French romanticism of Victor Hugo. Freili-
grath subsequently carried this to the farthest extreme.

In the long series of attempts to adapt the spirit of
the times to the form of the old German folk-song, the
four-line stanza is preëminent. The long-line stanza is
tried out and also the *G'stanzl* with its epigrammatic
brevity. Eichendorff utilizes the so-called *Schnadahuepfel.*
Heine seeks to master more skillfully the effects of the
Alpine dancing song (to Schottky, May 4, 1823). Fur-

thermore, the preference for the four-line stanza is supported by two currents that arise from very different sources.

It is Spanish literature, the most complicated and difficult metrical forms of which the early romanticists love to imitate, that made the four-line rimed stanza, together with the German folk-song, a favorite of romantic lyric poetry in its heyday. The efforts of the early romanticists offer the first incentive. Only certain forms of all that were essayed in this field were perfected. From these Spanish forms there emerged the trochaic four-line stanza, generally rimed, occasionally joined merely by assonance, and sometimes entirely rimeless. It is used preferably in poems of the romance type. Brentano's extensive *Romanzen vom Rosenkranz,* a work of his best period, [34] which was published very tardily (1852), used the polymorphous, trochaic, four-line stanza and achieved therewith moving passion as well as earnest, decorous solemnity. Heine, who, in his early years, in competition with Uhland, an excellent connoisseur of Romance poetry, wrote poetry in the Spanish style, elevated it in *Atta Troll* (1843) to the comic and the ironic as well as to deep-reaching, almost touching action and finally wrested from it the affecting moods of *Bimini,* a poem of resignation. Indeed, Arnim already knew how well the trochaic tetrameter, like its Spanish model, lent itself to comic action. He used it for the *Geschichte des Mohrenjungen* in the fifteenth chapter of the first volume of the *Graefin Dolores.* Immermann's *Tulifaentchen* made this stanza a favorite vehicle of the comic mood. It became very familiar to the German people through Scheffel's *Trompeter von Saekkingen* (1854).

Meanwhile, too, the four-line trochaic stanza with rimes

was suggested to German lyric poetry by Goethe's *West-oestlicher Diwan*. Goethe's last great lyric cycle was, as is well known, the result of the interest of the romanticists in the Orient. But rather than to the poetry of India, which the romanticists prized most highly, Goethe turned to the more original culture of Persia. The attempts on the part of the German romanticists to translate Indian metrical forms into German were decidedly fruitless as far as German poetry is concerned. Goethe, however, gave his *Diwan* only the most superficial oriental guise. The *Gasel* appears merely in isolated instances and even then is imitated most freely. He, too, perceived very well the charm of "measured rhythms," but he also discovered that they were "hollow masks, bloodless and meaningless" and very soon became nauseating (*Nachbildung,* 5, 22). And so he turned to simpler forms of his own discovering to finish the poems he had begun for the *Taschenbuch auf das Jahr 1804* (cf. K. Burdach, *Jubilaeumsausgabe,* 5, p. XXVI f.). Just like the "dear little poets" who followed the old Goethe when he began his easterly piping, so too Heine was quick to do homage to the rhythms of the *Diwan*. Though the *Gasel* was more assiduously cultivated after Goethe, and though Rueckert, who was according to Wilhelm Schlegel's sarcastic verdict "the cock of the walk in the Orient" (2, 218), was equal to the task of imitating the wealth of oriental rime-schemes, still, generally speaking, the poets of the later romantic generation copied merely the alluring exotic colorfulness of the Orient whereas Goethe was concerned merely with sampling the patriarchal atmosphere of the far East. Otherwise later romantic poetry was borne along by that mighty stream whose prolific source was the German folk-song.

Just as Goethe, for a long time, maintained a negative

attitude toward the *Gasel,* he also disregarded the sonnet, a favorite form of the romantic poets. None of the other Romance forms which Wilhelm Schlegel made accessible to the German language (see Part 1, p. 132) ever became as popular or was as frequently used. Though strongly knit together by its thesis and antithesis, the sonnet is a delicate form which several poets misused to the point of nausea. Arnim's riotous creative energy perhaps never went so badly astray as in his mass production of sonnets. After much hesitation, Goethe was finally won over to this form and he filled this ingenious vessel with the force of a mighty emotion. But the greatest glory went to Platen. Upon Italian soil, he brought to fullest fruition the resonant melodiousness of this Italian form and at the same time he breathed into it a strongly felt and actually experienced content.

II. GERMAN LEGEND AND HISTORY IN
ROMANTIC POETRY

THE metrical forms of the German folk-song brought forth a great train of poems which, together with the songs of the later romanticists, proved to be significant among the most powerful and vital creations of German romanticism, namely, the ballad and the romance. There was no new trail to be blazed here. The romances which Wilhelm Schlegel wrote around 1800 show decidedly, on the one hand, a return to the art of the *Goettinger Hain* and of the Storm and Stress and to the manner of Buerger and the youthful Goethe, and on the other hand, they are a continuation of the epic-lyric style which was common to Goethe and Schiller after 1797. But the romances and the ballads of Uhland and his Suabian school, of Rueckert, Platen, Chamisso, Heine, and of their numerous followers, who were as eloquent along the Rhine as along the Danube, hark back even beyond the youthful and the aged Goethe as well as beyond Schiller and, on the whole, they bear about the same relation to Buerger that Wackenroder's and Hardenberg's conception of the Middle Ages bears to the picture which the chivalrous dramas present of that same era.

The epic-lyric poems of the younger generation of romanticists are not confined merely to German antiquity. They revivify the Middle Ages in Romance and Moorish countries also; as they proceed down the centuries, they forsake the confines of Europe and tell tales of exotic lands, of noble savages, and of the chicanery of the European in his dealings with the aborigines. They vie with Byron in conjuring up before the reader's imagination the alluring colors and the overpowering fragrance of the Orient. In order to do justice to such strange corners of the world, they reached out after strange forms; this was the place where Spanish trochees could be utilized, and even the three-line iambic strophe (another conquest of Wilhelm Schlegel's) proved amenable, in Chamisso's hands, to exotic balladry. But alongside this foreign opulence, imported to beguile the senses, there developed, hale and hearty, a tremendous growth in the national, and at the same time artistic, glorification of old German customs and indigenous life and thought. What Moritz von Schwind presented to a smaller circle through the media of his art was likewise proclaimed to every German by means of the German ballad. Both gave glad tidings of that blessed golden age of German antiquity when human dignity, freedom, faith and piety still held sway; when German vigor, unimpaired, was permeated with the loftiest ideals to which the human soul aspires and with all the loveliness to which the human heart responds. There was called into poetic life a long gone golden age of German integrity such as was proclaimed to the contemporary world by Novalis and Friedrich Schlegel and Tieck—by the latter with particular effect in 1803 in the preface to his *Minnelieder* (see Part 1, p. 108). It was the age of German emperors, benevolent and mighty, of brave German knights, and of high-minded German women. It is the world which, like the Sleeping Beauty, the king's son in Uhland's *Maerchen* awakens to new life with a kiss; it is the world which the romanticist conceived to be the world of German

poetry. This world was unsuited to the crass colors of
the chivalrous dramas of the Storm and Stress. The
luminous tones of von Schwind's paintings predominate,
not the dazzling brilliance of burning fortresses nor the
musty darkness of dungeons. A silvery radiance illumines
the Middle Ages; the prophetic breath of spring hovers
over Germany's mighty past which has just been called into new being.

> We hear the German forest-murmurs,
> We breathe the air of German May.
> The glory of departed days,
> Bathed in moonlight, rises to our view.
> The winding horn in the ancient tale
> Sends a delightful shudder through our soul.

These lines, in which Geibel (1862) sought to express
the mood that had been called forth by Uhland's poetry,
are applicable also to the wealth of ballads which the later
romanticists wrote in Uhland's style, though, to be sure, in
Schwab's and Simrock's hands, all this became quite
bloodless and pale, and, greatly overdone, gradually suc-
cumbed to mere repetition and stiffness.

This romantic-mediaeval mood is apparent only in
isolated instances in Goethe's *Goetz* or Maler Mueller's
Golo und Genoveva. It is wholly foreign to Buerger's
ballads. The temperament of the generation of 1770,
more vital and robust, strove after more forceful effects
and did not hit upon the delicate, subtle shades of romanticism. Rather it was Schiller who approached these tones
in the *Graf von Habsburg.*

Nevertheless, it is very difficult to differentiate clearly
between the German Middle Ages as painted by the Storm

and Stress and as sung by romanticism, and in the field of the novel and drama it is even more difficult than in that of the ballad. The devices used in Goethe's youth were not scorned by the romanticists and the latter furthermore possessed that with which the generation of 1770 was unacquainted: the mood of Wackenroder and Hardenberg.

The material utilized by the historical poetry of romanticism had not been suggested by the Storm and Stress alone. Toward the close of the eighteenth century narrative writers, following the trend which Goethe's *Goetz* had inaugurated, had sought to familiarize their contemporaries with old German poetry and German folktales. J. K. A. Musaeus' *Volksmaerchen der Deutschen* (1782–6), Veit Weber's (Leonhard Waechter's) *Sagen der Vorzeit* (1787–98), and Benedikte Naubert's *Neue Volksmaerchen der Deutschen* (1789–93) are undeniably products of the Enlightenment. W. Pantenius (*Das Mittelalter in Leonhard Waechters* [*Veit Webers*] *Romanen*, 1904, p. 118) declares that Weber's return to the Middle Ages was actuated by far different reasons from that of the romanticists: "He did not submit himself affectionately and willingly to the charm of antiquity; it was rather antiquity which willy-nilly had to submit to him. He dragged it forth from its venerable repose and forced it to participate in the weal and woe of the declining eighteenth century. . . . The existing present was crowded into the past, into the Middle Ages, and extended or recast by the infusion of particular tendencies or Utopian qualities. . . . A decisive change in the revivification of the German Middle Ages could not come to pass until . . . the present had been definitely brushed aside." The same is true of Musaeus and Benedikte Naubert. But, thanks to the greater genuineness of the material which they handled, there are aspects in the latter, in which the ancient heritage emerges in a purer and less garbled form.[35] To be sure, they cannot compare with the genuine simplicity of the *Volkssagen* which the theologian Nachtigall collected under the pseudonym *Otmar* (1800); these were a joy and a delight to Arnim, and the Grimm brothers used them for their *Deutsche Sagen*. Even in that wide field of romantic poetry which dealt with legends and folk-tales, past and present were not always sharply distinguished. The romantic poets also used the present as their point of departure. But they merely wished to carry the present back to the creations of the past; they did not wish to prune and trim the latter to fit the spirit of the present, which had advanced beyond them culturally and spiritually. In spite of this, the eyes of the romanticist occasionally penetrate the nebulousness of folklore and legend with the clarity and acuteness worthy of a son of the Enlightenment. At times the differences between Musaeus and this or that member of the later romantic circle seems to disappear entirely. It remained for Tieck, from whose poetry primarily Uhland acquired his conception of the Middle Ages, to produce the most unusual combinations of the mood of romanticism and the spirit of the Enlightenment.

Two collections made by this protean, versatile personality reveal the marked antitheses in his attitude when representing the days of old in Germany: the *Volksmaerchen, herausgegeben von Peter Lebrecht* (1797) and the *Romantische Dichtungen* (1799–1800). Harking back to the German chap-books, they mark the beginning of romantic poetry of the German Middle Ages; they are the sign-posts for the vast majority of later romantic

poets. In these books Tieck proceeds from the devout and
faithful reproduction of the *Geschichte von den Heymons
Kindern* to the *Denkwuerdige Geschichtschronik der
Schildbuerger,* an undisguised satire on the world about
him. Here are found *Der gestiefelte Kater* and its sequel,
Prinz Zerbino, both of which abound in mad pranks, self-
parody, and destruction of the illusion. The *Wundersame
Liebesgeschichte der schoenen Magelone* is saturated with
the mood of romanticism. But in the dramatic poem
Leben und Tod der heiligen Genoveva this mood is in-
tensified; garish and sustained by a plethora of shifting
moods is this *missa solemnis* in which all the nations of
Europe join in doing homage to St. Genevieve (Minor).
In Maler Mueller's chivalric drama *Golo und Genoveva,*
the Storm and Stress dramatized in a far different manner the legend of this patient sufferer. Tieck was in possession of the manuscript of this drama and subsequently
arranged to have it published in its first unabridged
edition, but for all of that his own treatment of the subject
matter is not only thoroughly original but it also maintains primarily a genuinely romantic, religious atmosphere.
In *Kaiser Octavianus* (1804) Tieck hoped to achieve the
utmost; with consummate skill he sought to glorify the
enchanting moonlit night which enthralls the senses, and
to endow the wondrous world of folklore with all its
pristine splendor. Uhland bears witness to the spell which
the revivification of old folk-tales cast upon the youthful
writers of the day. His first pseudonym, *Florens,* was
derived from *Octavianus;* the awkward dramatic fragment of his youth, *Die Entfuehrung,* eloquently bespeaks
the influence of Tieck's work in that it depicts a half-
grown youth who is prone to build air-castles in the hope
that after living long in obscurity he, too, like Florens

in *Octavianus,* would eventually be recognized as the prince, the king's son, and achieve the splendor compatible with his supposed noble birth (A. von Keller, *Uhland als Dramatiker,* 1877, p. 131, cf. p. 149). In *Fortunat* (1816), the third of the great mediaeval dramas derived from chap-books, Tieck has already become more prosaic. His erstwhile love of romancing has disappeared and with it has gone also his vast facility with tone and color. *Fortunat* is the last drama in the collection *Phantasus,* into which Tieck gathered the creations of his romantic youth and in so doing also bade farewell to his youthful mental attitudes. *Fortunat* indicates that Tieck had reached the end of a definite period in his life and at the same time it represents a tacit admission that the wondrous world of mediaeval folklore had lost its charm for him; indeed, it had become common property.

Not only in the metamorphosis of old chap-books but in other ways also, Tieck sought to deck out the mediaeval world in harmony with Wackenroder's artistic conceptions. *Franz Sternbalds Wanderungen* (1798) expressly professes to be "an old German story." In the form of a novel patterned after the *Lehrjahre,* the story begins by reverently glorifying the artistic diligence of the old Germans. The introduction simulates Wackenroder's style so perfectly that many supposed Wackenroder to have written it. But before long Tieck loses his grasp upon this lofty tone; consummate actor though he is, he steps out of character and instead of playing the part of the lay-brother he portrays the sensuously passionate successor to Heinse. Friedrich Schlegel was quite right when he observed (*Athenaeumfragment* 418) that in depth and in the details of characterization *Sternbald* was not to be compared with *William Lovell.* But he did praise its facility and wealth of fancy, its gift for irony and the intentional variety and harmony of the tone-color; everything, he said, was lucid and clear; the romantic spirit seemed to be agreeably weaving dreams about itself.

The *Klosterbruder* was nearer kin to Novalis than to Tieck. The former had but to follow the dictates of his own spirit in order to glorify mediaeval German life in *Heinrich von Ofterdingen* (1802). To be sure, this fragment by virtue of its style and its intellectual designs demanded utter freedom from the trammels of the time element and it is debatable whether the continuation of Hardenberg's subjective novel, hovering as it does beyond the confines of time, would have achieved an historically more faithful atmosphere. At any rate, the notes for the prospective continuation mention names and circumstances peculiar to mediaeval life, to the era of the Hohenstaufens and the Crusades; these might have bound the narrative more closely to the earth and might have located it more definitely as to time. It was this very timelessness, however, which gave its style that peculiar quality which henceforth became a prerequisite in the external form of the romantic folk-tale. [36] Its childlike simplicity corresponded to that freedom of form from which Wilhelm Grimm, unlike the folklorists of the Enlightenment as well as Tieck, derived the fairy-tale style in the *Kinder und Hausmaerchen* (1812). As in his spiritual songs, Novalis here showed himself to be a master of quiet simplicity and in this way he cast a nimbus over those emotions which henceforth throughout the era of romanticism were bound up with the presentation of old German life.

But it was Fouqué who had at his command a more thorough knowledge of Germanic antiquity than either

Novalis or Tieck. Nordic poetry was more familiar to him than to the great majority of the romanticists. It was his novels, however, primarily his novel of adventure, *Der Zauberring* (1813), rather than his dramatization of the Sigurdsaga (1808–10), which captured the public fancy. Heine (7, 152) criticized Fouqué as an epic writer by saying that his knights consisted merely of iron and noble sentiments and had neither flesh nor brain; his feminine characters were mere pictures or dolls whose flowing hair curled sweetly about their flower-like faces; neatly arranged in proper sequence were tournaments, pastorals, duels, ancient costumes, insignificant adventures—a riot of superficiality. In *Der Zauberring,* however, there is a keen feeling of inner kinship with a heroic world of the past; Fouqué here created a story of his own ancestors. Moreover, the picture of the Middle Ages which the novel sketches was not a mere wild dream in spite of the fact that it encompassed the miraculous and the supernatural; indeed, it was effective enough to serve as a guide to later German poets. [37]

It remained, however, for Arnim's *Kronenwaechter* (1817), the most vivid of the romantic historical novels, to combine the miraculous with a more virile realism, a greater ability to depict living characters, and a more penetrating knowledge of old German life and thought. What Wilhelm Grimm in discussing the novel (*Kleinere Schriften,* 1, 229) says of all Arnim's creations is applicable also to *Die Kronenwaechter:* they are like a picture that is framed on three sides but not on the fourth; from the open side the artist proceeds to paint on and on until, heaven and earth having become indistinguishable, painful uncertainty arises in the reader's mind. And this is not due alone to the fact that the novel is unfinished. It is undeniably true that Arnim offered delightfully realistic and original pictures of the waning mediaeval and the dawning modern eras, splendid presentations of towns as well as of imperial cities, of the highways traversed by wandering apprentices, singers, jugglers, and mercenaries, of the imperial court, of the *Reichstag,* and of tournaments. But side by side with this gay world of rough and ready characters he placed—and rather more spontaneously than usual when he was concerned with having well-observed facts gradually trail off into the miraculous—his secret order of the *Kronenwaechter* and endowed it furthermore with externally supernatural powers quite out of harmony with the serious aims of the novel. This device of the supernatural which was inherent in the secret societies of the eighteenth century was used in many novels down to the *Lehrjahre* to heighten the effect of the action. Arnim sought to reflect the conditions of contemporary life and to offer his countrymen a solution of the most pressing problems of the day. With lofty idealism he pleaded the cause of the nobility while the modern age sat in stern judgment upon the social system which had been handed down to it from time immemorial. He also attacked those of his narrow-minded fellow-nobles who were opposed to all liberal reforms in state or society. According to Achim von Arnim, himself a nobleman from the margravate of Brandenburg, citizens were deserving of certain social and civic rights, to which the peasant also was to be taught to aspire. [38] The historical cast of the novel is derived in part from old chronicles. Arnim however, manipulated his material freely. From folksongs and old writings he had absorbed the spirit of the ancient days. So he felt justified in spinning out any material which he found at hand, just as legend molds and embellishes historical fact. He thoroughly believed in the creations of his own fancy and was not at all disturbed when reality seemed to discredit them. Three years after his novel had been published he became acquainted at first hand with the locality in which most of the action takes place. Because of his *Kronenwaechter* it gave him great pleasure to see it. On November 2, 1820, he wrote to Bettina how he had stood with beating heart at the gates of Waiblingen and had realized that it really looked quite different from what he had imagined. But he consoled himself with the thought that it must once have been as he had pictured it—three centuries make quite a difference.

Historical novels of this sort were quite contrary to the method of that novelist who, like the Pied Piper of Hamlin, was gaining a tremendous following among the German reading public at the very time of the appearance of *Die Kronenwaechter*. The strength of this novelist, Walter Scott, lay in the authenticity of his local color. Whatever he depicts—broadly enough to be sure—he has actually seen; and he knows also, especially of the Scotch Highlands, that they looked much the same three hundred or more years before the writing of his novels. Furthermore he recognized the fact that creative literature with a historical background is most effective when it ferrets out the bonds which persist in linking past and present. The romanticists had hitherto been striving toward quite contrary objectives: they, too, had opened lovely vistas, in part also with the purpose of leading the present back to them. But now they learned from Scott that a Scotchman presents Scotch antiquity most convincingly; that literature with a historical background is best essayed by a native of the country whose history is being portrayed. They might indeed have gleaned this fact from Kleist, the author of *Michael Kohlhaas* (1808), who also came from the margravate of Brandenburg. But Hauff and Zschokke, both thoroughly unromantic, were the first to introduce Scott's theory into the German historical novel. Hauff portrayed his native Suabia, Zschokke the land of his adoption, Switzerland.

Though E. T. A. Hoffmann's tales, for the most part, portray the present, the local color therein is minutely observed and faithfully depicted. Quite properly Hoffmann is deemed the successor of Kleist in a field of literary production which is, like that of Scott, most closely associated with the soil of the writer's homeland and the mode of life pertaining to it. Willibald Alexis, whose novels of the margravate of Brandenburg began to appear in 1832, had but to follow the lead of Kleist and Hoffmann in order to do for Brandenburg what Scott had done for Scotland: namely, to delineate in broad strokes the familiar routine of life in the surrounding country-side in the by-gone days and to present all classes of society which lived within this narrow sphere, stressing primarily those of their peculiarities which had persevered throughout the centuries. The great characters of history emerge from isolation and take part in the teeming life of their countrymen, who are plastically represented by a wide variety of types. The broad scope which Scott and Alexis give their novels is also present in Arnim's *Kronenwaechter*. Indeed, Arnim was one of the first representatives of the collectivistic tendency of the age and owed to this very tendency his understanding of the masses for which and through which he hoped to work effectively. Quite independently he arrived at a method of depicting people which went beyond the mere individual and gave artistic portrayal to the multitude.

To be sure, Arnim did not solve this problem any more definitely than did Scott or Alexis. Collectivistic portrayal was essayed again and again until at the end of the century the naturalism of Tolstoi and Zola attempted it from different angles.

Hoffmann's historical novel-writing is by no means confined to his native land. But even where he could not rely upon his own observations, his keen, well-trained eye could visualize the locality very definitely. Just as Schiller, in a distant land and without first hand observation, gives in a few bold strokes concise pictures of Genoa, Venice, and even Switzerland, so Hoffmann quite consistently creates the impression, in his delineation of Italy, for example, that the background of his story is thoroughly familiar to him. Neither do Tieck's historical novels of the Middle Ages depend upon first hand observation for their descriptions of the country or its customs. In order to compete with Scott and with Manzoni, whom he esteemed even more highly, Tieck lavished upon these historical novels and romances such penetrating research as would have been quite incomprehensible to him in the days of his youth. In no sense did *Sternbald* ever strive to reproduce the actual spirit of its time, and as it progressed it deviated more and more from the kindly, old German atmosphere of its early pages. H. Lebede has shown (Halle, 1909) how minutely and exhaustively Tieck studied his source material for the fragment *Der Aufruhr in den Cevennen* (1826) and how studiously he observed authenticity even in regard to miraculous elements. Religious fanaticism is the theme of the story. Other writers had already considered as promising novelistic material the wars which were fought at the beginning of the eighteenth century between the Camisards and the Catholic French government. Walter Scott's *Old Mortality* (1816) depicted similar religious struggles which had taken place in Scotland in the not distant past. Contrary to Scott, Tieck offered more than the revivification of mere history. He made religious fanaticism his central theme and sought to rise above narrow religious controversy. Here, too, Jacob Boehme was his mainstay. The pernicious consequences of religious fanaticism are likewise reflected in *Der Hexensabbat* (1831). Again adhering to documentary tradition, Tieck developed in this novel a detailed picture of the political and social conditions of the day. The story takes place in the time of Philip the Good. *Der griechische Kaiser* (1830), on the other hand, treats the genuinely dramatic situation produced by unjustified and consciously false pretentions to a throne. Schiller was not the only one who recognized the tragic force of such a situation. Tieck's story takes place at the time of the Crusades.

The great historical novel *Vittoria Accorombona* (1840) forms a worthy conclusion to Tieck's literary career and treads finally upon the soil which the artist knows at first hand. He seizes upon an historical problem with which the nineteenth century, for some time to come, was destined to be pre-occupied: the better understanding of the type of person produced by the Renaissance. Whereas to Victor Hugo the Renaissance was but the background for theatrical villainy, Tieck's novel was an attempt, at least, to fathom the uniqueness of that period.[39] That excellent Renaissance scholar, the art historian Karl Schnaase, said of this novel that it epitomizes the spirit and life of the Renaissance just as vitally as do the chief artistic productions of the age itself, and that it conjures up instantly and as with a magic wand the warm ardent spirit of that by-gone age which presented the soul of humanity in a new guise (*Briefe an L. Tieck,* 3, 372).

Closely related to Tieck's historical novels are his two attempts to exalt poetically the life of an artist. Even the *Herzensergiessungen* had attached great value to accounts of the external events in the life of an artist and had been the incentive to the novelistic treatment of these accounts. Arnim's story *Raffael und seine Nachbarinnen* (1824) attained only one of the objectives of the *Herzensergiessungen,* inasmuch as it merely showed how works of art are the outgrowth of amorous experiences. Tieck chose two favorites of romanticism: Shakespeare in *Dichterleben* (1824-9) and Camoens in *Tod des Dichters* (1833). *Dichterleben,* however, by no means fully compensates for that exhaustive study of Shakespeare which Tieck promised to produce but never did. In the first part—in which he presents the youthful Shakespeare in the midst of his forerunners and competitors—Tieck dealt with a field in which he was an outstanding scholar. And he was singularly successful in casting over Shakespeare something of the glory with which his dramatic idol had ever, in his estimation, been surrounded.

The dramatic form would have been much more suited to the romantic glorification of German history than the ballad or the novel, since the stage is much more effective for that purpose than the other forms. The barrier here was the unfamiliarity of the romantic drama with the stage. Tieck's *Genoveva, Octavianus,* and *Fortunat* remained merely literary non-stage plays; their fate was shared by most of the romantic works of similar purport and content. The romanticists, however, the earlier ones at any rate, knew how to arouse the interest of others in whatever they themselves were unable to carry to full fruition. Wilhelm Schlegel gave the first impetus to the movement. At the conclusion of his Vienna lectures (1809-11), supported by the national feeling of enthusiasm on the eve of the Wars of Liberation, he had uttered the dictum: "The worthiest form of the romantic drama is the historic." In his final lecture he solemnly exhorted the poets of Germany to pluck their laurels in this field. With the utmost precision he drew the line of demarcation which was to divide the subsequent romantic historical drama from the chivalrous drama, in other words, from the drama of the Storm and Stress and its followers. The new drama was to be truly national and was not to revolve about the events in the life of an individual knight or of lesser nobles who were without influence upon history as a whole. It was to be truly historic, to be created out of a wealth of knowledge, and was to transport the audience into the vast arena of history. "What pictures our history presents from the earliest days, from the times of the Roman conquests, down to the firm establishment of the German Empire! There ensued the resplendent, chivalrous era of the House of Hohenstaufen and finally, more important politically as well as less remote from us, there came the House of Habsburg, which has produced such a wealth of mighty princes and heroes. What a field for a poet with the ability of a Shakespeare for seizing upon the poetic side of mighty historical events!"

This being his attitude, Wilhelm Schlegel bestowed great praise upon Schiller's Swiss drama and evinced less enthusiasm for *Die Jungfrau von Orleans* with its ennoblement of the main features of the chivalrous drama. He left it to Madam de Staël to pay praise to the most illustrious example of the historic drama since the death of Schiller: Zacharias Werner's *Martin Luther* (1807). To his own detriment as well as to that of their author and of the stage, the two dramas which grew out of romanticism and were most worthy of fulfilling his wishes were unknown to him for years. These were the two historical dramas of Heinrich von Kleist, which were not published until 1821.

With *Kaethchen von Heilbronn* (1810) Kleist, too, breathed new life into the chivalrous drama. His use of the requisites of the chivalrous drama already makes apparent in this play much of the spirit of romanticism, and at the same time there is also something of the mood of Wackenroder and Hardenberg. *Die Hermannsschlacht* and *Prinz Friedrich von Homburg,* however, fulfill generously, item for item, all the demands that Wilhelm Schlegel had made. In these dramas the author does indeed reflect the illustrious past as in a mirror and proclaims what the Germans once were and what they ought to become again. Just as Schlegel wished, he "drove home to us the fact that unless we henceforth heed the lessons to be learned from history more than we have in the past, we Germans are in danger of disappearing entirely from the ranks of independent nations—we, at one time the first and most glorious nation of Europe." Schlegel had emphasized the fact that the upper classes had become estranged from the rank and file through their predilection for foreign customs and their zeal for foreign culture, and that furthermore internal dissension was consuming their finest efforts. All this we find reiterated, point for point, in *Die Hermannsschlacht*. It must have been clear to Kleist that the plight of the Germans prior to the Battle of the *Teutoburger Wald* was identical with the situation in Germany after Jena, when he wrote to his sister, November 24, 1806: "We are the subjugated nations of the Romans." In a single poetic vision he beheld past and present as one. The hopes which Kleist and all the romanticists placed in Austria prior to the Battle of Aspern and the faith that, united, Habsburg and Hohenzollern would overcome Napoleon, swelled, in *Die Hermannsschlacht,* into a great poetic battle-cry. But Kleist was still more effective when he turned from distant Cheruscan lands to his own native soil, conjuring up out of its recent well-known history the world of the great Archduke and eliciting from it the thundering line, "Down with all the foes of Brandenburg!" With the assurance of real genius Kleist here demonstrated the great truth which German historical writers learned, at a much later date, from Scott's novels: that an historical writer is most effective and history is presented most precisely when the author avoids the nebulousness of the remote and plants his feet squarely upon his native sod, and, instead of relying upon information gleaned from mere books, turns to that wealth of reminiscence which, buried deep down in the soul of his own people, still breathes the breath of life.

Wilhelm Schlegel perhaps had a similar idea in mind when he urged the poets of Austria to dramatize the history of the House of Habsburg in the Shakespearean manner. Among the Austrian poets who had joined the ranks of the romanticists, Mattaeus von Collin attempted to carry out Schlegel's suggestion (cf. J. Wihan, *Euphorion, Supplement* 5, 167 ff.). Schlegel's desires, however, were most happily realized in the works of that greatest of all Austrian dramatists, Franz Grillparzer, who was a follower of Joseph Schreyvogel, Schlegel's antagonist, and who, although he proclaimed himself a foe of romanticism, was nevertheless indebted to romanticism for much of his artistry. His dramas *Koenig Ottokars Glueck und Ende* (1825) and *Ein Bruderzwist in Habsburg* (printed in 1872) proved to the Austrians—who never had had any faith in themselves—that their territory, too, and that of their rulers contained material of artistic value, though, to be sure, the appearance of these dramas did not coincide with the prevalence of that spirit with which Wilhelm Schlegel had been imbued. Thus the most outstanding achievements to approximate Schlegel's exhortations or to result from them were destined not to be published or produced upon the stage before they had lost their immediate significance.

A bit of poetry taken from the history of Austria, likewise an historical incident in the Shakespearean manner, is the *Trauerspiel in Tyrol* (1828) by Immermann, a native of Magdeburg. After the victory had been won and Germany had been freed from the yoke of France, after everything, indeed, had come to pass that Wilhelm Schlegel had demanded, it was an inviting task for one who had taken part in the Wars of Liberation to dramatize in Shakespeare's style the immediate past and to erect a memorial to the national hero, Andreas Hofer. And yet, even Immermann was too late. Public opinion had already reversed itself; under the heavy pressure of the reaction the people began to do honor to the self-same Napoleon whose ruin both Schlegel and Kleist had most ardently desired. The *Trauerspiel in Tyrol* was followed in 1831 by Grabbe's *Napoleon oder die hundert Tage*, an historical drama of similar artistic style though of contrary political sympathies. Both dramas adhered so closely to the immediate past that Scott's principle, namely, that the author derive his material from that which is nearest and most closely related to him, was splendidly exemplified; but Grabbe, like Scott, sought especially to portray not only a definite historical personage but his whole environment as well, including the great and particularly the small. The masses, those who to a greater or less degree took part in the great historical events of the day, found expression in *Napoleon* as well as in Grabbe's other historical dramas. This new principle of dramatically revivifying a whole epoch is worked out still further by Georg Buechner. His drama *Dantons Tod* (1835) indicated, just as did Grabbe's *Napoleon,* Germany's interest in France two decades after Waterloo.

The Hohenstaufen dramas prove that the field of national history had not been abandoned and that dramatists were endeavoring still to make the Germans feel the glory that once was theirs. The initial effort was Friedrich von Raumer's *Geschichte der Hohenstaufen und ihrer Zeit* (1823-5). This book was in line with the endeavor of the romanticists, primarily Uhland, to glorify the German Middle Ages. After Raumer, Ernst Raupach was but one among several to "lay hands upon the Hohenstaufens, our beloved old Suabian kings," as Heine expressed it (7, 158). In his *Cycle of Historical Dramas,* which consisted of sixteen five-act plays, most of them with a preamble as well, and which was known under the collective title of *Die Hohenstaufen* (1837), Raupach proceeded to garb Raumer's figures from Friedrich Barbarossa to Conradin "in poetry as leathern as Russian muscovy." As early as 1828 Immermann had published his *Kaiser Friedrich der Zweite* and in the two years immediately following, Grabbe also appeared with a cycle called *Die Hohenstaufen,* a *Kaiser Friedrich Barbarossa,* and a *Kaiser Heinrich der Sechste*. But though the efforts of these three poets differed widely as to form, content, and artistic and political points of view, they all suffered from the lack of immediacy which perforce exists between our day and the Hohenstaufen period. The characters and events in Shakespeare's historical dramas had created the political and social world in which his contemporaries lived, whereas the German Middle Ages were but a remote historical fact to the Germans of the nineteenth century. We were not granted the creative dramatic genius that might have bridged this difficulty. The Hohenstaufen dramas demonstrate clearly the validity of Scott's fundamental principle. Modern poetry was unable to manipulate the history of the "dear old Suabian kings" as a whole. Their history could serve as no more than an isolated incident and for this purpose the ballad is the most appropriate artistic expression. Hence it is hardly praise to call Uhland's dramas *Ernst, Herzog von Schwaben* and *Ludwig der Baier* (1818–19) "ballad-dramas." This very epithet bespeaks their unfitness for actual production upon the stage.

But though, adroit dramatist that he was, Raupach may have erred in his dramas upon the Hohenstaufens, he must nevertheless be given due credit for having been the first to stage the Siegfried legend. His *Nibelungen-Hort* (1834) succeeded where Fouqué's Sigurd trilogy had failed. But perhaps even more significant is the fact that the staging of Raupach's dramatization incited Hebbel to create the greatest drama ever fashioned up to that time out of the *Nibelungen* material. And yet not even Hebbel was ordained to achieve the success that Richard Wagner attained with his music-dramas. Acclaimed beyond the confines of Germany, the *Ring of the Nibelungen* along with *Tannhaeuser, Lohengrin, Tristan and Isolde,* the *Meistersinger,* and *Parsifal* still remain the supreme realization of the hopes and dreams of the romanticists. To be sure, they do not quite belong to that historic type which Wilhelm Schlegel deemed most worthy for the romantic drama. Nevertheless they achieved that for which Wilhelm Schlegel and his companions hoped and strove: they breathed genuine life into the world of German antiquity and enshrined it not only in the German heart but in the hearts of all men the world over. Wagner revived ancient German poetry just as the fairy prince with a kiss awakened the Sleeping Beauty. There is much genuine romanticism in Wagner's art productions. The various attempts made at present to show that Fouqué (not only in his Sigurd trilogy) anticipated Wagner in many ways, merely reveal how closely romanticism skirted the ideal which the genius of Wagner was destined to achieve. [40]

III. ROMANTIC SATIRE

T HE romanticists, every one, were innovators who enjoyed the battles which their efforts begot. Brushing
aside what seemed to them antiquated, they sought to sup-
plant the old with conceptions of their own. To these ends,
being artists as well as innovators, they brought to bear
the power of their poetic eloquence. The diction in their
dialectics not infrequently reached a high plane of artistry.
The very compression of these utterances reveals a conscious sense of literary form, which even in prose tended
to create little masterpieces of epigrammatic wit. In these
epigrams the carelessness which was generally in evidence
whenever a romanticist gave his poetic fancy free play
vanished almost entirely. The poetic satires of the romanticists are, in particular, masterpieces in which the scintil-
lating spirit of romanticism discloses such dazzling vivacity as to win not only the approval, but even the admiration of those who are otherwise rather loath to follow
in the paths of romantic thought and speculation.

It has long been the custom of poets who wished to win
an audience for themselves and for a new idea in art to
offer their challenge in artistic form. At the very time
when romanticism was born, there had just begun to appear those inimitable epigrammatic masterpieces upon
topics of essentially literary interest, the *Xenien* of Goethe
and Schiller. These came out in the fall of 1796 and
hence were able to take note of the very first pronouncements of the Schlegels and to aim their wit primarily at

the younger of the two brothers and his bold, occasionally too extravagant utterances. The creators of the *Xenien* were two unique personalities who, from the heights of their mature understanding of the world and of art, weighed and measured their contemporaries. Though before and after 1796 Goethe and Schiller attacked in poetic or non-poetic form other writers besides the Schlegels, they surely never regarded such satirical efforts as anything more than an avocation. To the romanticists, however, such a conflict of personal opinion was of primary importance. Countless are the poems that were written merely for the sheer joy in the controversy. Even in works which with genuine artistry seem to strive after the noblest ideals, the tendency toward strife and satire makes itself felt. Few of the great romantic poems are without passages referring to literature as a craft. Kleist, to be sure, avoided alluding in his productions to his profession, but he is only one writer against the great number of those who again and again introduced bits of professional humor and thus exposed romanticism to the criticism that its productions were meant only for writers. As a matter of fact, it demands intimate knowledge on the part of the modern reader to understand all the allusions in romantic poetry to the controversies which were carried on incessantly by the writers of the time.

To a certain extent the Storm and Stress had exhibited a like tendency. Even Goethe competed with the friends of his youth by writing little dramas which entered into the general controversial spirit, and poems which, overstepping the confines of poetizing, lost no opportunities to make apt allusions or to deliver lateral thrusts. Such instances are found in *Claudine von Villa Bella* and in *Goetz*. Throughout *Faust* the author claims the right to strike at his opponents much in the manner of the *Xenien*. The Storm and Stress, not unlike romanticism, made war upon the Enlightenment and endeavored to consign it to the junk-heap. But whenever a rising generation of artists engages in warfare with the generally prevailing one and presumes to prove to the latter how antiquated it has become and how enmeshed it is in tradition, there are certain expressions which are found constantly recurring. The French romanticists of 1830 were animated by much the same spirit as the Germans of 1770 or 1800 when they made it their task to *épater le bourgeois;* they were like the Viennese revolutionists of 1890 when they began "dressing down the Philistines."

These assailants of the existing order were not merely destructive. Though apparently bent only upon overcoming the prevailing conditions, they did not fail at the same time to propound the innovations which were their chief concern. There is much that is constructive in the *Xenien;* there are many beacons pointing the way to the newer ideals. The controversial poetry of the Storm and Stress, and primarily that of Goethe's youth, reveals to us the attitude of the younger generation. A considerable portion of the philosophy and aesthetics of romanticism is perhaps most clearly and keenly reflected in the products of that artistic capriciousness which took delight in amusing itself with the weaknesses of the opponents of romanticism. There is a collection of romantic epigrams, written exclusively in prose, that embodies theories of the utmost importance. These epigrams are indispensable in the presentation of German romanticism. They are the aphorisms, which among the early romanticists were generally simply referred to as *Fragmente*. They were a favorite form with Friedrich Schlegel, and his brother took delight in using them like a keen-edged sword with which to make graceful and subtle thrusts at his literary opponents. The *Fragmente* of the Schlegel brothers may appropriately be considered later counterparts of the *Xenien*. In form many of them compete quite successfully with the terse brevity and telling force of the exquisitely edged couplets of Goethe and Schiller. Others, again, are considerably expanded and assume the proportions of little essays which with unique compression dispose in the smallest possible space of an entire argument, a book, or some person. There is nothing in the later years of the nineteenth century nor yet in modern journalism which really approaches the conciseness of these *Fragmente*. Their facility of expression is so apparent as to make it seem quite superfluous for a German to have tried to acquire further skill from a study of any French writer of the day. And yet the Germans bestowed great praise upon a certain Frenchman to whom they felt themselves indebted. This man was none other than Mirabeau's friend, Nicolas Chamfort. His ideas and comments on worldly wisdom were to Friedrich Schlegel a compendium of genuine wit, deep thought, and delicate perception, replete with mature good sense and sterling manhood and withal of such excellence and couched in such exquisite diction as to be incomparable and the consummate achievement of this type.

This verdict appears in the first collection of romantic *Fragmente* (No. 111). The collection was published in Reichart's journal *Lyceum der schoenen Kuenste* and was entirely from the pen of Friedrich Schlegel. He set the fashion and here, as well as subsequently, caught the spirit of the prose epigram most truly and accurately. The very first *Lyceumfragment* contains a thought which might

well have been found among the couplets of Goethe and
Schiller and which is expressed with a compression to
which the distich could hardly aspire: "Many are called
artists who are, properly speaking, nature's works of art."
Though the same idea was defended simultaneously in
the chapter on Piero di Cosimo in Wackenroder's *Herzensergiessungen* (p. 155), the entire content of this first collection of *Fragmente* is rich enough to justify all claims to
originality and uniqueness. Striking turns of speech suc-
ceed in hurling satiric wit at the vital spot of a much-
talked-of writer. "Voss in 'Luise' is a Homeroid; similarly
Homer in his translation is a Vossoid" (No. 113). When
finally the brothers had the first literary organ of their
own, the *Athenaeum,* Friedrich yielded the precedence to
Hardenberg's aphorisms. These appeared in the first volume of the *Athenaeum* in 1798 under the title *Bluetenstaub.* Novalis, as well as Schleiermacher, was at that
time engaged upon that really great achievement in the
line of early romantic aphorisms, the *Fragmente* of the
second volume of 1798, which are simply called the
Athenaeumfragmente, and which are essentially the work
of the Schlegels.

Novalis was much less prone than his associates to base
his aphorisms upon witty expressions which were meant
to sting and wound his opponent. He took delight in the
habit of jotting down in a few words the gist of his ideas
each day. Out of this teeming wealth of hasty memoranda
that booked each transitory thought without subjecting it
to a definitive test, from this collection of "thought-
splinters" which purposely looked at things from every
conceivable antithetical point of view in order to survey
them from all angles, the *Bluetenstaub* was composed.
After his death, the editors of Hardenberg's works made

several more selections. In fact the original notes are now available in their entirety, but one need search only the *Bluetenstaub* to find examples of genuine epigrammatic skill. Ricarda Huch has indeed aptly characterized Hardenberg's epigrams as they appear there, by saying (1, 48): "Suffusing the dark heavens with their delicate glow, they soar gracefully, like rockets, into the air and ere they have been definitely observed, they have already expired."

Schleiermacher's contributions, on the other hand, aim to be more than mere art. A keen dialectician seeks the word that expresses his ideas and observations most strikingly and which presents most accurately the last reaches of his penetrating and impartial vision. One perceives in Schleiermacher, indeed, an artist, who, to be sure, did not spare his opponents and even seemed to prefer somewhat rugged expression.

In the *Athenaeumfragmente,* however, Friedrich Schlegel formulated the germinal ideas of romanticism. He created winged words: "Good dramas must be drastic" (No. 42) ; "An historian is a reversed prophet" (No. 80) ; or the assertion—which occasioned much mirth—that the French Revolution, Fichte's *Wissenschaftslehre,* and Goethe's *Lehrjahre* were the greatest tendencies of the age (No. 216) ; or the terse statements about marriage *à quatre* (No. 34). He characterized individual writers such as Jean Paul (No. 421), and by means of his clever turns found himself in the closest proximity to the *Xenien.* Poetic gems of sarcasm are penned in prose: "If not too much of anything is equivalent to a bit of everything, then Garve is the greatest of German philosophers" (No. 317). Successfully he lived up to his own dictum: "Like a little masterpiece, a *Fragment* must be utterly isolated from the world about it and be a world unto itself, like a hedge-hog" (No. 206).

Wilhelm Schlegel was less concerned than his brother with the larger aspects of things. He revealed himself in the *Fragmente* as the sensitive connoisseur. For this very reason he was prone to confine himself to certain individuals and hence his satire was, relatively speaking, of a more personal nature. "Klopstock is a grammatic poet and a poetic grammarian" (No. 127). "Hogarth painted ugliness and wrote about beauty" (No. 183). "In his history, Johannes Mueller often glances beyond Switzerland into world's history; less frequently, however, does he observe Switzerland with the eye of a cosmopolite" (No. 224). The rule, inherent in the distich—and hence, also, in the *Xenien*—which demands antitheses in the lines and which places hexameter and pentameter in juxtaposition to each other like question and answer, like blow and counter-blow, also holds in these *Fragmente*. It is felt more strongly and is likewise more obvious here than in the utterances of his brother Friedrich. One 'seems to feel that the younger brother was primarily seeking a vehicle for a striking, clear-cut thought while the older brother sought the clear-cut expression for an opportune idea. With Friedrich terminological witticism hovered in the background. He gave scientific conceptions new and surprising interpretations. Many of his *Fragmente* took the form of definitions. "Moderantism is the spirit of castrated illiberality" (No. 64). "Genuine mysticism is morality in its greatest dignity" (No. 263). "Philosophy is seeking omniscience conjointly" (No. 344). Wilhelm, too, loved the form of the definition but he did not seek to make obscure revelations. He preferred to use a clever word which would prick the mind or at least surprise it.

In the *Ideen,* the last collection of *Fragmente,* which appeared in 1800 in the first part of the third volume of the *Athenaeum,* Friedrich's obscurity increased still more. His wit here took a different turn. He now called it the external phenomenon, the external flash of fancy, and from this conception of it he derived its divine quality as well as that quality in mysticism which approaches wit (No. 26). Now, for the most part, he merely whispered obscure presentiments into the ears of the initiated. At the same time, however, the *Ideen* contain statements of decided and penetrating character, particularly when they seek to determine the essential character and tasks of the German. These statements must be borne in mind in connection with what has been said above.

Just as the *Xenien* of Goethe and Schiller were met with the counter-*Xenien,* the *Fragmente* of early romanticism also evoked retorts. The victims of their shafts likewise felt themselves obliged to answer tit for tat as far as they were able. Kotzebue's "drastic drama and philosophic comedy for youths," which, referring to *Athenaeumfragment* No. 197, was called *Der hyperboreische Esel oder die heutige Bildung,* created the rôle of a representative of the "present-day culture" with its "impertinent arrogance," its "bombastic nonsense," its "utter worthlessness" out of perversions of the *Fragmente* and *Lucinde.* This might have been considered a clever stroke if it had not been presented with such utter crudeness and lack of delicacy. Though he was a versatile master of the stage, Kotzebue was no match for the romanticists in the art of writing parodies. *Der hyperboreische Esel* turned out to be nothing more than a melodrama at the end of which vice is overcome with nausea and virtue proceeds to banquet.

Parody was already used in a sort of continuation of the *Athenaeumfragmente* which may be found at the end of the second volume of this publication (1799), in the *Literarischer Reichsanzeiger oder Archiv der Zeit und ihres Geschmacks*. The *Reichsanzeiger* chose, out of the variety offered by the *Fragmente*, only those adapted to personal satire and adroitly concealed them in the form of booksellers' advertisements. Wilhelm Schlegel, who was practically the sole author, was able to give pleasing variety to his jest. The lack of consideration displayed in ridiculing prominent German writers resembles the *Xenien* far more than it does the style of the *Fragmente*. The climax of these malicious thrusts was reached at the close where, in keeping with the form of newspaper advertisements which had been adhered to throughout, a meeting of creditors was announced. Strictly in accordance with the custom of the day, upon the application of the poets whose intellectual property had been borrowed by the debtor, there was called under the heading *Citatio Edictalis* a meeting of creditors relative to the poetry of the aulic councillor and *Comes Palatinus Caesareus* Wieland, and any one who could *titulo legitimo* make similar claims was invited to come forward within due time and then forever afterward to hold his peace.

Under quite other circumstances and with wholly different aims and effects Schleiermacher had, in one of the *Fragmente* (No. 364), used for his *Katechismus der Vernunft fuer edle Frauen* the form of the Ten Commandments and of the Creed and had thereby proved at least this much, that he too was able to heighten the effect of his words by skillfully adapting them to a prescribed form.

Wilhelm Schlegel went further. A born translator, his delicate ear readily perceived any peculiar quality in poems which he disliked and he spared himself no pains in imitating any such qualities whenever he was bent upon making writers with whom he was at odds appear ridiculous. What is unquestionably his masterpiece in this field is likewise to be found in the *Athenaeum*—the *Wettgesang* by the three poets, J. H. Voss, Mathisson, and Schmidt von Werneuchen. The poem is delightfully prefaced by a detailed discussion in which the essential characteristics and persistent mannerisms in the poetry of these men are amply illustrated by numerous quotations. Voss's domestic, Philistine complacence, Mathisson's superlative elegance and diligent daubing of landscapes, Schmidt's song of praise to the commonplace are duly ridiculed. The song itself starts with twelve six-line strophes, each strophe devoting two lines each to Voss, Mathisson, and Schmidt. Then there ensues a dialogue in six four-line stanzas in which the three of them bestow extravagant eulogies upon one another. Finally they burst out in unison in a closing six-line strophe. Not only the content but the very diction itself is derived from the weaknesses of each of these three victims. Voss outdoes himself with clumsy laconisms; Mathisson's language is smooth, oily, and flat; Schmidt is dry and uncouth. Mathisson's tendency to fuse, with utter lack of style, the commonplace with the piquant is by no means overlooked. His collection of poems bearing the pompous title *Basreliefs am Sarkophage des Jahrhunderts* (1798) is duly scored against him. Voss begins:

> Mathisson, your delineation of nature,
> Sweet as honey, soft as wax,

Will never cease to delight
Until primitive Teutonic taste runs wild.

Mathisson answers:

Beplanting its slopes with potato-bulbs
You plow, oh Voss, into Pindus;
Boiled, the fruit will delight
Apollo in Elysium.

He is taunted by Schmidt:

I admire whatever I understand of you,
Mathisson! But your bas-reliefs
Which sprout at the bier—
Are they some sort of wall-pepper?

About this time Goethe, too, was experimenting in satirical mimicry of a similar nature. His *Musen und Grazien in der Mark*, which came out with the *Xenien*, was also meant to imitate the work of Schmidt von Werneuchen. This parody, which now bears the title *Deutscher Parnass*, appeared in the *Musenalmanach* of 1797 and among Goethe's poems it is, strange to say, incorporated among the *Cantatas*. Certain it is that this production by Goethe almost awakens the impression of having emanated from the time-worn lyre of the aged Gleim. But the very fact that the *Deutscher Parnass* was misinterpreted for decades and that its real meaning was not deciphered until almost a century had elapsed shows quite conclusively that in the field of mimic satire Goethe was no match for the facile translator, Wilhelm Schlegel. Furthermore, Schlegel's parodies bear the unmistakable imprints of conviviality. It is only when boon companions who are in the habit of forgathering at frequent intervals amuse themselves with satires of this sort that things develop, such as the many epigrammatic projects that occupy so much space in Wilhelm Schlegel's works (2, 149 ff.). Doubtless much that originated with others is embodied herein. The sonnet against Garlieb Merkel, Kotzebue's blatant shield-bearer (2, 201), is the result of just such friendly competition. A letter written by Caroline to her daughter Auguste on October 28, 1799, depicts graphically one such instance of excessive merriment. Merkel had spread the gossip in Berlin that the Grand Duke Karl August had reprimanded the Schlegels on account of the *Athenaeum*. "So Wilhelm and Tieck sat down last night and presented him with a nefarious sonnet. It was rare sport to watch how their eyes glowed at each other, and with what unrestrained gaiety this bit of justified *malice* was perpetrated. [Dorothea] Veit and I almost rolled to the floor from laughter."

It is quite possible that the bold travesty *Schillers Lob der Frauen* (2, 172) came about in much the same way. It begins:

Honor the women! They knit the stockings
Woolly and warm to wade through the swamps,
And mend worn pantaloons, too;
They cook their husbands nourishing soups
And dress the children their cute little dolls.
On a moderate week's wages they manage the house.

The early romanticists naturally had a different conception of woman's sphere from Schiller's. A purely artistic antithesis was also brought out by attacks such as these—an antithesis to Schiller's poetic style in general, as depicted not only in this poem but also in others of a similar nature. This difference in artistic taste quite naturally determined the reception which the *Song of the Bell* was accorded by the romanticists. Again Caroline informs her daughter (October 21, 1799) that all of them nearly rolled off their chairs laughing over the poem and that it was à la Voss, à la Tieck, and à la the devil, and at the very least was enough to drive one mad. As might be supposed, Wilhelm Schlegel's sarcastic verses did not spare the *Bell*.

There is much more in the nature of parody to be found among Wilhelm Schlegel's epigrammatic poetry. In thirteen none too chaste strophes, for example, based upon those favorite lines from Byron's *Had We Never Loved So Kindly,* he developed the conversation of a pair of lovers. Or he links together nine German translations of the refrain in the witches' incantation in Shakespeare's *Macbeth* and continuing in the same manner, as though stupefied by the hollow sound, adds to them nine insolent couplets. "Doodle, doodle with foul tootling! Spume rime and iambus fume!" it starts. Replete with parody is the sentimental-romantic drama entitled *Kotzebues Rettung oder der tugendhafte Verbannte,* which is contained in the manifold satire *Ehrenpforte und Triumphbogen fuer den Theaterpraesidenten von Kotzebue* (1801). Characters from Kotzebue's drama, old favorites of the public, are placed upon the stage to recite their favorite lines. The most telling character is one Kamtschadalin Puseltusel, a cynical counterpart to Kotzebue's too naïve Gurli, daughter of India.

Brentano did much the same thing in his *Gustav Wasa* (1800) by poking fun at a drama bearing the same name and written by Kotzebue. This satire was meant to be a

continuation of *Der hyperboreische Esel.* Indeed, Arnim
and Brentano had a natural inclination toward parody.
Even in serious moods they were prone to appropriate
and develop strains which had originated with others.
Arnim's *Kriegslieder* as well as many a line in the *Wunderhorn* were conceived in this way. This in itself at times
approaches satiric parody. Arnim was disposed to give
a free reproduction in German of national hymns, especially those of England. He did not hesitate in one instance
to attempt to translate into German even the nonsense
verse of humorous English war-ditties. In the second part
of the play *Halle und Jerusalem* (1811, p. 322 ff.), a
company of Englishmen who are besieged in Acre sing
a long series of verses according to the following scheme:

> Round is the table,
> The world is round,
> In friendship bound
> We sit, still able.
>
> Let the fool's cap sway,
> Let the dogs bay,
> Let the enemy make war—
> 'Twere better, they forbore.

Brentano consciously imitated other poets (2, 338 ff.).
He varied Goethe's *Wer nie sein Brot mit Traenen asz*
(2, 443 ff.). His particular delight, however, in which he
was more or less successful, was to make use of dialects
with which he had just become familiar. The spooky,
though jolly, story *Die mehreren Wehmueller und un-
garischen Nationalgesichter* (in Gubitz's *Gesellschafter*,
1817), which takes place in southern Hungary, used with

very pleasing effect the Hussar Latin which the Hungarians employed at a time when their own language did not yet aspire to the position it occupies today. At a sanitary cordon a Czech hussar bawls at Wehmueller, a painter: "You lie, *mentiris!* Have you not given the surgeon his picture, *non dedidisti Domino Chirurgo suam imaginem?* So that he 'looked through his fingers' [connived at the procedure] and let you pass, *ut vidit per digitos et te fecit passare?* You have come back from pestilence-stricken regions, *es returnatus ex pestiferatis locis!*" (4, 220). But the Viennese dialect, particularly, held Brentano under its spell. He sent the festival play *Viktoria und ihre Geschwister* (1817) into the world with a little dictionary which translated the Austrian idioms for the Germans and thus enabled them to understand the poem. This dictionary was, to be sure, not a model of accuracy; Brentano's quick ear was, however, most apparent in his choice of favorite Viennese expressions. *Bachsimperl* (a stupid fellow), *bagschirli* (droll, or more correctly, dainty), *balawatchet* (confused), *Batzenlippel* (a fellow that is worth but a *Batzen*), *Bofoesen* (slices of toasted wheat bread with brain), *Dampus* (a slight drunk), *Franziskerl* (pastil for fumigating), *Gfrisz* (face), *Goderl* (chin), *Goschen* (mouth), *Gugaschecken* (freckles), *mudelsauber* (neat)—these are but a few specimens of the dialectic treasure which Brentano assembled in this work.

In his treatise on Philistinism and in his fairy-tales also, Brentano used caricatures. Elsewhere he delineated the correspondence between a director of a theater and a poet. Arnim collaborated in this as well as in a contribution to Kleist's *Abendblaetter*. The latter article, which was printed in unchanged form only in Brentano's works

(4, 424 ff.), sought to note the opinions that are expressed before a picture by various visitors at an art exhibit. (The French woman, Madame Gyp, used this device also, but at a much later date). From the eminence of his skill in the art of parody Brentano was able to mock at *Die Versuche und Hindernisse Karls* (1808), which came from the circle to which Chamisso, Fouqué, and Varnhagen belonged, and which was jointly produced by four of its members in imitation of J. H. Voss as well as Johannes von Mueller.

But the greatest masterpieces in parody form are to be found in Tieck's satires. He was essentially the model followed by romantic writers in this field. A born actor, he was accustomed to playing rôles. Moreover, his unusual facility in extemporizing gave jests of this sort the spontaneity of real life. Steffens gives an account (*Was ich erlebte*, 4, 372 ff.) in which he relates that, at his request, Tieck wrote a piece extemporaneously in which the lover and an orang-outang were one and the same person. Steffens declares he had never seen anything like it.

E. T. A. Hoffmann's *Nachricht von einem gebildeten jungen Mann* in the fourth volume of *Phantasiestuecke in Callots Manier* (1815) and Hauff's narrative *Der Affe als Mensch* in his collection of fairy-tales *Der Scheich von Alexandria und seine Sklaven* (1826) are based upon the same theme. But Tieck does not have a real ape take the part of the lover. A hopeless suitor wins the daughter of an inordinate lover of nature and an eccentric collector of oddities by posing as an orang-outang which the London African Society had carefully brought up and educated. In his presentation of a youth who wishes to pass as a human ape with human impulses toward cultural development, Tieck is tremendously effective. The beast's voice is still somewhat inarticulate but if one listened attentively, one would hear some excellent ideas: ideas concerning human happiness, acacia plantations, chicory raising, and many other things pertaining to the betterment of the human race. With these recommendations the youth was presented to the old man. When the fraudulent ape arrived, he was not loquacious; yet in spite of his inarticulate speech his conversation was sententious and sentimental, replete with splendid ideas. When finally the truth leaked out, the father continued to call the son-in-law who had thus been thrust upon him, Mr. Orang-outang.

A human being mimics an ape that wishes to pass for a man. Thus romantic delight in confusing duplication and re-duplication ran its course. Simultaneously blow after blow was rained upon the platitudes of the Enlightenment and the mania for sheer utility. This was the native element of *Der gestiefelte Kater*. The hero of this mad play occasions great astonishment because, though but a tom-cat, he speaks and thinks like a human being. Then presently it becomes apparent that this creature, though dressed and demeaning himself like a human being, has claws and likes to climb trees. Everything is meant to mock the Enlightenment and its Philistines. While Tieck voices the observations of the tom-cat, he has the Philistines, who fill the auditorium and make remarks to one another upon all that they see and hear, converse as was their habit in smug and self-complacent language. Particularly he parodies the quibbling of Karl August Boettiger, the rector at Weimar, who had devoted an entire book to the glorification of his favorite, Iffland, and the latter's dramatic ability. The counterpart of Boettiger which Tieck created discourses in the rector's phrases on the acting of the artist in the title-rôle. Meanwhile touching scenes which had been inserted for their cheap effectiveness into the dramas of Iffland or Kotzebue are being parodied on the stage; the audience approves tumultuously, betraying thereby its utter lack of discrimination.

A compendium of spite, aimed at the literary, social, and indeed, also at the political conditions of the time, *Der gestiefelte Kater* is by no means unique among Tieck's productions. Since Tieck wielded this weapon habitually, those of his poems which forego satire are far more easily enumerated than are his almost countless lampoons written for the sheer joy in the onset. H. Guenther in his study *Romantische Kritik und Satire bei Ludwig Tieck* (Leipzig, 1907) gives a lengthy, well-ordered list of the objects of Tieck's attacks. Enlightenment, fashionable literature, classicism, romanticism, Young Germany were all flayed by him. As yet it is left to future research to determine the numerous ways in which Tieck's wit gave vent to his dissatisfaction with contemporary life. Practically every conceivable form of Tieck's art is implicated, whether it is a creation of pure satire—such as *Der gestiefelte Kater*—or whether it merely contains occasional thrusts. It seems to have been difficult for him to refrain from expressing his opinion upon the weaknesses, or what seemed to him to be weaknesses, of others.

Tieck was the typical native of Berlin who, as Goethe expressed it, "was born with his eyes open"—the guiding progenitor of the Berlin comic paper. It would almost seem that to destroy with cutting criticism was more natural to him than to submit to moods of poetic elevation. Indeed, might one not have expected him to ridicule the excessive enthusiasm of romanticism? Was not Nicolai's frigidity, his tendency and ability to turn the sublime into the ridiculous also more in keeping with Tieck's nature than the romantic tendency to apotheosize all emotion? His animated fancy, moreover, delighted in vacillating with genuine romantic glee from pole to pole. Theodore Fontane, though not a native of Berlin, was nevertheless genuinely imbued with a native's attitude toward life; but for all his vivacity he was less inclined than Tieck merely to flutter about like a butterfly. Yet he, too, felt these antithetical tendencies and proved in the lines *In Memoriam Nicolai* that although he sincerely hated Philistinism and ever remained untainted by it, he nevertheless felt in sympathy with Nicolai and was prone to become upon occasion a thorough-going Philistine.

Tieck's first satires were works which Nicolai printed and thoroughly approved of. From the melancholy, gloomy world of his first literary efforts Tieck sprang directly into blasé, ironic, soberly deliberate mockery; he became an advocate of healthy commonsense; he was all Nicolai could have wished. The *Straussfedern,* a collection of entertaining, instructive, and, above all, moral and censorious tales, had been published by Nicolai under different editorship since 1787. Tieck's contributions (1795–8) soon eclipsed his models in cleverness. If he was obliged to ridicule *Fermer der Geniale* or *Ulrich der Empfindsame,* Tieck gave his inclination to destroy free rein and intimated that he was subject to no illusions where meaningless albeit mellifluous words were concerned. *Peter Lebrecht. Eine Geschichte ohne Abenteuerlichkeiten* (1795) preserved the world-weary tone of the deliberate scoffer of Nicolai's school. A decided reversion was effected in the *Volksmaerchen, herausgegeben von Peter Lebrecht* (1797). No longer championing reason nor condemning the delusions of emotion, Tieck, at a stroke, glorified instead the national tradition of ancient artlessness, thus becoming at once a dangerous opponent of the narrow morality of the Enlightenment and playing off against the narrowness and incapacity of mere intelligence and intelligibility the days of yore, glowing with a portentous wealth of fancy. But he maintained the genuine mood of the folk-tales only a short time. *Der gestiefelte Kater* bears eloquent testimony of how his pungent satire blossomed forth out of the essentially natural soil of the fairy-tales and how his Berlin wit as shown in the *Straussfedern* now took clever shots in the opposite direction. It was even more natural still for him to adapt the *Denkwuerdige Geschichtschronik der Schildbuerger* to the present and instead of merely relating the follies which the *Schildbuerger* committed at some long gone time, to level his aim at the pedantic Philistine of the declining eighteenth century, to whom utility was the sum total of all activity. These *Schildbuerger* conceived of poetry as naught but the means of improving erring humanity. Rogues are not deterred by the spectre of the gallows; one reads them odes or shows them a dramatic scene in an infirmary.

The favorite butt of Tieck's satires against the Philistines was their constant effort to put poetry to practical purposes and their utter misunderstanding of the proper approach to it and to its real meaning. Now a real culture with romantic connotations threw down the gauntlet before pedantic Philistinism. In the "garden of poetry" in *Zerbino,* the dupe of the Enlightenment is innocently standing in the presence of the greatest writers in the world of literature and is seeking his own favorites in vain. Hagedorn, Gellert, Gessner, Christian Ewald von Kleist, and Bodmer are conspicuously missing. He beholds in the place of these the "notorious Jacob Boehm'" and Ariosto, who, thanks to Wieland, had been entirely disposed of. For, indeed, this greatest of all German poets had, so thought the Philistines, appropriated most of the best points in Ariosto's style and had incorporated them, greatly improved, into his own beautiful *Oberon*. At the same time he had invested the so-called stanzas with a charming originality by tearing them apart and knitting them together again in a freer, more delightful, and more artless form. In the realm of poetry Tieck was able, however, to proceed from destructive to constructive criticism. He was not satisfied merely to have expressed his approbation of the chap-books and their childlike simplicity in the *Schildbuerger* and in *Der gestiefelte Kater*. He did homage to those poets who were especial favorites of his and of his companions. Of Goethe he says (10, 280 f.) :

A flower-decked grove is prepared
For the artist to whom posterity does homage,
At whose coming German art awakened,
And who still has many a noble song to sing you,
To carry into your bosom the glow of poetry
So that henceforth you will understand;
The great Briton hopes to embrace him,
Cervantes yearns for him by day and by night,
And Dante is creating a gallant greeting.
Then these sacred four, the masters of the new art,
Will roam in harmony over the meadow.

In the folk-tales Tieck developed a form of burlesque drama reminiscent of Aristophanes, which served him well for a long time in his skirmishes in literary and social criticism. In *Ritter Blaubart: Ein Ammenmaerchen* he had merely inserted Shakespearean comic figures and wittily satiric allusions between scenes of intense seriousness. But, beginning with *Der gestiefelte Kater,* satiric comedy became his dominant theme and *Zerbino* and *Die verkehrte Welt* developed this tendency further. Tieck blazed the trail, and both the older and the younger romanticists followed eagerly. The final step in the development of these audacious sketches was to appropriate a form which Goethe had used in the days of his rebellious youth. During his last years at Frankfort Goethe had written farces in doggerel in imitation of Hans Sachs. Tieck, who thoroughly admired all of Goethe's early poetry, particularly loved these droll sketches. Thus once more the romanticists received from the Storm and Stress a medium not only for poetic expression but also for effective recrimination. *Ein Prolog* in the *Volksmaerchen* and *Der neue Herkules am Scheidewege, eine Parodie in Versen,* later called *Der Autor, ein Fastnachtsschwank* (13, 267 ff.) represent the initial steps in Tieck's adoption of the Hans Sachs-Goethe style. The second of these sketches proceeded from attacking those who lagged behind to ridiculing those who displayed too much zeal and haste in imitating Tieck. The following lines were addressed by Tieck (p. 314) to the *Bewunderer* (who was Brentano) :

Earnest effort and endeavor
They fancy may well be dispensed with.
Success they imagine will come while they slumber.
And they pose as Titans.
Yet they know that even brewing and baking
Are not effected by sheer genius.

Tieck was obviously aging and becoming peevish. He himself had been guilty of the very fault which he here censured in Brentano and in others who overshot the mark in imitating his style. Once more, in 1801, he commenced a bristling comedy which would have brought him still more dangerously close to the style of Goethe's early poetry. But the *Anti-Faust oder Geschichte eines dummen Teufels* (*Nachgelassene Schriften*, 1, 127 ff.) did not progress beyond a mere beginning. Haym (p. 824) curtly calls the fragment an attempt of a pigmy to slip into giant's clothes.

Meanwhile Wilhelm Schlegel had demonstrated with the *Ehrenpforte* for Kotzebue that he was capable of competing with *Der gestiefelte Kater*. But Schlegel's *Ein schoen kurzweilig Fastnachtsspiel vom alten und neuen Jahrhundert. Tragiert am ersten Januarii im Jahr 1801* (2, 149 ff.) proved fully how far superior Wilhelm Schlegel was to his friend Tieck in ability to follow a clearly defined pattern. Schlegel, a philologian, caught the spirit of Goethe's early farces much more accurately than did the extempore actor Tieck.

In 1799, about the same time that Tieck began to issue his translation of Cervantes' great masterpiece, *Das juengste Gericht. Eine Vision* (9, 339 ff.) was conceived. In this piece Tieck pretended to be dreaming of the Day of Judgment. To be sure, the victims of his satire fared badly, but he himself was destined also to feel the austerity of the judge. "You cannot deny that you scorned and underrated . . . distinguished and respected men . . . indeed, no one ever measured up to your demands." To which Tieck answers that his intentions were not at all wicked. "That is your everlasting excuse . . . when you do not know what else to say" is the next accusation against him. But the worst of all is when he is suspected of having anticipated and made ridiculous this very Day of Judgment. The charge takes him unawares; he is overcome by fear, when fortunately he awakes.

Das juengste Gericht is the final flourish to the audacious, satiric deviltry of Tieck's youth. But few of the satires which have been mentioned were written later. Tieck presently relinquished the role of universal satirist. When in *Phantasus* (1812-6) he collects the productions of his early romantic period, the comments which accompany each poem or group of poems afforded him convenient opportunity for recrimination against his adversaries, but it seemed of greater importance to him to show the way to an aesthetic enjoyment of life and, primarily, of art. He now sought to present the many-sidedness of romantic culture in its most charming aspect and to propound the duty of romanticism to educate Germans to an appreciation of German culture. The theater is no longer considered merely as a place for bold buffoonery, but rather as the indispensable medium for giving reality to dramatic art. Though up to this time he had rarely written reviews, in Dresden Tieck finally emerged as a reviewer of current plays. His *Dramaturgische Blaetter* (1825-6) are not satiric. His earlier manner of arrogant scorn gave way to rigid austerity. In the meantime he had evolved a new form in which to give vent to his feelings, namely, the *Novelle*. His very first attempt in this field, *Die Gemaelde* (1812), proves how decidedly the goal of his satire had shifted since the days of the *Volksmaerchen*. Far more zealously than in *Der neue Herkules am Scheidewege* he here attacks the after-growth which his own instigations had produced. This story does not renounce that period in his youth in which together with

Wackenroder he championed in laybrotherly fashion the art of Catholicism, but it does sit in stern judgment upon all mistaken enthusiasm for art and particularly upon such enthusiasm as has a religious cast. Others of Tieck's *Novellen* flay misuse of the word "religion," scourge social dishonesty, mock eccentricities of musicians, presume to see a moral disease in the tendency toward belief in ghosts and spiritualism, launch a defence of Goethe against the arrogance and ingratitude of the rising generation, deny the privileges of the nobility, satirize the Dresden group of poets, and denounce French romanticism, Heine, and Young Germany. E. T. A. Hoffmann's ghost-stories and the fate-drama after the manner of Muellner are subjected to ridicule. Much of this is merely parry and thrust in response to attacks which Tieck had brought upon himself. In these controversies Tieck is inclined to depict in the darkest possible colors the sad moral consequences which might issue from the loveliest and most elevating innovation. More and more he became an advocate of the waning age and a conscious adversary of the new. Much the same thing had happened to Nicolai.

The two types of satiric poetry which Tieck presented as models to the romanticists were fashioned in such an original manner that, generally speaking, the imitations patterned upon them admitted only of personal animus and specialized talent and could not attain a really new form. These two types were the dramatic farces in the manner of *Der gestiefelte Kater* and the stories with satirical side-lights in the manner of the *Schildbuerger* or his later *Novellen*.

Justinus Kerner's most ambitious poetic production, *Die Reiseschatten von dem Schattenspieler Luchs* (1811), is a decided advance in the development of these two forms. It was conceived in the spirit of that group which rallied about Uhland in his youth and declared war upon the *Plattisten* [people addicted to platitudes], as Uhland and his youthful friends called the backward champions of the Enlightenment. Blows were rained upon innumerable individuals, many of them quite unknown. J. Gaismaier (*Zeitschrift fuer vergleichende Literaturgeschichte,* N. F. 13, 492 ff.; 14, 76 ff.) had no small task in ferreting out the subjects of these allusions. The new idea was to clothe satire in the form of an account of a journey. It harked back to the books of travel current in the eighteenth century but combined with their sentimentality a very sturdy variety of wit and thus paved the way for the travel-pictures and letters of Young Germany. Heine's *Harzreise* (1826) was still a genuinely romantic satire aimed at the Philistine and was embellished by more or less concealed thrusts at contemporaries. Not until they had undergone further development did his *Reisebilder* achieve a higher and more independent point of view. Eventually, however, in the *Baeder von Lucca* Heine employs this literary form for the purpose of attacking Platen in the most personal and violent fashion. The dramatic interpolations in Kerner's *Reiseschatten,* though they suggest the puppet-play which adapts itself nicely to jests after the manner of *Der gestiefelte Kater* and which thrived in Tieck's environment, were, as a matter of fact, conceived as shadowgraphs. Kerner loved shadowgraphs, with which he had become acquainted in Tuebingen and in Vienna, and utilized them with great skill. He made them the poetic symbol of the travel-story in general, for his theory was that events should pass before the reader like shadows, like pictures projected by a *laterna magica.* Arnim put in a good word for shadowgraphs when he published his shadow-play, *Das Loch oder das wiedergefundene Paradies* (1813). To those, however, who relished the art of E. T. A. Hoffmann, the *laterna magica* became a favorite conception. Hoffmann himself bestowed great praise upon the puppet-play in the discourse *Seltsame Leiden eines Theaterdirektors* (1819). The significance of puppet-plays, finally, was very subtly and profoundly explained by Heinrich von Kleist in *Abendblaetter* (*Werke,* 4, 133 ff.).

Another writer to attempt the puppet-play was Eichendorff, but his endeavors remained unfinished and unpublished. He, too, accepted it in the sense of a literary and social satire. Indeed, he was ever inclined to articulate with the style of *Der gestiefelte Kater.* Inasmuch as he was rather an old man when he began experimenting in the field, he, too, like Tieck in his later days, gibed at characteristics which professed to be really quite specifically romantic. When the poetic forces burst into the land of the Philistines in *Krieg den Philistern* (1824, in *Dramatische Maerchen*) the invaders as well as the invaded are regarded from a humorous angle. *Meierbeths Glueck und Ende* (1827) is called a *Tragedy with Song and Dance.* This satire ridicules not only the fate-drama but also the decided preference on the part of German readers for Walter Scott and Scotch customs and landscapes. Even Grabbe as late as 1835 took a shot at the "great unknown," Walter Scott, in a scene in his dramatic fairy-tale *Aschenbroedel,* which he did not retain, however, in the final version. Grabbe, indeed, realized, when he was preparing this piece for publication, that attacks upon contemporary writers are soon obsolete. On the other hand, his comedy *Scherz, Satire, Ironie und tiefere Bedeutung* (1827), by virtue of its drastic humor, is still

very effective. The only portions which are no longer en-
joyable are those which allude to individuals or stupid
fashions in the literary world around 1825. The phenomena which he ridiculed have long since been forgotten
and Grabbe is often absolutely obscure, whereas Tieck's
caricatures present tangible human beings that continue
to live.

So, too, Platen's "Aristophanic comedies" require a
detailed knowledge of contemporary literature. He did
not always pause to give the names and specific works of
his victims when he spoke ill of them. The revival of *Die
verhaengnisvolle Gabel* (1826) which the court-theater
in Dresden ventured to produce in the fall of 1917 proved
that but few touches are necessary for the effective demonstration of the genuine theatrical spirit of this comedy.
The consummate artistry in *Die verhaengnisvolle Gabel*
as well as in *Der romantische Oedipus* (1829) consists in
letting the victims speak for themselves. Mimicking
parodies are used here just as in the literary satires of
the earlier romantic period. The very title of *Die verhaengnisvolle Gabel* indicates that it is an attack upon the
nonsensical fate-dramas. Deliberately the author conjures
up an utterly silly fabrication hinging upon fate. All the
fateful and accursed knives and daggers which figure in
the fate-dramas are symbolized by the dreadful fork
which leads an entire family to destruction. Written in
much the same spirit, the other comedy is a dramatization of the Oedipus legend such as only the most stupid
imitator of Shakespeare or Calderon could have contrived.
Shakespeare and the Spanish dramatists often present
the whole life-history of the hero. Hence Platen has a
romantic bungler write a tragedy based upon Oedipus
which opens with two mid-wives at the bedside of the

Queen Jocaste, who is in child-birth, but it is not until the third act that Oedipus, though still in the cradle, appears upon the stage. Thus Sophocles' *Oedipus Rex,* that perpetual model of tremendously compact and analytic tragic action, is meant to be out-trumped by an hyperbolic emphasis upon the time element. Finally Oedipus climbs into his own coffin. Thus, granted this immense extention of time, all the grisly details, which are incorporated into the legend but which Sophocles deleted from his stage version, are duly enacted. It was a clever idea not to present the author of this tragedy, who also appears as an actor at the beginning and at the end of Platen's play and who witnesses the production of his own botchery, as the typical romantic dramatist but rather to drag him in as a significant representative of romantic usage and then to proceed to caricature him as usual by accentuating his weaknesses. Inasmuch as Platen gave this monster the name of *Nimmermann* and definitely alluded not only to certain of his works but also to his friendly relations with Heine, he assumed the artistic onus of mimicking the most characteristic traits of his victim just as Wilhelm Schlegel contrived to do in his *Ehrenpforte.* Schlegel, who was very familiar with all of Kotzebue's works, gleaned from them whatever he could utilize in his satire and thus he achieved that striking similarity to the original which is the peculiar quality of caricature. Platen, on the other hand, was barely acquainted with Immermann's works; he based his Nimmermann on a preconceived notion of the original. Specifically he ordained his Nimmermann to be merely the representative of that whole mad tribe of poetasters who murdered the stage with their fantastic, feverish dreams. The very piece of Immermann's which is specifically mentioned and berated in *Der romantische Oedipus,* namely, *Cardenio und Celinde,* has technically very little in common with those excesses of romantic dramaturgy which are ridiculed by Platen's Oedipus parody.

Platen did not escape entirely the danger of offering, instead of satiric poetry, a rather destructive discourse upon those whom he attacked. Yet he ennobled these veritable castigations by their artistic form, which was based upon Aristophanes' parabases, and by the passionate zeal with which he defended his particular creed. This was rather more than the opportune thrusts of the romantic comedies or those of Grabbe.

The romantic novelist accepted literary allusions containing a more or less satiric gibe as a matter of course. Even Goethe's *Lehrjahre* had discussed questions pertaining to poetry and to the theater in such detail that a long line of writers who felt the need of unburdening themselves hailed the novel as a delightful excuse for discussing their trade. If a writer could deliberately produce a counterpart to the *Lehrjahre,* if Tieck could follow *Wilhelm Meister* with his novel *Der junge Tischlermeister* (1836), then quite properly Shakespeare's *Hamlet* might be offset by Goethe's *Goetz* and prolix discussions be offered to reëstablish the Shakespearean drama over against the accepted customs of the German theater. Jean Paul also suggested to his romantic imitators and admirers the peculiar habit of turning away from the narration of the story itself to discussions of problems of interest to authors. Because of the efforts of the romanticists to base German culture upon aesthetic values, and also, doubtless, because of the reactionary restriction upon the discussion of politics, it became the custom in society to discuss only problems pertaining to art and society. Hence it became more and more common in the novel to offer criticisms of the latest literary productions. In his collection of *Novellen* called *Die Serapionsbrueder* (1819–21, *Werke,* 9, 189 ff.) Hoffmann had already begun to ridicule "aesthetic teas." This same collection merely continued what Tieck's *Phantasus* had begun: it linked together a series of poems by means of discourses which properly belonged in the field of literary criticism and controversy. But even before Tieck, Arnim's *Wintergarten* (1809) had strung together a group of stories by interludes of a critical nature. Hauff, on the other hand, in his *Novelle, Die letzten Ritter von Marienburg* (1827), placed about a single historical narrative a frame which was meant to fix the social and literary conditions of its type of production. In Hauff, indeed, it is very apparent that at the time when romanticism was declining and gradually settling into rigid patterns the very problems of his trade offered ways and means to the author. In conscious imitation of Hoffmann, Hauff's *Mitteilungen aus den Memoiren des Satan* (1826–7) deliberately sought out sarcastic literary allusions. His novel *Der Mann im Mond* (1826) was perhaps the most voluminous parody in the realm of romanticism. In all probability, Hauff, accustomed to follow slavishly the track of H. Clauren, a copious writer who displayed much false wit and sensitivity, had at first merely faithfully imitated the latter's stupidity without any thought of satirizing it. Then it doubtless occurred to him that his story would bring him much greater honors if he announced it as an extravagant satire on Clauren. In this way the imitator assumed the dignity of a stern critic.

Previous to Hauff, romanticism had produced no narrative of similar proportions in the field of literary satire.

Presently Eichendorff sought to transmit to the *Novelle* the spirit and manner of his two comedies *Krieg den Philistern* and *Meierbeths Glueck und Ende*. In the story *Viel Laerm um Nichts* (1832) he conjured up characters, not only of his own creation in *Ahnung und Gegenwart,* but also from the *Lehrjahre* in order to depict the Philistine features of the days following the July Revolution, humorously and at times also with an ironic portrayal of the romantic spirit prevalent at that time. This was still within the borders of literature, whereas the story *Auch ich war in Arkadien* (printed in 1866), which soon followed, ridiculed political events of the July Revolution. *Libertas und ihre Freier* (printed in 1864) tarried within the realm of politics, having been directly inspired by the events in the revolutionary years of 1848 and 1849, and revealed the picture which the new era presented to the aged Eichendorff, who meanwhile had been becoming ever more strongly Catholic.

With a much broader outlook, though also in a fundamentally satiric spirit, and yet not merely with sheer literary jugglery, Immermann, whose *Tulifaentchen* (1830) mildly ridiculed many a delusion rampant in the world about him, portrayed contemporary life in two novels. *Die Epigonen* (1836), which took the form of family memoirs, betrays by its very title the temper of an era to which the past seemed richer and more significant than the present and which recognized in its own literary output and, primarily, in its own social life nothing more than pitiable echoes of an older, far lovelier melody. Immermann in his early days had ventured far in the field of romanticism and hence had been stigmatized by Platen as a romantic charlatan in the dramatic field. Immermann, thick-blooded though he was, lived to see ·the anguish that might accrue from the transvaluation of women according to the new moral code of romanticism. He aimed his satire at romanticists and pronouncements which harked back to romanticism. His picture of contemporary life is almost wholly destructive. Graecomania and demagogic spying, Teutomania and fraternal organizations, aesthetic tea-parties, the caprice of romantic nobility, affected piety and ardor for conversion, *Weltschmerz* and Nazarenism—all fare equally badly at his hands. Nevertheless Immermann recognized the outstanding problems of contemporary life: he considered how the established German nobility might strike a suitable balance with the technical mechanization of the future. Tieck's later *Novellen* also touch upon these topics. But in *Die Epigonen* and in *Muenchhausen* (1838–9) Immermann put to his contemporaries more definitely the problems that were demanding solution. *Muenchhausen*, apparently of a dual nature—now a veritable Witches' Sabbath of romantic reflection and counter-reflection and then again a homogeneously conceived achievement of indigenous art—resolved itself so naturally into two parts that the rustic tale *Der Oberhof* was subsequently detached, by another writer, from the rest of the story. Yet the extraordinary association of the romantic juggler, who had appropriated the name of the mendacious old Baron Muenchhausen, with the peasantry of the red Westphalian soil indicated two basic tendencies in German life of the time both of which demanded thoughtful consideration in their bearing upon the future of the German people. In its ironic delineation of contemporary life *Muenchhausen* encompassed the entire development from romanticism to Young Germany with a more comprehensive grasp and in greater detail than any other collection

of romantic satires and at the same time put some problems which are almost insoluble even to the modern interpreter.[41]

Side thrusts, made from sheer joy in combat, are found
even in a favorite medium of the romantic story-teller,
which—if indeed it did not from the very outset abandon
its naïve character and make sport of itself—seemed
hardly adapted to satire, namely, the fairy-tale. Novalis'
tale *Heinrich von Ofterdingen* attacks an antagonistic
philosophy of life. Brentano in his fairy-tales was still
more outspoken against his opponents. *Der goldene Topf*
(1814) was Hoffmann's original anti-Philistine fairy-
tale and he copied it repeatedly in his subsequent productions.

In imitation of Tieck, his comrades and followers developed the satire more and more, both in dramatic and
narrative form. Tieck left it to others to employ the
fiction of preservation of strict scientific truth in connection with personal attacks or caricatures of opponents
as a group. That philosopher who, though himself no romanticist, came to be one of the indispensable progenitors
of romanticism, namely, Fichte, blazed the new trail when
he published the pamphlet *Friedrich Nicolais Leben und
sonderbare Meinungen. Ein Beitrag zur Literargeschichte
des vergangenen und zur Paedagogik des angehenden
Jahrhunderts* (1801). Wilhelm Schlegel wrote the introduction and thus claimed it for romanticism; it was a
considerable advance beyond the wittiest of Wilhelm
Schlegel's discussions or his *Reichsanzeiger*. One of the
Xenien pityingly addressed Nicolai:

Poor empirical devil! You do not recognize the stupidity
In yourself: it is, alas, a priori so stupid.

Fichte a priori furnished the proof of Nicolai's stupidity. To be keen was not a difficult task for the creator of the *Wissenschaftslehre;* he was terrible in combat. In this instance he executed his "hero" with ironic humor. Was not the very fact that he specifically spoke of Nicolai as though he were already dead, or as though he belonged to the past, convinced apparently that Nicolai never could or would change, a thrust worthy of the pitiless art of Heine's attack?

Heine loved indeed to create an air of scientific accuracy in his pamphlets. This is proved by his *Schwabenspiegel* (1839), which was provoked by his anger at the attacks of the Suabian writers and their followers. And yet like Boerne in his little volume *Menzel der Franzosenfresser* (1837) he adheres much more closely than Fichte to the prevalent form of controversial literature. Fichte's anti-Nicolai might better be compared to Jean Paul's *Clavis Fichtiana seu Leibgeberiana* (1800), which was directed at Fichte himself. But Brentano, who was in more or less close touch with Jean Paul, was particularly fond of scattering his ironic thrusts throughout mock scientific treatises, in this respect, as well as in others, showing a decided spiritual kinship to Heine.

Brentano's masterpiece and model was *Der Philister vor, in und nach der Geschichte* (1811). Its dryly humorous, matter-of-fact description of the Philistine of that day is irresistible and proves conclusively Brentano's ability to charm a group of companions by means of his spiteful satire. Even Brentano's enemy Varnhagen explicitly states that Brentano created a veritable sensation when he delivered his discourse to that coterie which also gave rise to Kleist's *Abendblaetter*. Brentano anticipated the temper of this group in nuances which hitherto were

scarcely to be found in the satiric utterances of the romanticists against the Philistines. Finally politics also
entered in; and then it was that Brentano emphasized
more strongly than ever before his antipathy toward the
Jews, a feeling which he shared with Arnim.

In his *Geschichte und Ursprung des ersten Baernhaeut-
ers*, a tale in the chap-book style which appeared in Arnim's *Zeitung fuer Einsiedler* (1808), Brentano led up
to his discourse upon the Philistines. This story utilizes
the author's comprehensive knowledge of old German tradition and at first carries on Grimmelshausen's little
narrative essay *Der erste Baernhaeuter* (1670) but ends
in attacking the opponents of the Heidelberg group of
romanticists. The facetious tale, *Des Uhrmachers BOGS
wunderbare Geschichte* (1807), of which Brentano and
Goerres were joint authors, was, according to Goerres,
primarily an attempt on the part of the authors to satirize
themselves rather than their opponents. The name BOGS
is composed of the initial and final letters in the names of
the authors. The romantic quality of the tale is quite in
keeping with the spirit of the *Zeitung fuer Einsiedler*.

Hoffmann gratefully assumed the attitude of Brentano's satires toward the Philistines. His privy secretary
of the chancery Tusmann (in the *Brautwahl*) bears all
the palpable symptoms of Philistinism which Brentano
had demonstrated as such. Indeed the long line of Philistines which Hoffman portrayed was deeply indebted to
Brentano's work, particularly in the device of presenting
their speech and manners imitatively. On the other hand,
Hoffmann did not compete with Brentano by writing
mock scientific treatises. He preferred the story form.

It was remarkably seldom that Brentano utilized the
lyric form of expression for satire. His mocking quat-

rains *Und man wird Geheimrat!* (2, 455) stand almost
alone among his poems. Tieck also shunned the habit
which was particularly dear to his friend Wilhelm Schlegel. Schlegel, on the other hand, demonstrated to the romanticists how rigid lyric forms could be utilized in their
attacks. It was very natural that he should continue the
use of the distich in which the *Xenien* had been couched.
But preferably he presented his bellicose satire in the
delicate lines of the sonnet. In the long list of romantic
sonnets there are many of the satiric nature. The controversy to justify the German sonnet was itself fought out
in the form of sonnets. Arnim carried this far beyond
the limits of good taste when he conceived in ninety-four
sonnets the *Geschichte des Herrn Sonet und des Fraeuleins
Sonete, des Herrn Ottav und des Fraeuleins Terzine.* This
tale was published as a supplement to the *Zeitung fuer
Einsiedler.* Uhland, Chamisso, and Heine were inclined
to give the controversial sonnet a spirit of especial virility,
almost grotesque.

Other lyric forms of Romance origin were added,
Uhland using the *Glosse* and Chamisso, quite naturally,
the *Terzine.* At the same time every imaginable stanza of
German genesis was pressed into the service of satire by
the later romanticists. The encroachment of politics upon
literature gave rise to an ever increasing number of lyrics
with satiric animus. The germs of the political poetry
which came to fruition in the fourth decade of the nineteenth century are to be found in later romanticism. From
the controversial lyric in the field of literature down to
the poetry of contemporary politics, Heine displays an
extraordinary wealth of structural forms. Whether his
longer polemic poems utilized the Spanish four-verse
stanza (in *Atta Troll*) or the German (in *Deutschland:*

ein Wintermaerchen), the numerous forms with which
the romanticists since the days of Wilhelm Schlegel had
tormented their opponents submitted without struggle to
his pen. Nor did he eschew the parody. The inscription
of the monument dedicated to his *Tendenzbaer Atta Troll*
is strictly in imitation of the stumbling, telegraphic lines
of King Ludwig of Bavaria:

> Atta Troll, Tendenzbaer; morally
> Religious; devoted as a husband;
> Led astray by the spirit of the times,
> Primordial sansculotte;
> Dancing badly, yet harboring
> Sentiment in your shaggy, high breast;
> Evil-smelling at times;
> No talent, yet a character!

But though Heine's satiric somersaults are ever so
merry and though he ridicules his enemies ever so cleverly
with humorous rime-schemes ("Romantik": "Uhland,
Tieck"), even in his most successful efforts he does not
outstrip his erstwhile teacher, Wilhelm Schlegel, in the
mastery of structural form. The latter, a master of form
and a philologian as well, had the gift to achieve a gem
such as the *Triolett* to Garlieb Merkel (2, 200). Merkel,
being but superficially educated, had ignorantly confused
the triolet with the terzet. Schlegel opened Merkel's eyes
with a satire which was itself clothed in the intricate structural form of the triolet:

> With a little triolet (Triolett)
> I shall, little Merkel, serve you (dienen).
> Do you confuse the mighty terzet (Terzinen)

With a little triolet (Triolett)?
Oh, oh, and with such knowing airs (Kennermienen)!
I have already taught you the sonnet (Sonett);
With a little triolet (Triolett)
I shall, little Merkel, serve you (dienen).

Heine could not have produced a better masterpiece
even if he had been more concerned with clean-cut form
rather than with the desire to create the impression of
artless, extempore composition. But in this very renunciation of form Heine proved himself to be the more genuine
romanticist. Though he aimed directly for well-defined
effects, his structural manner is far more loose than that
of Wilhelm Schlegel. The rare precision of Schlegel's
technic, on the other hand, is hardly compatible with the
freedom and extravagance of romanticism.

IV. ROMANTIC IRONY AND NATURE PHILOSOPHY IN ROMANTIC POETRY

THE satiric poetry of romanticism was not concerned with irony merely in the general sense of the term; it endeavored to give intelligible expression to the idea of "romantic irony," even in the strictest sense of the word.

The early romanticists produced works abounding in romantic irony before Friedrich Schlegel ever developed his doctrine of irony or conceived of it as a fundamental principle in romanticism. Similarly many tales were being written, permeated with natural philosophy but without their having been necessarily conditioned by the natural philosophy of Schlegel, Schelling, or Hardenberg. In both instances Tieck offered illustrations of the romantic theory, which served the theorists splendidly, though the latter had by no means inspired them.

Tieck's versatility was destined primarily to give poetic expression in creative works to the daring aesthetic conceptions of his comrades. He rose generously to his task. Greatly deserving of recognition, therefore, are the services which he rendered in his spontaneous creative writings.

The most obvious, most direct form of romantic irony and the one most freely used by the romanticists is the destruction of the illusion. Friedrich Schlegel's definitions of romantic irony (see Part 1, p. 42 f.), by alluding to "the mimic style of an average good Italian comedian" (*Lyceumfragment* 42), did not overlook this quality.

As early as 1794, in his essay *Vom aesthetischen Werte der griechischen Komoedie* (1, 18), Friedrich Schlegel defended Aristophanes against the accusation that "he often destroys the illusion" and pointed out that such destruction of the illusion is inherent "in the nature of the comic impulse." "This destruction is not lack of skill but intentional unrestraint, effervescent joy in life. . . . Life's greatest animation manifests itself in activity and must destroy; if it finds nothing beyond itself, it turns upon a favorite subject, upon itself, a creation of its very own and does violence to it, not with the intention of destroying it but merely to give it animation. This characteristic of joy in life furthermore becomes significant in the comedy because of its relation to unrestraint." Destruction of the illusion was already gathering up the threads which were later to form the fabric of the conception of romantic irony and manifested itself as the essential trait in that ideal of comedy which the romanticists had in mind. Stimulated by Kant, Heydenreich, and Christian G. Koerner, this same youthful essay rejected the contemporary comedy which embellished the dramatic actions of serious domestic life with the charms of comedy, whereas genuine comedy, such as the Greek comedies of Aristophanes, instead of blushing for its joyousness, depicted a veritable orgy of it. [42]

Adhering unremittingly to these principles, the romanticists and Schiller, who doubtless, like Friedrich Schlegel, had been stimulated by Christian G. Koerner, waged unrelenting warfare against the affecting comedies of Iffland and his school. It was, however, only by virtue of Tieck's aid that this coterie was able to proceed from mere formulation of the conception of a comedy of pure joyousness to actual realization. Tieck's first attempt, which became the criterion of practically all romantic comedies, was, once more (see above, p. 201) *Der gestiefelte Kater, ein Kindermaerchen in drei Akten*. In this satiric play, which destroys illusion in every possible way, Tieck was certainly not inspired by Friedrich Schlegel. Indeed Tieck had long before learned how the stage can make sport of itself from the burlesque jests of Holberg and Gozzi, from Goethe's *Triumph der Empfindsamkeit*, and also from Shakespeare's *Midsummer Night's Dream*, the comical satires of Ben Jonson, and most particularly from the buffoonery of the *Hanswurst* plays. As early as 1795, in the puppet-play *Hanswurst als Emigrant*, which was printed for the first time in 1855 in Tieck's *Nachgelassene Schriften* (1, 76 ff.), the style of *Der gestiefelte Kater* is anticipated.

Der gestiefelte Kater surpassed anything that had thus far appeared upon the stage, in wilful destruction of the illusion and in boldly foiling the mutual understanding which habitually exists between the stage and the audience. It shows the stage as it is customarily seen by the audience after the curtain goes up, but the spectator is soon introduced by a revelation of the activities behind the curtain or by a raising of the curtain prematurely to scenes which ordinarily are strictly denied him. Moreover, in the play itself, the audience is seated out in front and assumes with its remarks, opinions, and general manifestations of its attitude an important rôle in the piece. The author speaks to the audience from the stage and naturally also to the actors and stage-hands. Thus the play itself discusses the play which the audience is witnessing, but within this play also the same play is being discussed. As in a series of mirrors, there is endless romantic-ironic reflection and re-reflection.

Tieck's romantic satiric dramas all follow this path. In *Zerbino* the hero himself by sheer force seeks to reverse the play. The scenes which had already been presented are being staged once more in reverse order, but thanks to the peremptory action of the author and his faithful aids a crisis is averted and the play goes on.

Wilhelm Schlegel's *Ehrenpforte* and Brentano's *Gustav Wasa* took Tieck for their model and imitated his raillery. Eichendorff and Grabbe did likewise. The jester in Eichendorff's *Krieg den Philistern!* divulges to the audience the author's true sentiments. Warningly the author behind the scenes cries: "For God's sake, don't tattle everything!" The audience retorts in anger: "Oh, what do we care about the author!" At the close of *Scherz, Satire, Ironie und tiefere Bedeutung,* Grabbe appears in person and is received with malediction: "He is as stupid as an iron crow; he berates all other writers yet he himself amounts to nothing; he is bow-legged, cross-eyed, and has an insipid monkey face!" Another character in the play accuses the vulgar assailant: "How bitter you feel toward the man who wrote you!" This buffoonery was not a new note in Grabbe's comedies. It was merely an exaggeration of that tendency toward grotesqueness which the older romanticists had manifested in their comedies. Tieck is mild and tame in comparison with Grabbe's mad ventures.

Puppet-plays and particularly shadowgraphs represent another step. Kerner's shadowgraphs delight in having one figure merge into another or in causing one figure to disintegrate into several. Such artifices are not difficult in shadowgraphs. This trend did not escape Uhland in his epilogue to Kerner's *Koenig Eginhard.*

Sooner or later this whole process of development was bound to complete the cycle and arrive again at its starting

point, Aristophanes. Platen's Aristophanic comedies utilized practically all of those jests pertaining to the stage
which Tieck and his followers had evolved. At the same
time, however, they seek to remain in closer spiritual
relation to Aristophanes and very especially to compete
with him in the art of metrics. But the metrical structure
of Aristophanes' comedies was a humorous counterpart
to the metre of the Greek tragedies and hence was in itself
contemporary satire. Platen, therefore, really caught the
spirit of Aristophanes only when he employed the metrical
forms of the German tragedies and not those of his prototype. Aristophanes, furthermore, had had the temerity to
attack a poet of the stature of Euripides while Platen
tilted only with the small fry. Again Aristophanes boldly
attacked all those phases of Athenian life and activities
which he opposed or, more accurately, the satirizing of
which he felt sure would win the approval of the more
narrow-minded of the Athenian citizens. He posed always
as the voice of the people, the advocate of the old order
against destructive innovation. Conversely, the romantic
satiric drama ridiculed the Philistine for his obsolescence;
it is comparable to a comic magazine that delights in
revolutionary tactics, whereas Aristophanes' humor supported conservatism. To be sure, in aesthetic matters
Platen, too, was on the side of the old order and opposed
to romantic innovations but his whole attitude was hostile,
as was romanticism, to Philistinism. Had he proceeded
into the larger field of political satire he would more
palpably have preserved his attitude of a progressive. It
must not be supposed, however, that it was his renunciation of politics which prevented Platen from measuring
up completely to his Aristophanic prototype. Political
satire was not unknown among romantic satiric dramas.

Der gestiefelte Kater had already experimented with it (cf. J. Wolf, *Revue germanique* 5, 158 ff.). That clothing a political satiric drama in the metre of Aristophanes is not sufficient to make of its author a German Aristophanes was proved by R. Prutz, who wrote the *Politische Wochenstube* (1843), a weak imitation of Platen's comedies, which achieved no particular distinction and has fallen entirely into oblivion.

Platen recognized in Aristophanes too much of his own ardent zeal. It was his ambition to uplift society to a finer understanding of art and he ascribed the same motives to the Greek dramatist. The spirit of the success which buoyed up the years following the Persian wars offered the Athenian dramatist a propitious atmosphere such as was entirely wanting in the case of the German writer Platen. Athens at that time was the first city in Greece. She was at the high tide of her achievement in art and literature. Calm and secure, she basked in the sunshine of success. Well might the people, as well as their champion Aristophanes, comport themselves with such consummate boldness and haughtiness. Compared with such effervescence, Platen's satire indeed seems timorous and restrained. [43]

The romanticists, to be sure, were quite well aware of the fact that the demands of a genuine comedy were not fully satisfied with satiric buffoonery which depended for the most part upon the destruction of the theatrical illusion. Platen himself perhaps was the only one who believed that his Aristophanic comedies really reached the goal which the opponents of the sentimental comedy had striven for. There was no dearth of attempts to liberate the comedy from backbiting in the form of literary satire. Thus Tieck at times imitated the comedies of that self-same Ben

Jonson whose "comical satires" were among the forbears of *Der gestiefelte Kater*. That the problem of pure comedy was ever a weighty one with the romanticists was shown by their keen interest in the prize contest which Goethe and Schiller announced around 1800 and which, wholly in the romantic sense, called for a comedy of intrigue free from sentimentality. Among the plays offered was Brentano's *Ponce de Leon*. [44] That spiritual blitheness and temperamental abandon which Schiller held to be the medium of pure comedy, that intoxication of joy which Friedrich Schlegel believed comedy ought to provoke, Brentano had hoped to achieve by way of puns and witticisms. Accustomed to play with words and sounds and willing in moments of deep spiritual emotion to link harmonious sounds in subtle combination, he gave his wit free play in *Ponce de Leon*. Beneath the involved form is a wealth of thoroughly humane art and of humanity artistically perceived. One is dazzled and stunned by the superabundance of wit. Rewritten in 1814 and called *Vaterlist oder Valeria*, the play failed upon a Viennese stage. In spite of additions which were meant to appease the temper of the times, too much of the original wit had been retained and the piece was doomed to failure. The word-play in *Ponce de Leon*, just as in Georg Buechner's *Leonce und Lena,* might be traced directly to Shakespeare, whose comedies stood particularly high in the favor of the romanticists. Eichendorff's later comedy *Die Freier* (1833), which was quite different from his satires, approached still more the manner of Shakespeare's *As You Like It* and, directly inspired perhaps by suggestions from Friedrich Schlegel, tended toward genuine comedy. [45]

At length, however, all the demands of both classicists

and romanticists for a masterpiece of humor were satisfied in Kleist's *Der zerbrochene Krug* (1811). Here finally was a comedy which, unlike the sentimental family scenes in which Kotzebue delighted, made its appeal not to the emotions but to the mind. The cruder effects of romantic irony were missing; humor had full sway. With strokes of real genius, sheer laughter was provoked even in situations where motives threatened to produce more earnestness than is compatible with comedy. The conclusion of *Der zerbrochene Krug* indeed also hints that an engagement is imminent. But whether or not Rupprecht would win his little Eve is by no means the problem in the play. The paramount question is: Will Judge Adam keep concealed the identity of the person who actually broke the pitcher? This is a problem purely of the intellect and precludes emotional effects.

Romantic irony in the form of destruction of the illusion is most noticeable in pieces meant for theatrical production. Nowhere in the realm of poetry are reality and make-believe called more into play than on the stage. To be sure, there are other types of literature which utilize destruction of the illusion and which, at a stroke, convey us into the poet's work-room and lead us behind the scenes. When Friedrich Schlegel demanded that "transcendental poetry" present the producing medium along with the product (*Athenaeumfragment* 238), he doubtless was thinking chiefly of the novel, which in his estimation "tinged" all of modern poetry (*Athenaeumfragment* 146). In Goethe's *Meister* (2, 171, 30), he thought to discern, behind the veil of poetry, the poet himself smiling with spiritual aloofness upon his creation. Friedrich Schlegel's demands, however, were much more clearly exemplified in Jean Paul's novels. The latter's humorous sallies often, as episodes, appear like inserted songs or, as an appendix, destroy the book (*Athenaeumfragment* 421). As a matter of fact, what the romantic novelists learned from Jean Paul was primarily "the irony of dropping out of the piece," as Brentano drastically termed it. Jean Paul delighted in following "steam baths of emotion" with "cold showers of satire"; he himself defines his humor as the result of the effervescence of the spirit of both when his negative electric philosophy and his positive electric enthusiasm are struggling to recover their equilibrium. A favorite form of Jean Paul's humor is to thrust the person of the author between the reader and the story and to give an account of his trade, his troubles as a writer, or his vexation with his work. In so doing Jean Paul is merely following long-standing practices in humorous literature which in prose or, preferably, in verse discussed, within the book itself, its origin and problems pertaining to printing and to royalties. Then finally the author, who has been pretending that he is merely a faithful copyist and that the bulk of his story is merely a manuscript which has been turned over to him, gets to know in person the characters which he himself has created, while they themselves read what he has written about them. Cervantes, English comic novelists like Smollett, and English humorists like Sterne use these devices; German story-tellers (Miller, Musaeus) follow in their wake. Wieland's verses, following a variety of leads, are a veritable chart of the manifold devices by means of which an author can infuse himself and his reflections into his own production. It was Sterne primarily who showed his countryman, Byron, and his whole school, as well as Jean Paul and the romanticists, and finally indeed all the writers of books of travel from M. A.

Thuemmel to Heine and, beyond these, Young Germany and the writers of our own day the way in which a novelist can reduce the epic sequence to a minimum and weave the thread of a meagre story into a preponderance of self-expression, self-portrayal, and personal opinions. In the four hundred and twenty-first *Athenaeumfragment* Jean Paul is accused of being "unable to tell *one* story well, what one would call just passably well." Before long, however, this perverse non-epic style found favor with the romantic novel. Even *Lucinde* shows strong symptoms of out-doing Jean Paul in the use of all genres except the one of epic sequence of events in narration. *Lucinde,* too, might well be censured because its author had not the gift of story-telling.

But the literary mannerism of Sterne and Jean Paul was carried to the extreme and even surpassed in Brentano's exuberant novel *Godwi*. As in Jean Paul, the most unusual surprises occur, such as when the pseudonymous author Maria meets with the individuals portrayed in his story; beholding his hero, at length, he cries in astonishment: "So this is Godwi of whom I have written so much . . . I had imagined him to be quite different." The book itself—just as in Jean Paul—is cited by chapter or page. Godwi, for instance, explains: "This is the pond into which I fall, Volume 1, page 266"; or he asks Maria: "What did you wish to do with the candles on page 281 ?"; or there is reference to the passage "where Werdo Senne sings on page 126." The reflections and re-reflections which according to Friedrich Schlegel's theory are peculiar to romantic irony are still further augmented when the author, Maria, himself dies. He is said to have been bored to death while engaged upon the second part of his story. A fragmentary sequel describes his fatal illness. It was impossible for a poet, thought the romanticists, to rise more energetically beyond himself than to have himself die and then recount his own death.

These jests continue for decades throughout romantic-ironic novels and hence are deserving of detailed study. Toward the end of Immermann's *Epigonen* (1836) the author joins the circle of characters in his story; the participants read what he has written about them and through misinterpretations a most embarrassing situation ensues. Immermann's *Muenchhausen* (1838–9) is concerned with the book-binder just as Sterne and Jean Paul had dragged in the printer. Immermann's novel begins, ostensibly because of an error on the part of the binder, with Chapter Eleven; the first ten chapters are finally inserted after Chapter Fifteen. An exchange of letters between the author and the binder must not be omitted. Doubtless this buffoonery with the book-binder was aimed at Pueckler-Muskau's *Briefe eines Verstorbenen* (1830–1), which printed letters numbering from twenty-five to forty-eight in the first volume and followed these with the first twenty-four letters in the second volume. Hoffmann's Kater Murr in jotting down his *Lebensansichten* uses partly as a writing pad and partly also for blotting purposes "chance sheets of waste paper" that belonged to the biography of the orchestra conductor, Johannes Kreisler. Accidentally these pages are printed along with his own; hence Murr's accounts are terminated repeatedly in the midst of a sentence and alternate with pages from the life of Kreisler.

These jests seem stale and ineffective to us. Intellectual pyrotechny of this sort fulminates too quickly and we are left merely with the impression that the disorganization has been almost purposeless. Yet romanticism learned to derive startling effects from the interruption of mood. It became the task of Heine to combine romantic irony in prose and poetry with the technic of French wit and to use the romantic device of disrupting the mood in order to produce effective end-lines. At the end of the poem *Seegespenst* (*Nordsee,* 1, 10), the poet, fascinated by the sight of his beloved, whom he beholds in the depths of the sea, is about to plunge into the water; the atmosphere has been so well wrought that the action seems plausible; but the captain detains him with words so utterly prosaic that at once the mood of the entire poem crumbles when he says: "Has the devil seized you, doctor?" In *Der goldene Topf* (1, 184) E. T. A. Hoffmann used the very same jest, but Heine alone achieved an effective denouement with it. Gellert in his day had already used a closing line which, in imitation of the French, destroyed with a witticism the mood which the poem had been at pains to create. Heine makes of this a romantic device by turning the thrust upon itself, upon the ego of the poet, and by calling into play the antithesis both to the conventional attitude of Philistinism and to poetic enthusiasm. Heine's prose is fully as effective. Sterne is fond of using the dash and the aposiopesis. Several lines of dashes cryptically indicate experiences better left unsaid. Heine pretends that the censors had deleted his text. Thus the entire twelfth chapter of the book *Le Grand* consists almost wholly of dashes, the censors supposedly having left only these words of the text: "The German censors —— —— blockheads —— ——." Neither Sterne nor Jean Paul nor romanticism had derived such clever buffoonery out of their implications of the printer. In his prose, Heine prepares his thrusts pages ahead. The application of the dog's prayer, "Oh hound, you hound . . . you are

not sound . . . ," to King Ludwig of Bavaria (8, 61)
owes its effectiveness chiefly to the fact that it had been
woven in fully twelve pages back (p. 48).

Romantic irony attains its most calculating effects in
Heine. He was an artist of extraordinary virtuosity of
form who found in romantic irony a tool splendidly
adapted to his peculiar wit and artistic propensity. With
the utmost art he gives the impression of artlessness. [46]
Romantic irony, however, releases the capriciousness of the
artist, giving him free rein gleefully to destroy his own
creations. Heine fosters this illusion of capriciousness and
joy in destruction but at the same time the effects of this
apparent capriciousness are calculated with the utmost
precision. Even Brentano, kin though he is to Heine, both
as a man and a poet, in poetry and in prose, has neither
the telling force nor the assurance of Heine's wit. It
sufficed him as it did all the romantic ironists, Tieck
included, to precipitate the reader, à la Jean Paul, from a
steam bath of emotion into a cold shower of satire. Romantic freedom is preserved by the constant flux of antitheses. But there is ever present the spirit of negation.
The destruction of the mood in romantic irony seems to
us, for the most part, crude; hence Heine's finesse is as a
pricking stiletto to a clumsy sword.

Heine considers all romantic devices from the artistic
point of view; he utilizes their utmost artistic possibilities
but it never occurs to him to attempt to realize those more
fundamental demands which theoretically they were meant
to fulfill. Though he was a romantic ironist, he touched
but lightly upon the problem of "transcendental poetry."
Romantic nature philosophy was apparently of more importance to him; he was keenly appreciative of the artistic
possibilities in giving nature life and an all-pervading soul,

and in personifying the phenomena of nature. His virtuosity as an actor exceeded that of Tieck. Every mood which his muse demanded he portrayed without ever himself succumbing to it or being enslaved by it. Heine presents the entire gamut of romantic poetry but rarely, and then only in his earliest attempts, does he himself believe in the romantic moods which he aims to create. With more and more abandon he revels in the magic garden of romantic poetry. Precisely for this reason he derives from it far greater artistic effects than the romanticists, to whom the spirit loomed larger than the form, to whom life was more interesting than art. For this very reason he soars beyond romanticism because he absorbed all that was good in it without himself being engulfed by it. Compared with Heine, the majority of the genuine romanticists are mere dilettantes. For he has "architectonics in the highest sense, that power to put into practice, which creates, forms, and constructs"; the out-and-out romanticist "has but a vague notion of this and invariably succumbs to the material rather than mastering it" (Goethe, *Schema ueber den Dilettantismus,* Weimar Edition, 47, 326). Romantic art is not infrequently crushed by the burden of thought put upon it. To Novalis, a distinguished and genuine poet, it seems quite possible cryptically to reveal in his fairy-tale *Ofterdingen* the most mystic and most personal convictions in the field of natural philosophy. His tale of Hyacinth and little Rosebud proves, to be sure, his ability to create delightfully refreshing fairy-tales even though he freights them with spiritual and ideational profundity. Poetically, however, *Ofterdingen* does not come into its own; it devolves into a painful struggle to give artistic form to his speculations in the fields of cultural history and nature philosophy.

With artistic facility Heine achieves the goal which the romanticists also had in mind: to metamorphose nature, inorganic as well as organic, into a personified, spiritualized realm of poetry. His point of departure is Goethe, in whom the romantic theorists likewise found a practical example of their poetized "physics." From the days of his youth Goethe's lyrics, by personifying and spiritualizing nature, had been creating that new mythology which the romanticists were seeking. Goethe assumed the privilege of creating mythology in the same way that primitive peoples formulated their mythology: he endowed nature with his own emotions. Simultaneously Hoelty created a new mythology of spring. Both continued to develop what German folk-songs and the lays of the minnesingers had ever carried out in practice. It is indeed an ancient lyric device to carry over into the world of plants and animals all our human joys and sorrows. The Persian sings of the nightingale wooing the rose just as in the German folk-song the wild young lad must pluck the rose or the little owl complains that the bough upon which he wished to rest eluded him. The poetry of the seventeenth century, rich in blooms and blossoms, leads romanticism on: Brentano is fascinated by the song in which the reaper Death mows down the flowers; enraptured, conscious of his own genius, Lenau emulated the nature symbolism of Friedrich Spee (*A* 1, p. 338 ff.).

Lenau perhaps adheres a little closer to romantic theory than does Heine. He would combine nature and humanity into something "organically alive" which would represent symbolically the sublimer spiritual unity of natural and human life. His nature mythology is obviously indicative of keener and more sensuous observation than is Heine's. All the human traits with which a fond contemplation of nature can endow abstract conceptions, such as spring or springtime at the hour of dawn, he conceives of as an entity: he sees these conceptions conduct themselves as human beings, rejoicing, grieving, dying. Heine's spiritualized magic garden is wholly fanciful, breathing here the sultry fragrance of oriental vegetation and there the bracing air of the German woodlands. Now the violets giggle and caress and now the lotus flowers raise themselves tremblingly toward the moon. The firmament takes part; the sea, a favorite field of Heine's fancy, offers him the most daring and drastic combinations of the habits of humanity and the processes of nature. Free creative fancy here turns into mythology: in the genuinely Heinesque myth of Luna and Sol (*Die Nordsee*, 1, 3), or where the symbols of Christianity are applied to animal life (*Neuer Fruehling*, 9).

In romantic circles the fairy-tale became the peculiar field in which the new mythology of natural philosophy found poetic expression. Goethe's *Maerchen* (1796) in the *Unterhaltungen deutscher Ausgewanderte* was an enticing model. In an artistic sense Goethe was here toying with the possibility of profounder interpretation. Misinterpreting the wealth of similes in which the *Maerchen* abounds, fancy guessed at significant observations, and conjectured what Goethe himself never implied. Novalis, and Chamisso, also, in *Adelberts Fabel*, actually try to deck out a skeleton of ideas with the fanciful garlands of the fairy-tale; with the symbols of the fairy-tale they would discover new truths. The romantic magician is to prove himself to be a philosopher, a philosopher of nature.

Tieck disposes more readily of the fundamental aspects of nature philosophy. The theme of his fairy-tales, expressed in terms of natural philosophy is: There is no insurmountable barrier between man and nature; nature is pervaded by a feeling which is essentially kin to human feeling; in humanity a part of nature still survives. This poet is more concerned with delineating the force of nature in humanity and the human element in nature in their oppressive and destructive light than with revealing the liberating element in a natural philosophy which strives to put a soul into nature and a natural conformity to law into human existence. In Tieck's *Maerchen* his characters are destroyed by the horror which is aroused in them by their strangely contradictory attitude toward nature.

Again it must be conceded that Tieck's conception of nature and humanity and consequently also the leading motif in his fairy-tales had been formulated by him before he had ever heard of romantic nature philosophy. Just as *Der gestiefelte Kater* appeared at the psychological moment to exemplify the new theory of irony and pure comedy, so too there appeared simultaneously in 1797 Schelling's first pronouncement in the field of natural philosophy and Tieck's *Der blonde Eckbert*. With this poem Tieck begins a series of fairy-tales based upon nature, which he continued in *Der getreue Eckart und der Tannenhaeuser* (1799) and in *Der Runenberg* (1830) and subsequently in various attempts of lesser importance. In these stories Tieck's conception of nature and his nature philosophy gradually drew closer together. The realm of the miner, dear to the pupils of the Freiberg geologist, A. G. Werner, and transfigured by Novalis in *Ofterdingen*, is now also appropriated by Tieck and becomes a favorite locale where nature is endowed by romanticism with a soul. Thus *Der Runenberg* so nearly approximates the physical science of the romanticists that H. Steffen, Schelling's faithful pupil (*Was ich erlebte,* 3, 22), could trace it to his own experiences and to an account which he had given Tieck of his impressions gained on a voyage from Copenhagen to the rocky coasts of Norway. But the distinctive difference still persists: the nature philosophers strove to endow nature with consciousness, whereas Tieck would fain implant in the soul of man gloomy delusions derived from nature. They proceed from opposite poles: on the one hand the subconscious is elevated to the sphere of consciousness; on the other, fancy delves into the disturbing depths of the subconscious. This was brought about by Tieck's inmost emotional experiences; it developed gradually and even before *Der blonde Eckbert* it found expression in the fairy-tale *Nadir* in *Almansur* (1790) and in the story *Der Fremde* (1796) and is suggested in other youthful works. [47] Constantly repeated with slight variations, the lines pertaining to *Waldeinsamkeit* in *Der blonde Eckbert* are so typical of Tieck's way of expressing the lure, the ingratiating quality, and at the same time, the horror of a lonely forest that Wilhelm Schlegel might well refer to them jocularly as containing the quintessence of Tieck's poetry. The lines read as follows:

> Forest solitude,
> I delight in it,
> Today, tomorrow,
> Forever.
> Oh, how I delight
> In forest solitude.

Similarly in *Der blonde Eckbert,* there is a constant recurrence of a spiritual phenomenon born of Tieck's youthful habit of self-analysis: close friends suddenly appear to be strangers. While he was a student at Halle, Tieck wrote Wackenroder a letter (June 12, 1792) in which he recounts just such an experience and stresses the point that such occurrences are not infrequent with him. In real life it was his friends who seemed demented, but in the story the hero, Eckbert, becomes insane upon discovering that in the very moment of greatest trust, he cherishes a feeling of hostility towards his friends. As is well known, Tieck's youthful soul was ever tortured by fear of insanity.

The tendency to depict in his earliest works the utmost depths of paralyzing horror brought Tieck into close proximity to a low type of popular literature which flooded the market toward the close of the eighteenth century. The stories of chivalry and robber-knights which followed in the wake of the Storm and Stress led to these tales of horror. A common trait in these stories is the entanglement of the defenseless characters in the toils of an incomprehensible, apparently supernatural and all-powerful alliance. Schiller's *Geisterseher* (1789), which Tieck imitated in *William Lovell*, was the model which these tense, exciting novels sought in vain to match. In these stories, as in Schiller, the marvels of which they treat usually turn out to be sensory deceptions. F. J. Schneider (*Die Freimaurerei und ihr Einflusz auf die geistige Kultur in Deutschland am Ende des 18. Jahrhunderts*, 1909) sees in this phenomenon the literary embodiment of a conception which had sprung from degenerate Masonry: all-powerful superiors use their own judgment and manipulate their inferiors like balls in a game. Among the poetic devices derived from Masonry is the secret society which, intangible itself, directs from afar the life of the character. Goethe uses it, primarily in the *Lehrjahre*, and it is found also in the literature of romanticism. Arnim's *Kronenwaechter* (see above, p. 171) likewise contains such a secret society. Nor does Tieck overlook this arsenal of intensely exciting devices and in his early years is occupied with marvels that are thoroughly unromantic and which turn out in the end to be naught but illusion. Following in his footsteps, other romanticists also fostered this false notion, as though the grotesque presentation of horrible marvels were indeed romanticism, whereas these stories had already flourished in the popular literature of the period prior to romanticism. Tieck, however, did reveal to romanticism that marvel which is not mere illusion but which is inner experience, which rests not upon conscious misperception but upon mood. This is compatible with the soul of romanticism. The spirit of romanticism ever sought to penetrate through the mass of sense impressions to the ultimate secret which lay buried behind these myriad perceptions and, dreamily presentient, to grasp the truth not in the trite and obvious every-day things but in the realm of the super-sensual. Animate and inanimate nature, mute in the presence of others, becomes articulate to the romanticist. Thus spirits, elves, and fairies become quite self-evident, more self-evident indeed than are the Philistines who day after day cross the path of the romanticists. It was in Shakespeare that the youthful Tieck recognized this primitively related world as the world of sensuous reality. The treatise with which he accompanied his study of *The Tempest* (1796) discussed also the supernatural in Shakespeare's plays, especially in *A Midsummer Night's Dream*. Tieck was especially adapted by virtue of the nervous delicacy and subtlety of his sight and hearing to express romantic supernaturalism artistically by means of his own resources, augmented possibly by others borrowed from Shakespeare.

No German artist previous to Tieck had perceived the sensuous charm in the rustling and whispering of the lonely forest, in the flickering, glimmering rise and fall of light and shade as did Tieck (see above, Part 1, p. 126).

The spell of the forest is superseded in Fouqué's *Undine* (1814) by the spell of the water. In material Fouqué transcends Tieck, but he has but one narrative to tell and but one moving event to deck out in romantic trappings and yet he does not achieve the penetrating emotional effects which lie hidden in Tieck's naturalistic fairy-tale. [48] Hoffmann's fairy-tales are far more daemonic; here the conscious and the subconscious are inextricably wrought together. Like Tieck he knows the mood which springs from that feeling of uncertainty whether an experience is reality or a mere figment of the imagination. Hence the congeniality existing between his *Bergwerke von Falun* (1819) and Tieck's *Runenberg*. Hoffmann's tale, however, is further conditioned by the development of the romantic conception of magic which harks back to Gotthilf Heinrich von Schubert. It was Schubert, to be sure, who gave Hoffmann the material for his *Bergwerke von Falun.*

Brentano's tales base a story, sometimes wittily, sometimes seriously, upon a single word. From the name of a cliff along the Rhine he fabricated the legend of the lovely Lore Lay. This has its roots in nature philosophy.

V. THE PSYCHOLOGICAL ASPECTS OF NATURE. HEINRICH VON KLEIST

I N the later era of romanticism nature philosophy inclined more and more toward neurological investigations. Schelling's theory that nature is conscious intelligence led his disciples to investigate those realms in which this ascent to consciousness is effected. Before investigating the subconscious basis upon which conscious human life is founded, it was necessary to comprehend the intermediary stage which separated organic nature from rational existence. The romanticists called such psychological investigations studies in the "night side" of nature. Such was the basis of Tieck's fairy-tales. The impetus which Ritter and Novalis gave the movement led to further study. Through Mesmer, Ritter came to delve into the study of animal magnetism and believed that in somnambulism he had hit upon one of its phases (see above, Part 1, p. 64). In his final investigations he had even resorted to the divining-rod. Steffens, Burdach, Carus, and primarily Schubert, trod more or less cautiously the same precarious path. Schubert's *Ahndungen einer allgemeinen Geschichte des Lebens* (1806–21) and his *Geschichte der Seele* (1830) are especially concerned with the subconscious seat of psychic disturbances, with the mysterious phenomena of somnambulism, and with the unintelligible concatenation of conscious and subconscious activity which seemed to consign the human soul to a place on the unstable fringe of the world of nature and of reason.

Schubert, particularly in his *Ansichten von der Nachtseite der Naturwissenschaft* (1808), offered his poetic confrères a veritable store-house of psychological problems which demanded presentation in artistic form. His *Symbolik des Traumes* (1814) left nothing to be desired by these literary magicians. This treatise actually attempted to present a scientific study in the spirit of Hardenberg's magic idealism and *Hymnen an die Nacht*. In sleep, dreams, dreamlike states, and in ecstasy are revealed the phenomena which are inaccessible to waking consciousness. Schubert was convinced that in the dream the soul approached eternity far more readily than was possible for a mere waking human being. [49] Justinus Kerner even believed that he could discover new sources of knowledge in epilepsy and insanity. At the present time Hans Prinzhorn (*Bildnerei der Geisteskranken,* second edition, 1923) is promulgating a similar theory.

The psychological aspect of science might well command artistic expression, inasmuch as Goethe himself had used it in his *Wahlverwandtschaften* (1809). This novel is based upon natural philosophy. The chemical theory of elective affinities, of *affinitas* or *attractio electiva,* is not only symbolically applied to spiritual processes; it is assumed that in the spiritual realm, just as in nature, there is *one* harmonious law. All nature, Goethe felt, was homogeneous and even in the free, bright realm of reason traces of vehement, depressing necessity are ever to be found. Goethe here entered and studied the field which the romanticists characterized as the "night side" of nature. It is said, indeed, that Schelling suggested this novel to Goethe. It is not only the title and this particular idea, however, which have the connotation of natural philosophy. The story deals with a host of psychological phenomena;

magnetism and somnambulism, as conceived by Mesmer, Ritter, and Schubert, are treated exhaustively. Ritter's experiments with the divining-rod, of which Goethe had learned through Schelling's publications and from conversations with Hegel, were also woven into the story; Ottilia is represented as having magnetic proclivities, as a somnambulist, or—as modern pneumatologists say—as a good medium (*A 2,* p. 416 ff.).

Immediately after Goethe's novel, the magnetizer and somnambulist reappear in Arnim's *Graefin Dolores* (1809); Arnim's *Kronenwaechter* (1817) and his short story, *Melueck Maria Blainville,* are supplied with similar motifs. The dead Biondette in Brentano's *Romanzen vom Rosenkranz* is resuscitated by "metallic discs." In the *Phantasiestuecke in Callots Manier* (1814–5) Hoffmann presented his "magnetizer." In his *Bergwerke zu Falun* he dilated upon the magic motifs of Schubert, upon whom this work was modelled. *Die Automate* (7, 95) makes special reference to Schubert's "views" upon the antiquity of the human race, when it was still in its original, sacred harmony with nature and when nature still sustained from out of the depths of her being this marvelous creation of her own begetting. At that time she conceived man as if in the flowering of infinite enthusiasm, with sacred music. Even now audible sounds in nature, which terrify even the calmest observer, may be heard in the aerial music or devil's voice in Ceylon. Hoffmann himself claimed to have had an experience of a similar nature in the vicinity of the *Kurische Haff.* In *Der unheimliche Gast* (8, 94 f.) he is again mindful of the devil's voice. The *Phantasiestuecke* (1, 317) proceed to allude to the voice of the "subconscious poet" which Schubert's *Symbolik des Traumes* discusses. *Die seltsamen Leiden eines Theaterdirektors*

(4, 40) linger over the phenomenon of the "speaking conscience": "The *spiritus familiaris* leaps beyond the bounds of subconsciousness and, an independent being, discourses in sublime fashion." This inner voice is so distinctly audible as to seem to proceed from the lips of another person. The conception of the "double" is here anticipated in Schubert's observations (see above, Part 1, p. 25 f.).

But rarely has another romanticist made the subconscious as tangible as did Hoffmann. By so doing he seemed to achieve an unbridgeable dualism. From the beginning his own life was disunited and so it remained. Tenaciously and energetically Hoffmann asserted himself and maintained his creative life though engaged in a most prosaic occupation. In person he was small, ludicrous, almost homely, but—a magician according to Hardenberg's conception—he recreated himself by means of his poetic fancy and at times, through the media of art, he forsook the uncouth habitation of his soul and soared into the realms of beauty. Typical characters in his fairy-tales are similarly metamorphosed and we may quickly discover in them Hoffmann's own features: the lanky recorder Lindhorst in *Der goldene Topf* with his peculiar phrases, and his damask dressing-gown, and his great, staring eyes which gleam from out of the bony cavities of his lined and haggard face as from a case. Suddenly, however, he is transformed into the awful figure of a Salamander prince with a diadem and regal robes. He lives a double life; and like Lindhorst so also are old Liese, the apple woman, and Serpentina, Lindhorst's daughter, characters in the spirit world. Similarly in *Klein-Zaches,* Miss von Rosenschoen is the fairy Rosabelverde and Doctor Prosper Alpanus is a magician and a pupil of Zoroaster; in *Meister*

Floh the coquettish Doertje Elverdink is really Princess Gamaheh of Famagusta and the daughter of King Sekakis but her admirer George Pepusch is the thistle Zeherit. [50] It is given only the elect, such as the student Anselmus in *Der goldene Topf* or Peregrinus Tyss in *Meister Floh,* to penetrate the disguise and recognize the essential soul. The truth is perceived by them through their inner feeling, while the Philistines, such as the co-rector Paulmann and the registrar Heerbrand, reject and call delusion every interpretation that transcends the bounds of normal human reason. Alcohol, at best, can for a few moments give them vision. Primitive romantic conceptions here find artistic expression. The fundamental concept is Novalis' faith both in the sheer magic of poetry, which enables man to transcend his sense perceptions, and in a state of artistic ecstasy, which reveals the simple truth far more directly than any amount of thinking. Thus Hoffmann's dualism likewise resolves itself into romantic monism. Albeit he led a double life and ever in his tales contrasted life as viewed from a merely rational standpoint with life as conceived by the romantic seer, he found reality only in a poetically conceived world. The feudal estate which accrues to the student Anselmus after his marriage to Serpentina appears to him to be indeed the Atlantean wonderland in which the harmony of all living things is realized. Though repeatedly termed a fantast, Hoffmann also had the ability to see, strictly in the sense of Schleiermacher and Friedrich Schlegel, the infinite in the finite, and his finite world was most accurately observed. His powers of observation anticipated the realism of the last decades of the nineteenth century, notably the ability of Keller and Otto Ludwig to depict original characters. As with a magnifying glass he studies peculiar phenomena and unusual, uncanny people; the subtlety of observation and empathy with which he leads from the eccentric to the marvelous rises in the sketch *Des Vetters Eckfenster* to the penetration of the most intimate spiritual revelations.

This gift for observation causes Hoffmann to depict localities much more precisely than the majority of his romantic associates. Because he transplants his marvel into a realistically conceived environment, because he develops it slowly but steadily out of sheer eccentricity, he achieves the surprising technic of making the marvelous vital and credible in the midst of the routine of prosaic life in localities such as Berlin and Dresden, which everyone may visit. For this very reason he succeeds in depicting the marvelous as an actual experience. To be sure, Arnim in *Isabella von Aegypten* (1811) and in *Die Kronenwaechter* also sets the world of the miraculous directly beside realistically conceived actuality. Chamisso's *Peter Schlemihl* (1814) alone, however, approaches the artistry of Hoffmann in having the miraculous proceed from mere oddity and thus achieve credibility. Unlike even Chamisso, Hoffmann was the first writer who—long before the contemporary novel proceeded to such naturalistic "boldness"— dared to mention in his stories the names of actual streets and places in Berlin. Indeed this seer and magician is one of the first writers to introduce Berlin into better class literature.

As antithetical as their talents are otherwise, Heinrich von Kleist has Hoffmann's keen, realistic eye and his tendency toward the psychological aspects of nature. As a matter of fact, the antitheses between them, as well as those existing between Kleist and romanticism, are prone to be exaggerated.

If a leaning toward philosophy and the consciousness

of having such a leaning characterize the romanticist, then Kleist is at least as romantic as Hoffmann. In the case of Kleist, however, these qualities are differently motivated. Kleist's crucial intellectual experience was the staggering impression which Kant's theory of reason made upon him. The letter to his betrothed, Wilhelmine von Zenge, written on March 22, 1801, is the most important evidence of this experience. His philosophy of life, akin to the theses of early romanticism and to Novalis and acquired as a "mere boy," was: After death we continue to develop in another world, proceeding from whatever stage of perfection we achieved on earth. Gradually it became his "religion" never to pause even for an instant here below and to strive unceasingly for ever higher planes of cultural development. Culture seemed to him the only goal worth striving for; truth, the only riches worth having. It was Kant who robbed him of the firm conviction that he could know the truth. He sought to explain to his fiancée his interpretation of Kant's critique: "If everyone wore green glasses, he would of necessity maintain that everything he saw was green—he would never be able to determine whether his eyes presented things to him as they really were or whether something was being added which did not pertain to the things seen but to his own eyes. Thus it is with reason. We cannot tell whether that which we call truth is really truth or whether it merely seems so to us. In the latter case, the truth which we acquire here no longer exists after death—and all our efforts to accumulate such possessions as will follow us beyond the grave are in vain" (5, 204). Piteously he tells how the comprehension of this new idea wounded him to the very depths of his inmost being: "My greatest, my only ambition has vanished and I have no other."

And so, through Kant, Kleist suffered an experience such as culminated in the dictum of the *Erdgeist*, and wholly in the spirit of Faust he wrote to his sister (March 23, 1801): "Everything that is called knowledge nauseates me." [51]

But few of the early romanticists were so painfully affected by the implications of Kant's doctrine. Nevertheless their thought and endeavor were based upon Kant. There is a startling similarity between the deductions which Tieck's William Lovell and Kleist made from the doctrine of the limits of human reason (see above, Part 1, p. 23 ff.).

This experience formed the basis of almost all of Kleist's creative work. Researches based upon a remark which Goethe once made have shown that Kleist in his dramas and novels first develops a state of emotional confusion and then proceeds to resolve it. This emotional confusion is almost always based upon the uncertainty which a human being feels when confronted by the unanswerable question: "What is truth?" The theme of Kleist's creative work might be stated: What spiritual conflicts ensue because of the impossibility of comprehending the truth? What, ethically, are the consequences of the theoretical limitations of man? Errors in judgment precipitate ethical crises. Delusion causes the Schroffensteins to murder their children. Alkmene does not know that she has embraced Jupiter disguised as Amphitryon; the Marquise von O. . . . does not suspect who is the father of her child; indeed, for a long time, she mistakes her own condition. Kohlhaas has mistaken conceptions of what is right. Penthesilea actually believed that she overcame Achilles. Baron von Strahl thought that Kunigunde, who appeared to him in a dream, was his destined bride. The uncertainty whether his nocturnal coronation at Natalie's hands was mere delusion or an actual fact led Homburg into dire complications. In *Der zerbrochene Krug* the problem takes a humorous turn. Because the senses are so unreliable, this game with truth can be carried on indefinitely.

"If you kill each other, that is just an oversight," the Schroffensteins sneeringly remark (verse 2705). Kleist's poetry is replete with such "oversights." Only rarely is one of these "oversights" compensated for or resolved by having the character rise above himself. The purging-process through which the Prince von Homburg passes leaves him free to rise victorious above all his former groping and errors. More often, when the situation finally resolves itself, it precipitates the final consequences of the tragic conflict: Penthesilea commits suicide; Kohlhaas with spiritual elevation composedly ascends the scaffold. Eventually all are purified as was Homburg, but he was not obliged to pay for the boon with his life.

Inasmuch as human reason errs, true happiness is possible only in the idyllic state of unconsciousness. This idyllic phase is most clearly revealed in Kaetchen's undisturbed being. The acquisition of consciousness leads to misunderstanding, leads to emotional confusion. The bright glare of consciousness plunges Alkmene and Penthesilea into tragedy. The final goal is romantically revealed to be a spiritual harmony which germinated from consciousness and which vanquished all earthly frailties.

Meditation upon the uncertainty and unreliability of the senses naturally led Kleist to the study of the "night side" of nature. On that account Schubert is of such importance to him. Hence he delves into Schubert's thirteenth lecture on the "night side" of natural science for his "Kaetchen" material. Baron von Strahl, on the other hand, is the mag-

netizer; Kaetchen, the somnambulist. Besides Schubert,
Jung-Stilling and the physiologist Johann Christian Reil
doubtless assisted in creating Kleist's two somnambulistic
characters, Kaetchen and the Prince von Homburg. [52] Reil
impressed upon him the untrustworthiness of the senses
and thus engendered Kleist's philosophy in which, because
of Kant, the central idea had become the limitations of
human sense perceptions.

VI. THE PROBLEM DRAMA AND NOVEL

KLEIST'S great talent was able to sustain the ponderous intellectual burden with which his themes were freighted. Unlike many of the romanticists, he did not founder in his effort to interpret life in dramatic form.

The antithesis which existed between the romantic drama and the stage had been brought about by a sequence of causes. The antagonism which the romanticists harbored from the outset toward the dominant theatrical producers, notably Kotzebue, made a modest approach toward the contemporary theater very difficult indeed. Anyone who, like Tieck in *Der gestiefelte Kater, Die verkehrte Welt,* and *Zerbino,* had vented his spleen upon the more or less necessary stage devices which experienced producers traditionally permit, had not simplified his own problem when he wished to write a drama which would stage well and be constructive rather than merely destructive. The romanticists of Tieck's type had tarried too long in the ranks of the opposition and were now unable to assume theatrical leadership successfully. Their task was rendered more difficult on account of their opposition to the dramatic masterpieces of Schiller. Here genuine artistry was combined with the ability to sway the contemporary stage. Though the romanticists had rejected whatever was distasteful to them in Schiller, their own favorite dramatists, Shakespeare and Calderon, offered the wherewithal with which to replace whatever had been surrendered. Grillparzer, at any rate, demonstrated how a German masterpiece suitable for theatrical production could derive inspiration from the Spanish drama and even outdo Schiller. Otto Ludwig's sharp eye, on the other hand, perceived the advantages which would accrue to a modern dramatist from a close study of Shakespeare, provided he remained ever mindful of the line of cleavage between Schiller and Shakespeare. Despite Shakespeare and Calderon there failed to bourgeon in the romanticists that theatrical artistry which was intrinsically a part of Schiller.

Schiller in his youth had instinctively felt, and later had consciously concluded from his studies of the ancient drama and of the old and new theory, that tragedy, thanks to the peculiar restrictions of stageable productions, depended upon a sharply defined, accurately calculated coherence of antithethical facts. From the beginning, the antithetical trait in Schiller's mode of thought pointed to this ideal. In a tragedy, of all places, unrestrained skirmishing, idle dawdling with the plot, and foolish prolixity were mistaken as long as the author had not clearly established the sequence of events which was to lead to the conflict. In the very first wave of enthusiasm which the astounding wealth of Shakespeare's enchanting art evoked around 1770, his ability to depict life was deemed greater than his capacity to create really tragic situations. Thereupon Lessing (*Hamburgische Dramaturgie,* Chap. 38) and Schiller (to Goethe, May 5, 1797) referred to the opinion of Aristotle that in tragedy everything depends upon the coördination of the episodes (*Poetics,* Chap. 6). But the majority of the Storm and Stress writers, with Goethe and *Goetz von Berlichingen* at the head, believed in spite of Lessing, just as did the romanticists, in spite of Schiller, that the secret of tragic poetry lay not in precision of structural lines but rather in tone-color. Calderon rather than Shakespeare led the romanticists to develop high coloring. The introduction with which Tieck in 1828 prefaced his dramas (1, p. XXVI ff.) reveals how important he deemed the formal array in which he decked his dramatic works and how little he troubled himself about the structural development of the tragic conflict itself.

To be sure the Shakespearean research of the romanticists had long since freed itself from the errors which before and immediately after the *Hamburgische Dramaturgie* had crept into the fathoming and evaluation of Shakespeare's dramatic form.[53] Inasmuch as Friedrich Schlegel and his fellow-workers attacked the problem with such subtlety, their researches were of little service to the active stage. Friedrich Schlegel's theory of the *Centrum* (see above, Part 1, p. 56), the acceptance of a *Mittelpunkt,* which is supposed to dominate each of the Shakespearean dramas, this doctrine of organic aesthetics gave no clue how episodes might be coördinated into insoluble tragic conflicts. Indeed this doctrine was inclined to cause the romanticists to strive above all else after the decidedly artistic and most characteristically Shakespearean touch of attuning the entire drama to one mood. Nor could this subtle theory prevent romanticism from giving first place, even in the tragedy, to its favorite problem, the presentation and fathoming of the riddle of life.

In his Viennese lectures of 1812 (2, 136) Friedrich Schlegel said of Shakespeare : "Were understanding, penetration, and profundity of observation, insofar as they are essential in grasping life characteristically, the poet's prime distinction, no one could very easily compete with him in this respect." The dramas of romanticism presented life but not with the precision of Shakespeare's insight.

Strictly dramatic form in the sense of Aristotle, Lessing, or Schiller was precluded from the beginning. The demand that romantic poetry reunite all the diversified genres of poetry immediately became a matter of prime importance in Tieck's dramas. His task was simplified by his own predilection for dramas containing epic interpolations (*Pericles,* Shakespeare's *Winter's Tale*) and for the profuse lyric ornamentation of the Spanish stage. Johann Ranftl (*Ludwig Tiecks 'Genoveva,'* 1899, p. 141 f.) is quite right in his surmise that, regardless of his external dramatic form, Tieck thinks epically because his creation is to him a poem that is read and not a drama that is to be staged. Following A. F. Bernhardi's suggestions (*Berlinisches Archiv der Zeit und ihres Geschmacks,* 1800, 1, 457 ff.) Ranftl himself (p. 149 ff.) pointed out the artistic plan of *Genoveva* by showing the symmetry in structure and the consistent use of contrasting effects. "The apparent confusion is developed according to secret higher laws." For all that, there is no trace of genuine architectonics. Tieck lays claim far more decidedly than Shakespeare to the privilege of formlessness.[54]

"The entire background of life" (Tieck's *Schriften,* 1, p. XXXIX should be reflected; the riddles of human existence should also be discussed in the drama. Romantic thought—as we have already seen—tended from the very beginning to center upon the problem of adjustment to life. The final and most sublime solution of this problem was found in Schleiermacher's attempt to see mundane existence, the finite, as a reflection of infinity and to love the infinite in the finite. This romantic-monistic attempt at reconciliation with the world, however, remained for the most part merely an ideal on the part of the romanticists. In spite of it, they felt themselves constantly at odds with life, which, contrary to their expectations, would not be poetized. Though like Goethe they spoke glibly of the "art of living," they were for the most part merely dilettantes in it. *Wilhelm Meisters Lehrjahre* became the Bible of romanticism insofar as the hero persevered in his "false tendency" of trying to realize poetry in life; but when at length he abandoned this tendency for the art of real living, Goethe's novel, in the eyes of the romanticists, became a mere "Candide against poetry." Tieck's novel, *William Lovell* (1795–6), in which the author, before the theory had ever been formulated, apprehended poetically the protean quality of romanticism, was fundamentally more akin to the romanticists. Tieck's Lovell and Jean Paul's problematic natures are the first in a long list of heroes in romantic novels who display their amateurishness in the art of living under the same circumstances as Wilhelm Meister. Goethe's Eduard is also of this type. They are tormented by the question of the why and the wherefore of existence and grope for the means of attaining a definite attitude toward life. And still not one among them has the stamina to shape his life with rigid discipline; they drift, seemingly at the mercy of fate. *Die Wahlverwandtschaften* was the first book to suggest to the romanticists the desirability of a more definite conduct of life. Forthwith Arnim's Graf Karl in the *Graefin Dolores* manifests the more decided characteristics of a genuine nobleman of the old school. Eichendorff, though, still has the hero of *Ahnung und Gegenwart* (1815) end, like a good Catholic, in complete renunciation of active life because he himself doubtless had become too serious to acknowledge the free ethics of the first romantic novels and was unable to devise the way in which his hero could gain a mastery over life. Only in humorous satire was Eichendorff able to transcend the older romantic point of view. In this mood he created his *Taugenichts* (1826).

The problems of life which the romantic novel never wearied of depicting—problems which persisted down to Gottfried Keller's *Gruener Heinrich*—are the main theme of the romantic drama also.[55] But that which created for the novel a rich and fertile background became an obstacle in the drama. The romantic novel is as varied and interesting as the romantic drama, because of its depiction of life, is lacking in tragic force.

In architectonic finish, to be sure, the novels which followed in the wake of Goethe's *Lehrjahre* did not equal their model. Though this novel of Goethe's was much freer in composition than *Werther* and the *Wahlverwandtschaften,* the romanticists, where they did not actually make "delightful arbitrariness" their guiding principle, allowed themselves even more shilly-shallying without the least compunction. It was impossible to acquire a more rigid technique in the art of narration from Jean Paul, who, together with Goethe, was the chief germinative influence in the development of that type of romantic novel which dealt with the theme of education. Paula Scheidweiler (*Der Roman der deutschen Romantik,* 1916) would explain the difference between the *Lehrjahre* and the novels of romanticism with the aid of Schiller's terms, "plastic" and "musical." Her subtle observations raise the question whether she has not diverted these two aesthetic conceptions from their original meanings and interpreted them too much in the sense of comparison of moods. Romantic narratives are prone to formlessness; they strive very ardently after the structural possibilities of music. And they attain, moreover, especially in the hands of a musician such as E. T. A. Hoffman, the artistic effects of musical composition. Hoffman's tale *Der goldene Topf* not only carries forward the action by

means of the *leitmotif* but *leitmotifs* are also used to designate plainly the subdivisions in a structure which, though
it does not strive definitely for symmetry, nevertheless
carries the ever-changing moods through twelve chapters
in artistic ebb and flow.[56] Other romanticists carried their
disregard of form even farther. The drama courted danger
by following, out of principle, as it were, the free play
that is ordinarily accorded to the art of narration.

Nor did the longer epic poems strive after definiteness
of form. The romanticists should have proved to the
world how much more capable they were than Wieland,
whom they thoroughly scorned, of achieving the style of
the so-called romantic epic, and of competing with Ariosto.
Their efforts, as a rule, however, did not progress much
beyond a beginning. In close connection with the chronicles
of Pseudo-Turpin, dating from around the year 1100,
and in harmony, at times, with Ariosto, Friedrich Schlegel wrote his heroic poem *Roland* (in his *Poetisches
Taschenbuch* for 1806; cf. E. Wieneke, *Patriotismus und
Religion in Friedrich Schlegels Gedichten,* 1913, p. 48 ff.).
His brother did not proceed beyond the first canto of a
poem called *Tristan,* derived from Gottfried von Strassburg. Immerman's poem *Tristan und Isolde* (1841) sped
along with greater verve; it was almost completed when
Immerman suddenly died. Because of Wilhelm Schlegel's
stimulation, Tieck's sister, Sophie Bernhardi von Knor-
ring, began at an early date a work based upon a Middle
High German chivalrous poem by Konrad Fleck, which she
finally finished as *Flore und Blanchefleur* in 1822. Fouqué
also learned from Wilhelm Schlegel. He tried his hand
at turning mediaeval and allegorical material into modern
epics. Uhland's *Fortunat und seine Soehne* likewise remained unfinished. Thus the trifles of Ernst Schulze were

destined to become the accepted specimens of romantic narrative poetry. Platen's *Abassiden* (1833) reverted to the Orient and the atmosphere of the *Arabian Nights;* they displayed their author's skill in versifying just as Rueckert, in numerous epic attempts at imitating the atmosphere of the still more remote East, demonstrated his ability to adapt the German language to the subtleties of oriental words and rimes.

These romantic narrative poems were largely made up of elaborations and free translations. Not one could rival Herder's *Cid* (1805), which was merely a more pretentious demonstration of Herder's long acknowledged skill in translating into German the folk-songs of foreign nations. Herder at the same time gave the romanticists a model which was not only useful to them but which also followed the trend of their inclinations. His *Cid* is a series of ballads. In much the same way Friedrich Schlegel developed his *Roland,* except that he imitated the Spanish verse form even somewhat more accurately than did Herder's *Cid*. It was apparently easier for the romanticists to amalgamate a series of ballads than to attain the more rigid form of the greater epics. Brentano soon abandoned the teeming wealth of poetic ideas out of which he had planned to fabricate the myth contained in his *Romanzen vom Rosenkranz*. This fragment appeared so late that it was not apparent how much it anticipated Heine's midsummer night's dream, *Atta Troll* (1843), in which Heine for the first time proceeded from lyric cycles to a relatively fixed series of ballads. Possibly Heine had in mind poems after the manner of Byron's *Beppo* or of Musset's *Namouna,* ventures in the field of the comic heroic epic, which were less inclined than his own poetry toward satire. The winter's tale, *Deutschland* (1844), developed into an out-

and-out political satire. The glorified dirge, *Bimini,* approached more nearly the demeanor of Brentano's *Rosenkranz.*

Lenau's epic ventures, *Faust, Savonarola, Die Albigenser,* which were published around 1840, tended toward a less hampered, still looser articulation between the ballads. To some measure only they preserve that uniformity of meter which rules in Heine's epics and which may be observed in the cycle of patriotic romances by Lenau's comrade, Anastasius Gruen. So, too, Eichendorff's later epic songs, *Julian, Robert und Guiscard,* and *Lucius* (1853–7), display less diversity in verse form. The multifarious variations in external form correspond to the ebb and flow of animated and animating moods. In final analysis, the epic poem was merely assuming that privilege which Tieck's musical lyrics had already claimed (see above, Part 1, p. 129 ff.).

Of all the problems of life that were treated by the novel and drama, only one, the question of free will, led to the exercise of stricter observance of dramatic form. Hence, albeit in an ill-balanced, hardly praiseworthy sense, the fate-motif nevertheless became a means of familiarizing the romanticists with the contemporary stage. The fate-dramas of the romanticists were actually effective as stage productions.

The fate-tragedy is one of the peculiar fruits of romanticism. The romanticists themselves disowned it inasmuch as it contained a decidedly non-romantic element. It combined Schiller's doctrine with ideas and forms which were romantic, and exaggerating both, ended in sheer externalities. The first attempt at a fate-tragedy, however, was made by a highly gifted poet [Schiller, in his *Braut von*

Messina], and Grillparzer's *Ahnfrau* approached genuine art.

The close connection between the fate-tragedy and romanticism is indicated by Tieck's youthful efforts, *Der Abschied* (1792) and *Karl von Berneck* (1795). Tieck's youthful fatalism, which is still strongly apparent in *Der blonde Eckbert,* his speculations upon the involuntary restraint endured by human beings whose lives are directed by an inscrutable force of nature, anticipate accurately the work of Zacharias Werner, Muellner, and Houwald. Certainly the suffocating atmosphere that paralyzes all volition and which dominates in the fate-tragedies has its rise in those conjectures which also conditioned the previously mentioned works of Tieck (cf. above, p. 241 ff.). Tieck's antithesis to romantic philosophy (which sought to instill the light of the soul into nature rather than to infuse the restraining influences of nature into human existence) is even more apparent in these dramas than in the tales. Tieck continues to disport himself blissfully among horrors, while the Schlegels, Novalis, and Schleiermacher are trying to wing their way into the freer spiritual realms.

Even the boldest and most speculative of the romantic thinkers were in very real danger of allowing themselves to be dominated weakly by circumstances. Kant's rigid ethics was essentially foreign to them; they harkened to the voice of nature which spoke within them; they hesitated to deny the desires of their emotional life because they recognized therein the manifestation of the law of their own personalities. The difficulty of grasping the law of their own personalities, though, often caused the romanticists to seem like creatures of instinct, without will. Ricarda Huch (*Romantik*, 1908, 2, 126 f.) upbraids them for not consciously moulding their lives as an artist handles his medium; they do not live but are lived; she here quotes a statement which Karoline von Guenderode uttered against Bettina: "To me you are the clay which a god, creating, treads beneath his feet."

As a matter of fact, the romantic philosophy of life will be found to rest wholly neither upon the doctrine of free will nor upon that of utter lack of freedom. Novalis seems to grant the human will limitless power and at the same time is inclined, like Friedrich Schlegel and Schelling, toward Spinozism. The difficulty and the possibility of the task of combining Spinozism and free will in romantic thought is touched upon in certain of Hardenberg's *Fragmente* (3, 109, 289, 296). These obscure intimations consistently point to a combination of determinism and free will. Similarly Klingsohr in *Ofterdingen* says (4, 166 ff.): "An innate belief in human mastery over fate" (i.e. in the control of a human being by means of a fate that has been humanly tempered and is intimately akin to him) is indispensable to a poet, "because, if he ponders it deeply, he cannot imagine fate otherwise." But then Klingsohr continues (and here Goethe also serves as his model): "How far removed is this happy certainty from that anxious uncertainty, the blind fear of superstition. And so, too, the cool, inspiriting warmth of an artistic disposition is the very counterpart to the wild fever of a languishing heart." Though tremendously carried away by Spinoza, Goethe did not allow himself to be driven from determinism to superstition. But Novalis, like Goethe, sought to know how much responsibility devolved upon a human being who professed determinism and, in his capacity as a poet, he sought that point at which the gloomy mistaken beliefs contained in the previously mentioned works of

Tieck could be overcome, even though fate, in the loftier
sense of the poet, is not gainsaid.

Naturally the problem of free will is the pivotal point
in the speculations of Schleiermacher, the greatest ethical
thinker of romanticism, who had already treated it in a
youthful essay. He, too, like Spinoza and Leibnitz, Lessing and Hume, Goethe and Hegel, renounced absolute
freedom of the will. But his determinism had already been
definitely formulated before he knew Spinoza and independently also of the doctrine of predestination advanced by the Reformed Church (Dilthey, *Leben Schleiermachers,* I, 139). He was convinced that a moral emotional
life, which presupposes unhampered freedom, offered humanity no more than a chimerical possibility of arriving
freely at conclusions, whereas it made coherent effort at
improvement quite impossible. Furthermore he believed
that only through an understanding of the compliance of
human actions with rule could one attain that spontaneity
of achievement which develops along with character itself.
In his *Monologen* he treats the question in the light of the
development of Kant's ethics, to which he had meanwhile
devoted himself (see Part I, p. 50). Without renouncing the basic deterministic point of view, the fourth *Mono-
log* reaffirms his belief that for a true will there is no fate.

Schleiermacher felt that each individual in his own peculiar way represented a compendium of humanity, combining its elements in a manner peculiar to himself alone.
The task therefore of every human being is to strengthen
and fashion his own individuality. Having achieved this
goal, one is no longer disturbed by the thought of his own
happiness. He who ceaselessly pursues happiness becomes
the slave of destiny. Hence man must free himself of such
a desire. It is a question of achieving free, harmonious

fruition for the living forces within us; of granting to our lives the full measure of virtue which is implanted in us. "Such a conception of the will dispels the idea of fate." "Joy or sorrow, or whatever else the world may designate as weal or woe, are equally welcome to me because each in its way fulfills its purpose." Thus freedom is made to rest upon the renunciation of eudemonistic desires.

In spite of the antithesis to Kant, this is stern and rigorous ethics. To observe that law which is latent in every human heart is a serious and difficult task. But this very observance vouchsafes to the human soul its freedom. The moral necessity of the freedom of the will, as Novalis says, here actually merges with determinism.

Just as well as, through Schiller, genuine tragedy grew out of Kant's categorical imperative, so too it might develop from ethics such as this. Schiller, in his creative prime, delineated the character who, visited by misfortune, rises at the very moment of destruction to free self-determination; physically he is vanquished but morally he is the victor, inasmuch as he has conquered himself. Schleiermacher's ethics did not consist merely in renouncing the desires and inclinations of the heart, inasmuch as it demanded more than the recognition of a universally binding categorical imperative, more than mere subjection to the moral law. Of greater moment, according to Schleiermacher's ethics, is a tragic hero who is plunged into misfortune but who then, having become indifferent to happiness, begins to fathom himself and to unfold the living forces inherent in himself and to grant his life the full measure of virtue which is implanted within him. Kleist's Prince of Homburg underwent just such a process. A youthful, passionate, heroic nature, he was on the point of losing and denying himself. But as soon as the decision whether he should live or die was left to the Prince himself, as soon as the Archduke caused him to be his own judge, Homburg responded to the heroic qualities in his nature and made that decision which alone was compatible with his deepest personality. A similar situation is found in Goethe's *Egmont*. Egmont, also, unmindful of the law of his own personality, was in danger of cowardly surrender; but he, too, after a struggle regained the poise which was inherently his. He not only was willing to die, as was Homburg; he actually did surrender his life.

Subjective tragedy could very well follow in the wake of the romantic law of freedom and necessity. The fact, however, that romanticism had stripped death of its terrors was doubtless somewhat detrimental to external tragedy. A group of writers who, in the spirit of Hardenberg's *Hymnen an die Nacht,* saw in death only the awakening to a higher life could hardly use the terrors of death to create a tragic effect upon the stage (cf. Wendriner op. cit., p. 110 ff.). And yet the romanticists knew the beauties of this world. Schleiermacher, whose doctrine of freedom demanded the renunciation of happiness, had described the glory of the finite world too effectively to admit of a general desire to flee voluntarily from its enticements into a supernatural paradise.

Zacharias Werner's sophisticated nature was perhaps the least adapted to rise to Schleiermacher's demands. From the very outset Werner was bent upon cloaking his own peculiar tendencies in the imposing mantle of obscurity and upon recasting, with the aid of Hardenberg's language, his sensuality into the form of a religion. Superstitiously he fabricated daily oracles for himself; later, upon the basis of whether or not it would rain upon a certain day, he foretold his own eternal salvation. Yet, in constant fear, he kept his eye open for the fate which lay in wait for him. Pitifully conscious of his guilt, he felt in every trivial event a premonition of his inevitable punishment.

And yet, Werner, of all the romanticists, had the most decided talent for the stage. A practical man, such as Iffland, recognized, in spite of the veil of obscurity which enveloped Werner's first attempts, that the latter knew the stage. In Werner's *Luther* he saw his expectations fulfilled and, bending all his energy as actor and director, he made a decided success of the play.[57] Goethe, too, was soon convinced that Werner was destined to be the successor of Schiller, provided he abjured his freakishness. Grillparzer also concurred in this opinion. In order to get the intractable Werner off on the right foot, Goethe decided to set him a very definite task and not only to impress strongly upon him that this time he was to omit "all his infernal nonsense" but also to prescribe to him the theme, the action, the number of characters, and the scope down to the last detail. The efficacy of a curse was to be presented.

Goethe in this connection was thinking of Schiller's dramaturgical principles. Schiller felt that his theory of the necessity of a strictly tragic combination of events, as exemplified in the classic drama, was best presented in works in which the motivation rested upon situations dominated by fatalistic compulsion. Hence the word "fate" is used so frequently in his later dramas. To be sure he was not concerned with determinism but with rigid motivation. Nevertheless his search for a subject-matter which offered the advantages of Sophocles' *Oedipus Rex* led him at length into the fatalistic motifs of the *Braut von*

Messina. Thus Goethe might well recognize in the operation of a curse the "mainsprings of Greek tragedy."

Werner's conception of fate, to begin with, was far more superficial and ill-balanced than Schiller's. The latter sought to present that mighty, gigantic fate which exalts man though it crush him; in his dramas—strictly in accordance with Kant—the moral freedom and self-determination of the hero was to manifest itself at that very moment in which the hero was physically at the mercy of external circumstances. Werner, on the other hand, depicted characters in *Der vierundzwanzigste Februar* who—as has very aptly been said—were hypnotized by fate like somnambulists. Self-determination vanished into thin air; the actions of his characters were dependent upon time, place, and curse-laden properties. Wholly detached from man was a malicious force which entered his life to hold baleful sway and against which all resistance was without avail.

The same superstitious attitude was rampant in the imitations of *Der vierundzwanzigste Februar.* Instead of the intended fate-drama, we have a drama of chance. "Where is he," we read in Grillparzer's *Ahnfrau,* "who might presume to say: 'This I wish, thus it shall be!' Our deeds are but random throws in the dark."

The fate-dramas, led by Werner's *Der vierundzwanzigste Februar,* were much more effective on the stage than the majority of the romantic dramas. Schiller's dramatic principles, diverted by Goethe to the fate-dramatists, here bore good fruit. Their success upon the stage left nothing to be desired. Tieck, however, thought that Werner, whom he disparaged (*Krit. Schriften,* 4, 158) as "a follower" of Schiller, was mistaken in his innate adherence to Schiller. At the same time, however, he admitted that Werner "was possessed of great talent" and that he "naturally had just enough excellent gifts to allow him to soar like a shining meteor" (same as above, p. 214). In Tieck's estimation, though, the fate-drama stood "upon a peculiar level of raw barbarism, such as history had never before offered, not even in Paris during the Revolution, and certainly not upon the stage" (p. 144).

It has become a veritable commonplace to say that Tieck, the dramatic critic, is the opposite of Tieck, the poet. As a matter of fact, by rejecting the tactics of the fate-drama, Tieck repudiated similar youthful efforts of his own. To be sure, he was not directly responsible for the fate-tragedy of the nineteenth century. His own youthful efforts hardly influenced it. Its immediate sources were Schiller's example, Goethe's desire, and Werner's temperament. This concatenation gave Tieck, along with Boerne and Platen, a certain right to condemn the fate-tragedy. As early as 1795, the introduction to the story *Das Schicksal* (14, 3 f.) spoke most rationalistically of fate and chance. Two decades later, in the prologue to *Fortunat* (1816), Tieck jested about Fortuna and her servant, Chance. Fortuna is accused by six complainants of having plunged them into misfortune. She is able to prove, however, that each one of them of his own accord has turned her gifts to poor account. The enlightened secretary remonstrates with Chance, saying that for a rational human being chance does not exist. Chance, however, causes the tables to be upset, and all the documents are destroyed in a sea of black ink. This prologue was perhaps the first public statement which Tieck made against the fate-tragedy. It introduced a piece of work which revealed but little technical dramatic skill, having been written in a period during which Tieck still thought, dramatically, in a thoroughly romantic sense and was, therefore, more concerned with the meaning and regimen of life itself than with any matters of dramatic technique.

Zacharias Werner's freakish mysticism, "all his infernal nonsense," was in last analysis nothing more than an attempt to realize the prevalent romantic desire to solve the riddle of life in the drama. He, too, endeavored to make the stage his pulpit that he might preach therefrom his "religion." For this very reason, inasmuch as he did not try to depict life as broadly and impressionistically within the limits of a play as is possible in a novel, Iffland and Goethe considered him more adept, theatrically, than the majority of his fellow-romanticists. Tieck's *Genoveva* and *Octavianus,* on the other hand, tend to elaborate suggestions found in their source-material into explicit, dramatically purposeless delineations of life, which merely retard the action of the play. His *Fortunat* is nothing more than a half-dramatized novel of the romantic *Wilhelm Meister* variety. It tells of youths who enter upon life imbued with erroneous notions and who, being mere amateurs in the art of living, repeatedly come to grief. Father Fortunat does finally achieve something resembling the art of living but his son Andalosia can not give up and ever retains his restless, endlessly searching, craving, and yearning spirit and goes to ruin.

Similarly, Arnim's *Halle und Jerusalem* (1811)—to give another illustration—attempts to depict the profusion of life itself. This piece, the material for which Arnim derived from Andreas Gryphius, consists of two parts, and the hero, Cardenio, is twin brother to the typical hero of the romantic novel. The two female characters, Olympia and Celinde, between whom he is placed, are counterparts of similar antithetical pairs to be found in those novels which treated of education and training in life. Cardenio's experiences are brought about by the limitations with which a genial nature restricts itself when it tries to fashion life after a pattern of its own. So he is driven into tragic situations by his opposition to the world, its baseness, and its conventionality. This piece, also, makes the mere thought of actual presentation seem ridiculous. It follows the unhampered course of a novel and utilizes the monologue and dialogue form merely to preserve the semblance of dramatic action. Even the interpolation of lyrics is indicative of the *Lehrjahre* and its limitations. How little the demands of dramatic technique were appreciated at this time is revealed by a letter which Jacob Grimm wrote to Arnim (January 22, 1811) in which he states that *Halle und Jerusalem* revealed a decided dramatic talent on the part of its author, whereas *Kaetchen von Heilbronn* had convinced him that "Heinrich Kleist ought to write no more dramas." From the Aristotelian standpoint Arnim was utterly devoid of dramatic talent. Indeed, how could the severe technique of the stage be observed by a writer who, as Brentano tartly but correctly stated, allowed his poetry to "run riot like wild game" (to Arnim, p. 266)? He is quite successful in animating an individual scene with dramatic life; and here and there in his dramas—as in his novels and romances—his keen and penetrating eye also gleans a secret from life. The device of the youthful Goethe and of several of his Storm and Stress companions, notably Lenz, the same device by means of which Gerhart Hauptmann won the greater part of his public, is also Arnim's: he endows his characters, who probably never rise to the demands of the dramatic action, with moods and words which had never before been presented in quite the same way but which appeal to us as the simple revelation of the universality of human emotion. But re-

peatedly the reader wonders what connection these penetrating observations have with those passages in the drama
to which Arnim has attached them.[58]

It is, indeed, a step forward, compared to the untheatrical efforts of the romanticists, when Fouqué tardily—at
the close of the second part—created a unifying bond to
envelop his *Held des Nordens* (1810) and made of the
Sigurdsaga a concatenation of guilt and reconciliation.
Gudruna thus inaugurated this inclusive attitude (*Ausge-
waehlte Werke, 2,* 180):

> We were the sacrifices and we knew it not.
> Now they lie dead. Now through me has transpired
> That which had to be; soon I shall follow them.
> Can you not see? Are you unaware
> Of the bloody gleam rising in unbroken spirals
> From Sigurd's funeral-pyre,
> Dazzling and encircling the race
> Whose deeds of crime laid him, the hero, low?
> Such a deed is not easily atoned for.
> It reaches out after the guiltless and cries for justice
> As long as wife or child of the evil-doer lives.
> Annihilation is its final goal.

The romanticists were lured, even more by the Spanish
drama than by those of Shakespeare's plays which treat of
the lives of kings, to depict the life and death of their hero
or heroine. One of Tieck's works is called *Leben und Tod
der heiligen Genoveva.* He even dramatized the *Leben und
Tod des kleinen Rotkaepchens* (1800). Fouqué once used
the title *Historie vom edlen Ritter Galmy und einer
schoenen Herzogin aus Bretagne* (1806). All of these are
merely dramatized versions of old narrative material, but

externally and internally the essentially epic character is unmistakably evident. This elaboration of old epic material was the more likely to repudiate the ethos of the tragedy inasmuch as religious veneration and archaeological interest would make the author cautious about attacking it and rearranging it too energetically. Fouqué's revision of the Sigurdsaga may be deemed just as authentic as the majority of Oehlenschlaeger's Nordic poems. The latter in *Aladdin* (1808) manages to have the problem of life staged and experiments with a dramatized version of the *Lehrjahre*.

For the same reason a poem such as *Genoveva* comes in conflict with the precise dramatic action. To elaborate the romantic-mediaeval, religious atmosphere was in final analysis of far more importance to Tieck and many of his successors than mere form. Solger subtly observed how this ulterior motive caused a premeditated and intentional something to creep into *Genoveva* which detracted from its artistic effectiveness. He was justified in saying in his letter to Tieck, November 23, 1816 (*Schriften,* I, 465 f.), that while Tieck was engaged upon this drama, this peculiar religious attitude was not altogether his "actual condition" but that he was consumed by an intense longing to feel this attitude. "This is likewise apparent in the form, which is everywhere dammed by narration and in which the dramatic element is too widely diffused. Form, after all, is never mere chance; with a definite intention you sought in this instance to transport us into the genial and innocent atmosphere of the days of yore; and certainly you would never have presented and expressed the attendant circumstances so carefully to us unless you meant to accentuate their antithesis to something else by means of which discord enters into our consciousness and makes us ponder. . . . The characterization of individuals, as well as of the whole period, often seems premeditated to me." [59]

Even as a dramatic critic Tieck had but the vaguest conception, in Schiller's sense, of a definitely calculated, clearcut sequence of dramatic action. This is evident from the expressions which he himself used when speaking of authoritative stage technique. Thus he lauded F. L. Schroeder for his masterly ability in the development and disposition of characters and situations, and in furthering the action in every scene and speech (*Krit. Schriften*, 4, 200). The very same expressions were subsequently applied to Schiller's early dramas (p. 203), which Tieck prized very highly and to which he paid great praise for their "wealth of genuine dramatic talent and of that theatrical instinct which gives life and action to everything which we see in reality and in our imagination." "With every speech the action progresses, every dialogue has theatrical force, the suspense rises, everything which takes place off stage and between acts vivifies the scene which is actually enacted." In this "progression," in this "vivification by means of dramatic action" he recognizes "gifts with which the poet must be endowed by nature, inasmuch as they cannot be acquired. Once possessed they need but to be developed." These observations are doubtless subtle and hit upon important peculiarities of dramatic talent, but not upon the vital point. This is as explicit as Tieck ever became in discussing the secret of dramatic art.

The unadaptability of the romantic drama to the stage is partly attributable to the fact that the romanticists felt as much akin to Goethe as they felt alien to Schiller. Later, after his dramas had repeatedly shown that he was a student of Goethe's novels, Tieck declared that Goethe's tragedies were really not adaptable to the stage (*Kritische Schriften,* 4, 198 ff.). "In order to attain theatrical effectiveness, Goethe's marvelous nature would have had to sacrifice as much in his poetry as he would have gained thereby." In his capacity of stage-director, Goethe blamed the romanticists for their alienation from the stage; oddly enough Heinrich von Kleist fared worst with Goethe in this respect. Goethe's letter to Kleist, February 1, 1808, concerning *Penthesilea,* censures the tendency of the romanticists to wait for a theater which is yet to come. "A Jew awaiting the Messiah, a Christian awaiting the new Jerusalem, and a Portuguese awaiting Don Sebastian are not more irritating to me." Although the leading spirit of the theater at Weimar confessed to the creed of his theater-director, which demanded that to achieve the proper effect one must confine oneself to the proper medium, Goethe, as a poet, in the last decades of his productivity, adopted the position which Tieck assigned to him. On June 27, 1810, Goethe admitted in a letter to Kirms: "Inasmuch as I am engaged upon so many other projects, I hardly think that I shall ever again turn to theatrical activities, which offer neither joy, nor pleasure, nor advantage." The novel was more attractive to him than the drama; in the former he could give his genius free play while in the latter he was faced by the restraining demands of effectiveness, which were not always self-evident to him. And so he added by way of further explanation: "I now prefer the novel to anything else because everything which is disadvantageous to the dramatist becomes advantageous to the novelist."

Toward the end of Goethe's dramaturgic activities, poetry and the stage became so absolutely antithetical in his estimation that he could deny Shakespeare's rôle as a dramatic poet. Shakespeare's name and glory, he declared in 1816 (37, 46 f.), belong only in the annals of poetry; theatrical traits (Goethe calls theatrical "that which the eye at the same time accepts as symbolic") in Shakespeare are but "scattered jewels separated by great stretches of untheatrical material." Since this was Goethe's one-sided conception of the term "theatrical," his objections to Heinrich von Kleist, as well as his praise of Zacharias Werner, seem more comprehensible. If Goethe had not, in addition, discovered in Kleist's masterpiece that pathological tendency which was hateful to him, he might have come to an understanding with the artist in Kleist. For Goethe himself, at least in his old age, approached romantic usage the moment he decided, in spite of all, to choose the dramatic form. Thus to him, also, poetry upon the stage came to be more important than theatricality. In the long gone days of his youth he had been hailed as the German Shakespeare. Subsequently he gradually turned the dramatic field over to Schiller. His futile attempts to bring Schiller's *Demetrius* to a successful finish doubtless made clear to him that there was in Schiller's dramatic equipment a certain element in which he himself was lacking. His last dramatic efforts, however, completed and fragmentary, are conceived romantically in respect to both form and content. His wealth of forms and his deep, comprehensive grasp upon life bespeak the romantic tendency. And so at the close of the first part of *Faust* and in carrying out the second part, he achieved the most to which the nondramatic program of the romantic drama could aspire. With romantic diversity in form, combining antique and modern, *Faust,* the consummate masterpiece and demonstration of progressive universal poetry, unfolds the profoundest problems of life, delineating primarily the evolution of the romantic yearner whose insatiable striving for the infinite is doomed never to be satisfied, but who is ever borne upward toward infinity by the eternally feminine (*A 2,* p. 382 ff.).

It will ever be the chief glory of the Storm and Stress movement of the eighth decade of the eighteenth century that it gave rise to the greatest poetry of the German nation and of the German language. Romanticism may ever boast, however, that this achievement was brought to a conclusion in harmony with romantic theory. If, on account of *Faust,* there is something of the glory of the sunrise resting upon the Storm and Stress, romanticism, in the light of Goethe's poem, is glamorously illumined by this same heavenly body when its daily course is run.

VII. CONCLUSION

THE first edition of this presentation of German romanticism appeared eighteen years ago. Within the narrow limits of a relatively bulky little volume of the series *Aus Natur und Geisteswelt,* it sought to trace the creative products of German romanticism back to its aesthetic and philosophic theories. The task was, as it is now phrased, to fathom romantic poetry in the light of the spiritual development of the movement. As is commonly apparent in researches of this sort—a point which I also brought out concerning Rudolf Unger's valuable, directive study *Literaturgeschichte als Problemgeschichte* (Berlin, 1924) in the *Deutsche Literaturzeitung* (1925, column 1258)—the creative products of the movement did not fare as well in my brief volume as the spiritual concepts which conditioned them. To be sure, space also was lacking in which to discuss the former at greater length. In subsequent editions, however, these were accommodated at the expense of the philosophical speculations of the romanticists. When at length the book was divided into two volumes, it became possible to apportion approximately equal space to each division: the philosophy of the romanticists and their creative works. This happened in the fourth edition, in the difficult days of 1918, which fact precluded for practical reasons any essentially new revision.

The fifth edition of the first volume came at a still

more troublous time, in 1923, when the value of the mark was steadily declining. That edition was nothing more than a slightly altered anastatic reprint.

In the meantime I have delved more and more into the problems of the artistic form of creative works. The first edition was an initial and bold attempt to synthetize researches in literary history. As such it was strongly, and at times bitterly, opposed by those of my professional colleagues who thought to find true salvation in analysis. But meanwhile, in spite of its condensed form, there were many who received my book enthusiastically. Interest in so-called "synthetic" research and presentation has been mounting steadily since then. With due thanks I acknowledge assurances from many sides that I was instrumental in promoting this new tendency. Indeed, these very controversies between those who would analyse and those who would synthetize made it increasingly clear to me that the former, who were prone to accuse the latter of insufficient dissection, had themselves not yet attained the proper "vision," that is, a really exhaustive analysis of creative works of art. For the most part they had not yet passed beyond the stage of what I call the "elementary mathematics" of research in form.

I was aided in my project to grasp and express more accurately the essentially artistic quality in poetic works by the more recent researches in the history of the fine arts. I am most indebted to Heinrich Woelfflin and his book *Kunstgeschichtliche Grundbegriffe* (Munich, 1915). My publication *Wechselseitige Erhellung der Kuenste, ein Beitrag zur Wuerdigung kunstgeschichtlicher Begriffe* (Berlin, 1917) presents some results of my endeavor to approach the artistic form of poetry by utilizing conceptions which were already current in the field of art. In so doing I referred to the many who had labored in the same spirit and mentioned most particularly the earliest pioneers and fellow-workers, chief among them Carl Steinweg and Fritz Strich.

Woelfflin, in two lists of five concepts each, characterized the antithesis between the Renaissance and the baroque in the plastic art of the sixteenth and seventeenth centuries. He assumed the right to present antithetical art conceptions which manifested themselves at various times and places and suggested tracing similar antitheses in the other arts. The next step was to apply those conceptions which in Woefflin's estimation characterize the baroque and whose earmark is loosely-knit form to the poetry of the German romanticists. Fritz Strich, in a very helpful article on the lyric style of the seventeenth century (in the *Abhandlungen zur deutschen Literaturgeschichte, Franz Muncker zum 60. Geburtstage dargebracht.* Munich, 1916, p. 21 ff.), proved that valuable information was to be gained by so doing. In demonstrating how happily the characteristics of the German baroque-lyric of the seventeenth century corresponded to Woelfflin's categories of the baroque, he pointed out in various places the kinship between the baroque-lyric and the poetry of German romanticism. Theodor Spoerri (in the periodical *Wissen und Leben,* 1919, 12, 762 ff.) presently fitted the peculiarities of romantic expression into Woelfflin's categories of the baroque.

George Simmel's book, *Rembrandt, ein kunst-philosophischer Versuch* (Leipzig, 1916), made clear to me, however, that it is misleading to apply unqualifiedly the term baroque to German romanticism and its artistic expression. This term is easily taken to connote the conception of intoxication, exaggeration, immensity, the conception which Wilhelm Worringer emphasized so strongly when he placed the essence of the "Gothic" over against that of classicism. Simmel points out that Rembrandt's art was born of much less inner tension. He characterizes Rembrandt's delineation somewhat as follows: renunciation of conventional form and adoption of a wholly personal one; a seizing upon the inner life at that moment in which it flashes to the surface; not an imprisoning of life in a form which has its own peculiar privileges and demands.

Simmel does not indicate how far such a creative method agrees with the German classical and romantic theory of an organic work of art. It is obvious, however, that whoever, rather than confining the subjective life within a conventional form, makes his external artistic form the simple, direct expression of the subjective life is doing exactly what the aesthetics of German classicism and romanticism intended by playing off the organic form against the mechanistic. That is what Wilhelm Schlegel did in his Viennese lectures (6, 157 f.) apropos of Shakespeare's art. To him organic form was veritably a significant external phenomenon, the speaking physiognomy of all things, unmarred by any disturbing inconsequentialities, and one which bears true witness to the essential qualities latent therein. He adds: "Organic form . . . is an inherent quality; it proceeds from within and reaches its culmination simultaneously with the complete development of the seminal idea." On the other hand, Wilhelm Schlegel conceived of a form as mechanistic "if through any external influence it is joined, regardless of its suitability, like an accidental appendage, to any thought-material whatsoever."

This is but another of the countless paraphrases of the

doctrine of the organic work of art which was advanced repeatedly by the German classicists, by Goethe and Herder, as well as by the German romanticists (cf. particularly, Part 1, p. 20). My entire presentation of romanticism, its philosophy and its poetry, is based upon this conception. That it harks back to the aesthetics of Plotinus is duly mentioned in the present work (particularly Part 1, p. 59); I emphasize repeatedly that on decisive points Plotinus agrees with German romanticism. In an essay published in 1915 (now: *A 2*, p. 1, ff.) I endeavor to explain Plotinus' conception of the beautiful. Since then I habitually cite Plotinus as the forerunner of organic aesthetics when I speak of German arch-classicism or German romanticism.

Nor did I fail in my first essay to utilize Simmel's researches in order properly to interpret romantic form. In the Dutch periodical *Neophilologus* (4, 115 ff.) I sought to show in 1919 how accurately Simmel's remarks upon Rembrandt fitted the essential quality of Goethe's early poetry, especially his lyrics, as well as a large, indeed the greater part, of romantic poetry. This essay was reprinted in abbreviated form in 1922 (*A 2*, p. 85 ff.). An essay written in 1921, *Zwei Moeglichkeiten deutscher Form,* develops the subject still further. This article has also been reprinted (*A 2*, p. 114 ff.).

I maintain that two antithetical methods of forming a work of art may be distinguished within German romanticism. The first is rather calm and simple and lays no claim to emotional intensity. The other is more soaring, pathetical, and at times grotesque, and ever inclined to hyperbolic expression. The current conception of baroque, or, as Worringer terms it, of Gothic, is applicable only to the latter. The former conforms to the demands of organic aesthetics. It presents a subjective quality without ever doing violence to it. It subjects it neither to a conventional form which is a law unto itself nor does it persist in maintaining high tension or assuming a posing attitude such as is peculiar to the baroque on account of its tendency toward pathos.

Furthermore I maintain that this same, relatively simple code of expression is the essential characteristic of most of Goethe's poetry. Goethe, indeed, is one of the founders of organic aesthetics. To be sure, at certain times, he approaches the forms of ancient classicism and hence becomes conventional in method. But relatively very few poems in the wealth of Goethe's output followed to any great extent a tendency to adopt the forms of the ancient classics (cf. above, Part 1, p. 8).

Goethe's poem *Auf dem See* is my favorite illustration of his determinative method of form. It reveals better than the Roman elegies what Goethe really had in mind and what new ideas he had to give to German, as well as to non-German, lyric poetry. Tieck's lyrics in *Magelone* (cf. above, Part 1, p. 129 ff.) contain essential characteristics of *Auf dem See*. In such of Goethe's early poems the German romanticists recognized immediately the mode of expression toward which they had been groping. And if, contrary to others, I emphasize the fact that Goethe and even Schiller have much in common with German romanticism, and if I prove this fact repeatedly in my presentation of romanticism, upon this present point there exists between the classicist Goethe and the lyrists of German romanticism an agreement which admits of but one distinction: Goethe is the greater artist and is perhaps more visually minded than many of the romanticists. Assuredly he was the model of the German romanticists and became the guarantor of the organic method of fashioning a work of art.

I see no unbridgeable chasm between the German classicists and the German romanticists, least of all between Goethe (also Herder; cf. above, Part 1, p. 15 ff.) on the one hand and the romanticists on the other. And so at the very outset I feel rather hostile toward any attempt to conceive of German classicism and German romanticism as two poles which, though they belong together insofar as poles complement one another, are nevertheless felt to be far removed from one another.

The very title of Fritz Strich's *Deutsche Klassik und Romantik oder Vollendung und Unendlichkeit* (Munich, 1922; second enlarged edition, 1924) indicates this polar antithesis. For the very reason that I agree with so much that the book offers, I must here indicate wherein I differ.

In recent years comprehensive presentations of German romanticism have been appearing in rapid succession. Strich's book towers high above the rest. It is a vigorous step toward the attainment of new and more precise conceptions to be used in determining the characteristics of poetic works. It seeks also to subordinate to definite conceptions not only long reaches of poetry but also of philosophy, the foundation upon which poetry is built. It aims, furthermore, to trace an historical sequence to a few fundamental facts conditioned by the spiritual nature of man and also to evolve such a sequence from them. By applying Woelfflin's categories to poetry, the various arts shed mutual light upon each other. Strich here specifically acknowledges his indebtedness to Woelfflin (second edition, p. 401).

Woelfflin was censured for not having subjected each of his two lists of five categories to an all-embracing concept. Immediately these two all-embracing concepts, the one to head the list of the Renaissance categories and the other that of the baroque categories, were supplied from existing polar antitheses in the field of psychology. Strich was the first to apply these two lists to basic facts in the spiritual activity of man.

Strich sets out from the yearning of man for eternity. Unlike other living things, a human being not only lives, but he knows that he is experiencing life. Hence he endeavors to escape from transitoriness; he seeks to incorporate himself into transitoriness in such a way as to share its permanence.

Eternity, however, may mean the eternity of completion or the eternity of infinity. That which is complete in itself and endures perforce untouched by change or transformation is eternal. Similarly that which is infinite and can never end is likewise eternal because it is never complete: it is the persistence of infinite variation, mobility, and development; of the infinite melody, of the steadily rising tide of everlasting creative time which knows neither end nor completion.

Here is an all-embracing concept. And ranged under it are two polar concepts: completion and infinity. Whereever classicism—and hence also, according to Woelfflin, the spirit of the Renaissance—emerges, Strich presumes to recognize completion. Parallel to Gothic (according to Worringer) or to the baroque (according to Woelfflin) he sees infinity. Strich also reduces to his terms, completion and infinity, other polar antitheses which have been used for some time to indicate the various possibilities in creative art.

Strich refers expressly to Woelfflin's antithetical pairs of categories. Where Woelfflin granted to the Renaissance among other things definite form, a multiplicity in which every constituent art is complete in itself, in other words, clarity, and to the baroque, indefinite form, undifferentiated oneness, and hence, obscurity, Strich recognizes in the characteristics of the former, completion and of the latter, infinity.

Completion he conceives to be the goal of German classicism, and infinity, the goal of German romanticism. With keen penetration he traces the categories of Woelfflin's Renaissance column in the works of Goethe and Schiller primarily, and those of the baroque column in the works of the German romanticists. He utilizes Woelfflin's conceptions, granting them at the same time the larger background which accrues to them on the one hand from his own conception of completion and on the other from his conception of infinity. He does not neglect to reiterate again and again how great was the endeavor of the German arch-classicists to create something which would be complete in itself and how very apparent in the works of romanticism was the striving toward the infinite. Strich pursues his contrast into the very details of classic and romantic word-formations.

No one will gainsay Strich when he says there is in romanticism a striving toward the infinite. Previously in the pages of this book this romantic striving has frequently been taken into account (especially Part 1, p. 28 ff., 71 ff.). But the question is : Is this tendency wholly alien to German classicism? Why then, if not after Goethe, do we call this very striving the "Faust spirit"? And did not Schiller characterize his own being when he declared that there was in the sentimental poet, as well as in the sentimental human being, in the idealist, a striving after ideals that are unattainable inasmuch as they lie beyond the world of the senses? Furthermore it would be easy to prove that others, notable among them the German romanticists, attributed this striving for infinity, which Strich accords the German romanticists and, antithetically, withholds from German classicism, to the German people in general. Occasionally, indeed, it has been applied to the so-called "modern" in contradistinction to the so-called "ancient"; to occidental peoples in contrast to the supporters of the antique. Should then Goethe and Schiller, according to Strich, be denied their due as having created and felt as true Germans?

To escape this consequence Strich has but one alternative: to range at least the youthful Goethe on the side of romanticism and thus afford him and his art participation in the striving for infinity. On the other hand, Strich touches but lightly upon the fact that romanticism along with baroque, Gothic, form is content with lesser pathos or indeed renounces entirely emotional striving for infinity. Thus he missed the actual point of contact between Goethe and German romanticism: the need, on the part of both, of an unexaggerated poetic form, of a simple, straightforward method of expression, of a mode of exposition which grants the inner life a wholly individual, artistic frame-work uninfluenced by conventional turns. Strich does not really get at the problem of organic aesthetics. He is far removed from the three-fold cleavage which I suggest above. He makes no mention of the essential characteristics involved in artistic self-contemplation which constitute the bond between Goethe and German romanticism.

Just as Woelfflin and I, Strich seeks to defend romanticism from the unqualified accusations of formlessness. Convinced that there is form not only in the form of completion but also in that of infinity, he establishes two extremes in artistic structure. But the many subtle observations that Strich makes upon the more indefinite form inherent in the tendency toward infinity have not saved him from the accusation that the form which he ascribed to the German romanticists is after all nothing else than formlessness. Th. A. Meyer makes this accusation (in the *Deutsche Vierteljahrsschrift fuer Literaturwissenschaft und Geistesgeschichte,* 1925, 3, 231 ff.). If on the other hand, as I maintain, romanticism in Germany agrees with classicism, particularly Goethe's, in prizing organic form and if the romanticists like the classicists conceive their creations in conformity thereto, then the accusation of being without form which is aimed at the romanticists loses somewhat of its force. For logically the same accusation would have to be made also against Goethe and a large part of our classicism. In other words: the song *Auf dem See* is open to all of the objections which Th. A. Meyer makes against Strich's distinctions. For it, too, has form only in the sense of organic structure. But Meyer, also, it seems, does not care to hear about such a mode of construction.

The theory of the organic work of art cannot be conveniently set to rule for the benefit of either poet or critic. It appeals but slightly to reason. To French rationalism it might well seem to contain aesthetic mysticism. It transfers into the field of art the concept of the inherent conformity to rule to be found within any organism. This very thing had already been done by Goethe and Herder. Certain it is that romantic ethics is also concerned with the organic conception (cf. above, Part 1, p. 78 f.). Whatever is conditioned by the inner law of personality, Schleiermacher calls ethical. It is difficult properly to comprehend this inner law. It is quite possible to deceive one-self. There are enough instances in romanticism to prove that both in life and in poetry the desire to follow the dictates of the true self led to immorality. For this very reason, doubtless, Goethe's novel *Die Wahlverwandt-schaften,* with its strict lesson in Kantian morality, has become the conscious reaction to romantic ethics as a whole (cf. *A 2,* p. 429). As easily as the concept of organic morality can lead to immorality, so, too, the doctrine of organic aesthetics might well lead to formlessness.

Perhaps the difficulty of expressing in definitely under-standable terms the conception of the organic work of art is the reason why, even to this day, when speaking of Goethe and romanticism, this subject is avoided. But did not German arch-classicism as well as German romanti-cism express this conception in such a way as to make it not only intelligible to reason but also to give very defi-nite guidance to one particular art?

This is the art of landscape gardening. The antithesis between the regularity of a baroque park and the later art of gardening which did not force a tree into an unnatural contour is often cited in explaining the fundamentals of organic aesthetics, even by the youthful Goethe and par-ticularly by Schiller. The symbol, the favorite illustra-tion which recurs again and again, is the tree which de-velops unhampered, according to its own inherent laws.

I venture to use this symbol even there where the form happens to be destroyed by apparent lack of restraint. A well-known characteristic in the construction of the longer romantic poems is the lack of balance between the parts to each other and to the whole. Unconcerned about the harmonious proportioning of space or consistent sym-metry, the romanticist was prone to allow one part to develop unduly. Arnim's *Graefin Dolores, Die Kronen-waechter,* and *Halle und Jerusalem* (see above, p. 171 f., 280 f.) are but the extremest, most palpable illustrations of this tendency. Even Brentano, who censured his friend Arnim for such careless construction, himself gives evidence of the tendency to linger over details at the expense of the perspicuity of the whole, not only in the *Romanzen vom Rosenkranz* and in his *Maerchen* but elsewhere. Does Goethe do otherwise in his *Mummenschanz* or the *Klassische Walpurgisnacht* in the second part of *Faust?*

Oskar Hagen's subtle book *Deutsches Sehen* (Munich, 1920) informs me that expatiation upon non-essentials is a characteristic of German art; he observes it in Duerer and can offer illustrations from the poetry of the German Middle Ages. A Latin, such as Leonardo da Vinci, fashions his works according to a well-planned scheme; he determines the proper balance of each part before he sets to work. It is repellent to a German to fashion a work of art according to predetermined measurements. Even a German such as Duerer, though he was inclined in the sense of conventional form to subject himself and his art, like the painters of antiquity, to geometric symmetry, simply cannot overcome the tendency to give disproportionate space to details. This is proved by his engravings.

And so to return to the symbol of the tree: a tree which unhampered by the gardener's implements follows merely its own inner law and the course of nature may develop one or the other of its branches asymmetrically to the others.

This characteristic of Duerer is also inherent in romantic painting. Schwind, for example, is an important illustration of the antithesis in construction between genuinely German and Romance art. He, too, is but slightly concerned with that clear-cut general effect which is achieved by means of an outline based upon rigid calculation and the elimination of all unnecessary details. If Hagen says it requires a magnifying-glass to do justice to Duerer's delicate details, the same may be said of Schwind. But in using a microscope one loses sight of the work as a whole and of its construction.

Romantic painting particularly demonstrates from another point of view how important the symbol of the tree and of plant-life in general has been to that art whenever it sought to assume artistic form and arrangement. Runge's *Tageszeiten* develop the individual picture, arrange it within the frame, causing the picture to assume shape from within with plant-like growth. Brentano as a draughtsman occasionally does the same. But at the same time Runge's *Tageszeiten* are conceived in very good proportion. Nevertheless, they remain true to the organic idea inasmuch as their fundamental structure is analogous to that of a plant.

All of this is presented in greater detail in my study *Gehalt und Gestalt im Kunstwerk des Dichters* (in the *Handbuch der Literaturwissenschaft* of the Athenaion Publishing Company, Wildpark-Potsdam). This study (p. 328 ff.) contains, too, reproductions of pictures which in this instance are quite indispensable. It also discusses in greater detail wherein I differ with Strich's book. But it dwells recurrently and with sufficient length upon German romanticism so that it may be recommended as an indispensable supplement to this sketch. I refer to it briefly here and shall not burden the text with specific quotations (cf. also *W*, p. 118 ff.).

In *Gehalt und Gestalt* the conception of organic art is

dwelt upon at greater length. It also defines more closely that German type of art which is neither baroque nor Gothic. I would not say of this more tranquil German type, as Strich does, that it aims unmistakably at infinity. Organic art opposes the ideal which demands limitations, but it no more rises to infinity than—to use the tree-symbol here also—a tree grows into infinity. Romanticism can also be Gothic, can lose itself in infinity; but when it creates organically it confines itself to a smaller sphere and seeks to preserve the simpler proportionateness which was ever pleasing to the romanticists in the old German masters and in Goethe. Novalis particularly had this in mind.

One more possible objection is yet to be considered. We are in our day rather cautious whenever the question arises as to the extent to which an artist actually achieves the goal to which he commits himself in moments of artistic self-contemplation. The chapter *Kuenstlerische Absicht* in *Gehalt und Gestalt* (p. 67 ff.) points out how incapable an artist is of giving a definite and unequivocal evaluation of his creation and its decisive traits. In other words, the actual basis of an attempt to determine the character of a work of art is not derived from the artist's reaction to his own work but our reaction to it. An artist is prone to deceive himself in discussing his work while he is engaged upon it and especially in discussing it after it is finished. But does this make everything which our classicists and romanticists have uttered concerning the creative activity of an artist of no account in the proper understanding of the artistic works of classicism and romanticism? The present tendency is to draw this conclusion, indeed to advance it particularly against every attempt to understand classic or romantic art in the light of the classic or romantic doctrine of the organic work of art. It is even taken to be pure self-deception that Goethe, or any of the romanticists, should have presumed to have endowed his work with the inner necessity of any natural organism.

I cannot concur in this point of view. I refuse to accept it not merely because I am in a position to demonstrate which characteristics of classic and romantic art correspond to the conception of an organic work of art. Far more is at stake. Such a point of view overlooks entirely that feeling of assurance which was the strongest support for Herder and for Goethe and perhaps even more for the romanticists when they sensed in any phenomenon a hint of its being conditioned by nature and natural inner laws. Thus any historical development became to the romanticists the result of a necessity which corresponded to or was closely akin to the immutable laws in the process of becoming in nature. This is the source not only of the romantic conception of history, of art, and of morality. Thus also romanticism in Jacob Grimm conceived of language, and in Savigny and Adam Mueller of law and political science; from these premises it opposed all untraditional structural forms which granted reason unlimited power to fashion and recreate (cf. *Zeitschrift fuer Buecherfreunde,* 1922, p. 14 f.).

In the *Festschrift Heinrich Woelfflin, Beitraege zur Kunst- und Geistesgeschichte* (Munich, 1924), Strich expands his point of view into *Die Romantik als europaeische Bewegung.*

It is not my intention either in this conclusion or in the notes to cite all the recent researches in romanticism or the romanticists. It is, moreover, becoming more and more the fashion nowadays not to trouble about previous

researches. Whoever wishes to find them can easily do so:
in Paul Merker's thankworthy summary *Neuere deutsche
Literaturgeschichte (Wissenschaftliche Forschungsbe-
richte,* Volume 8, Gotha, 1922), and in the *Jahresbericht
ueber die wissenschaftlichen Erscheinungen auf dem
Gebiete der neueren deutschen Literatur* (Berlin, 1924;
there are three volumes embracing the years 1921–1923).
The best insight into the tendencies and antitheses of the
more recent researches in romanticism is afforded by
Julius Petersen's *Die Wesensbestimmung der deutschen
Romantik* (Leipzig, 1926). I call attention specifically to
the bibliography contained in the appendix to Petersen's
book. It completes the data which I have offered here.

The following books mentioned in Part 1, p. v ff.,
have appeared in new, and in part, enlarged editions:
the first volume of Dilthey's *Leben Schleiermachers* (published by Hermann Mulert, Berlin and Leipzig, 1922),
Karl Joël's *Nietzsche und die Romantik* (Jena, 1923),
and Carl Schmitt's *Politische Romantik* (Munich, 1925).

Paul Kluckhohn's *Die deutsche Romantik* (Bielefeld
and Leipzig, 1924) presents a survey of the entire field
of romanticism. Kluckhohn's *Persoenlichkeit und Gemein-
schaft* (Halle, 1925) discusses the romantic conception of
the state. Eleven numbers of Wilhelm Kosch's *Geschichte
der deutschen Literatur im Spiegel der nationalen Entwicklung von 1813–1918* (Munich, 1922 ff.) have appeared thus far. Philipp Funk in *Von der Aufklaerung
zur Romantik* (Munich, 1925) offers a history of in-
cipient romanticism in Munich.

The two volumes which have thus far appeared of the
Geschichte der deutschen Literatur nach Gattungen, which
is being published by Karl Viëtor, have taken up romanticism in Viëtor's *Geschichte der deutschen Ode* (Munich,

1923) and in Guenther Mueller's *Geschichte des deutschen Liedes* (also Munich, 1925).

Conceived very definitely as a problem in historical development is the penetrating study by Rudolf Unger: *Herder, Novalis und Kleist, Studien ueber die Entwicklung des Todesproblems in Denken und Dichten vom Sturm und Drang zur Romantik* (*Deutsche Forschungen*, Vol. 9, Frankfurt am Main, 1922).

Georg Stefansky's *Das hellenisch-deutsche Weltbild, Einleitung in die Lebensgeschichte Schellings* (Bonn, 1925) is supplied with a rather lengthy index of relevant literature. Critical notes are appended. To be sure this thankworthy "Directory of Source-Material" proves how simple it has become to overlook the obvious.

Josef Koerner in his *Romantiker und Klassiker* (Berlin, 1924) specifically discusses only "the Schlegel brothers in their relation to Goethe and Schiller." He utilizes a wealth of newly discovered material. He had already made use of this material elsewhere. With great care he proves and presents everything which transpired between the two classicists and the two romanticists. There are doubtless those who will feel themselves disillusioned by Koerner's conclusion. One would be pleased to find less of pettiness in the relations of these four men. It is everyone's privilege, however, to overlook the details of their social connections and to penetrate only into the inner relationship existing between the two parties. Thus it will be gratifying to discover that in spite of personal bickerings there is nevertheless harmony upon the most important points. The *Briefe von und an Friedrich und Dorothea Schlegel* (Berlin, 1926), published painstakingly with explanatory remarks by Koerner, weld together a mass of hitherto unknown material bearing upon the history of romanticism.

Paul Kluckhohn's treatise *Novalis und Friedrich Schlegel* (*Deutsche Rundschau* 191, 159 ff.) reproduces a copy of the *Ideen,* written in Dorothea's hand with marginal notes by Hardenberg. K. J. Obenauer offers some studies in Hardenberg in the volume *Hoelderlin, Novalis* (Jena, 1925). Other publications upon Hoelderlin and Kleist shall not be cited here.

Alfred E. Lussky (*Tieck's Approach to Romanticism,* Borna-Leipzig, 1925) endeavors to trace the steps by which Tieck became a romanticist. Konrad Burdach (*Die Entdeckung des Minnesangs und die deutsche Sprache* in the *Sitzungsberichte der Preuszischen Akademie der Wissenschaften,* 1918, p. 845 ff.) reveals much information in proving the service or lack of service which German romanticism rendered in the proper evaluation of the Minnesong (see above, Part 1, p. 108). The meaning of Gothic as used by the romanticists is developed by Heinrich Luetzeler in Volume 2 of the *Wallraf-Richartz-Jahrbuch* of 1925.

The entire third number of the second volume of the *Deutsche Vierteljahrsschrift fuer Literaturwissenschaft und Geistesgeschichte* (1924) is dedicated to romanticism. In this magazine (1, 419 ff.) Elisabeth Blochmann's article *Die deutsche Volksdichtungsbewegung in Sturm und Drang und Romantik* seeks to show wherein the Storm and Stress differs from romanticism.

NOTES

[1] Cf. Albert Koester, *Die allgemeinen Tendenzen der Geniebewegung im 18. Jahrhundert.* Leipziger Universitaets-program, 1912.

[2] This connection, which I barely touch upon here, I sought to prove in the *Germanisch-Romanische Monatsschrift*, 1, 416 ff. and in *Ilbergs Jahrbuecher*, 37, 186 ff. (*A*, p. 1 ff.). Cf. Chr. F. Weiser, *Shaftesbury und das deutsche Geistesleben*, 1916 (and my article in the *Deutsche Literaturzeitung*, 1916, Column 2067 ff.); G. Simmel, *Rembrandt*, 1916; E. Cassirer, *Freiheit und Form*, 1917.

[3] Cf. Fritz Mauthner, *Woerterbuch der Philosophie*, 1910, 2, 561.

[4] Cf. L. Zurlinden, *Gedanken Platos in der deutschen Romantik*, 1910; H. F. Mueller, *Ilbergs Jahrbuecher*, 36, 69 ff.

[5] P. Vogel, *Das Bildungsideal der deutschen Fruehromantik*, 1915.

[6] Cf. A. Poetzsch, *Studien zur fruehromantischen Politik und Geschichtsauffassung*, 1907, p. 81.

[7] Cf. my study, *Das Prometheussymbol von Shaftesbury zu Goethe*, 1910.

[8] The gradual growth of solipsism in the Eighteenth Century as evidenced by Goethe's *Werther*, Jacobi's *Woldemar*, Moritz's *Anton Reiser*, and Tieck's *Lovell* is ingeniously worked out by F. Brueggemann, *Die Ironie als entwicklungsgeschichtliches Moment*, 1909. The "Doppelgaenger" motif is discussed by J. Cerny, *Jean Pauls Beziehungen zu E. T. A. Hoffmann*, 1907–8, 2, 10 ff. Cf. also F. Wuestling, *Tiecks William Lovell*, 1912.

[9] Cf. *Euphorion*, 15, 610 ff., 792 ff.; F. Bulle, *F. Hem-*

sterhuis und der deutsche Irrationalismus des 18. Jahrhunderts, 1911.

[10] *A*, p. 384 ff.; A. Schier, *Die Liebe in der Fruehromantik,* 1913.

[11] Cf. C. Enders, *F. Schlegel, Die Quellen seines Wesens und Werdens,* 1913.

[12] Cf. M. Dessoir, *Vom Jenseits der Seele,* 1917.

[13] Cf. Ritter's, *Fragmente aus dem Nachlasse eines jungen Physikers,* 1810, i, p. XVIII.

[14] Concerning Hardenberg's relation to Plotinus, cf. P. F. Reiff, *Euphorion,* 19, 591 ff.

[15] Cf. J. Koerner, *Niebelungenforschungen der deutschen Romantik,* 1911, p. 80 f., 139 ff.

[16] An even finer distinction is made by W. Brecht, *Heinse und der aesthetische Immoralismus,* 1911, p. 53 ff.

[17] Cf. P. Kluckhohn, *Euphorion,* 20, 87 ff. and C. Enders, *F. Schlegel,* p. 364 ff.

[18] Cf. Johannes Nohl, *Euphorion,* 19, 612 ff.

[19] Cf. J. Koerner, *Nibelungenforschungen der deutschen Romantik,* 1911.

[20] Cf. F. Gundolf, *Shakespeare und der deutsche Geist,* 1911; cf. *Jahrbuch der deutschen Shakespeare-Gesellschaft,* 48, 259 ff.

[21] Cf. E. Muennig, *Calderon und die aeltere deutsche Romantik,* 1912; J. J. A. Bertrand, *Cervantes et le Romantisme allemand,* 1914; G. Richert, *Die Anfaenge der romanischen Philologie und die deutsche Romantik,* 1914.

[22] E. Firmenich-Richartz, *Sulpiz und Melchior Boisserée als Kunstsammler,* 1916; cf. *Goettingische gelehrte Anzeigen,* 1918, p. 447 ff.

[23] *Ph. O. Runges Zeichnungen und Scherenschnitte in der Kunsthalle zu Hamburg.* With an introduction by G. Pauli, 1916.

[24] Cf. A. Peltzer, *Goethe und die Urspruenge der neueren deutschen Landschaftsmalerei,* 1907; H. v. Kleinmayr, *Die deutsche Romantik und die Landschaftsmalerei,* 1912.

[25] Cf. *Jahrbuch der Goethe-Gesellschaft,* 1, 3 ff.

[26] Cf. W. Hilbert, *Die Musikaesthetik der Fruehromantik,* 1911; H. Goldschmidt, *Die Musikaesthetik des 18. Jahrhunderts und ihre Beziehungen zu seinem Kunstschaffen,* 1915.

[27] E. Wieneke, *Patriotismus und Religion in F. Schlegels Gedichten,* 1913; R. Volpers, *F. Schlegel als politischer Denker und Patriot,* 1917.

[28] Cf. R. Fester, *Rousseau und die deutsche Geschichtsphilosophie,* 1890, p. 151.

[29] Cf. Friedrich Schultze, *Die Graefin Dolores,* 1904, p. 23 ff.; H. Becker, *A. v. Arnim in den wissenschaftlichen und politischen Stroemungen seiner Zeit,* 1912.

[30] Cf. F. Lenz, *Agrarlehre und Agrarpolitik der deutschen Romantik,* 1912.

[31] Cf. R. Saitschik, *Hochland,* 10, 1, 257 f., 447 ff.; 10, 2, 129 ff., 309 ff., 456 ff.

[32] Cf. K. Bode's conclusive study: *Die Bearbeitung der Vorlagen in "Des Knaben Wunderhorn,"* 1909, esp. p. 733 ff.

[33] Cf. Josef Nadler, *Eichendorffs Lyrik: Ihre Technik und ihre Geschichte,* 1908.

[34] Cf. Guenther Mueller, *Brentanos Romanzen vom Rosenkranz,* 1922.

[35] Cf. *Germanisch-Romanische Monatsschrift,* 7, 471 ff.

[36] Cf. *Germanisch-Romanische Monatsschrift,* 7, 403 ff., 465 ff.

[37] Cf. also Konrad Burdach, *Vorspiel,* 1925, 1, 267.

[38] Cf. K. Wagner, *Die historischen Motive in Arnims "Kronenwaechtern,"* 1908–10; see above, Part 1, p. 139 f.

[39] Cf. Walter Rehm, *Das Werden des Renaissancebildes in der deutschen Dichtung,* 1924; O. Weibel, *Tiecks Renaissancedichtung in ihrem Verhaeltnis zu Heinse und C. F. Meyer,* 1925.

[40] Cf. Walzel, *Richard Wagner in seiner Zeit und nach seiner Zeit,* 1913, p. 84 ff.

[41] Harry Maync, *Immermann, der Mann und sein Werk,*

1920, p. 464 ff., 610 ff., blazes the trail toward the proper interpretation.

[42] Cf. *A 1*, p. 89 ff.; M. Pulver, *Romantische Ironie und romantische Komoedie*, Freiburg Dissertation, 1912.

[43] Cf. C. Hille, *Die deutsche Komoedie unter der Einwirkung des Aristophanes*, 1907; W. Suess, *Aristophanes und die Nachwelt*, 1911; R. Schloesser, *August Graf von Platen*, 1910–13, I, 686 ff.; II, 121 ff.; *Zeitschrift fuer den deutschen Unterricht*, 30, 481 ff.

[44] Cf. G. Roethe, *Brentanos "Ponce de Leon": eine Saekularstudie*, 1901; *Deutsche Literaturzeitung*, 1902, col. 788 ff.

[45] Cf. A. Renker, *G. Buechner und das Lustspiel der Romantik*, 1924; O. Demuth, *Das romantische Lustspiel in seinen Beziehungen zur dichterischen Entwicklung Eichendorffs*, 1912.

[46] Cf. Walzel, *R. Wagner in seiner Zeit und nach seiner Zeit*, p. 73.

[47] Cf. R. Benz, *Maerchendichtung der Romantiker*, 1908, p. 102 ff.

[48] For romantic literature concerned with elementary spirits (they play an important rôle in Heine's poetry and studies) cf. O. Floeck's study (1909) and Julius Haupt, *Elementargeister bei Fouqué, Immermann und Hoffmann*, 1923.

[49] Cf. F. R. Merkel, *Der Naturphilosoph G. H. Schubert und die deutsche Romantik*, 1913.

[50] Cf. R. Buchmann, *Helden und Maechte des romantischen Kunstmaerchens*, 1910; P. Sucher, *Les sources du merveilleux chez E. T. A. Hoffmann*, 1912; M. Pirker, *Euphorion*, 20, 261 ff.; Walther Harich, *E. T. A. Hoffmann: Das Leben eines Kuenstlers*, Fourth Edition, 1923.

[51] Among the numerous discussions of Kleist's "Kant experience," there needs to be emphasized only: Ernst Cassirer, *Idee und Gestalt*, 1921, p. 153 ff.

[52] Cf. S. Wukadinovic, *Kleist-Studien*, 1904, p. 150 ff., 186 ff.

[53] Cf. M. Joachimi-Dege, *Deutsche Shakespeare-Probleme*, p. 158 ff.

[54] Cf. *Jahrbuch der Deutschen Shakespeare-Gesellschaft*, 52, 28 ff.; *W*, p. 318 ff.

[55] Cf. K. G. Wendriner, *Das romantische Drama*, 1909.

[56] Cf. *Zeitschrift fuer Buecherfreunde*, New Series, 8, 270. *W*, p. 172 f.

[57] Cf. Jonas Fraenkel, *Z. Werners Weihe der Kraft*, 1904. About Werner in general: Paul Hankamer, *Z. Werner*, 1920; Franz Stuckert, *Das Drama Zacharias Werners*, 1926.

[58] F. Schoenemann, *L. A. von Arnims geistige Entwicklung an seinem Drama "Halle und Jerusalem" erlaeutert*, 1912; R. Kayser, *Arnims und Brentanos Stellung zur Buehne*, 1914.

[59] Cf. W. Liepe, *Das Religionsproblem im neueren Drama von Lessing bis zur Romantik*, 1914, p. 83 f.

INDEX

305